Erik S. Lunde and Douglas A. Noverr, Film History

Selected Course Outlines and Reading Lists from American Colleges and Universities

Film History

edited by Erik S. Lunde and Douglas A. Noverr
Michigan State University

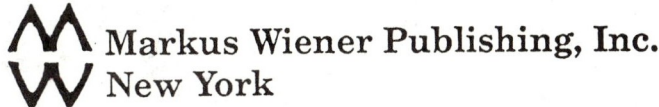 Markus Wiener Publishing, Inc.
New York

© Copyright 1989 by Markus Wiener Publishing, Inc.

All rights reserved. No part of this book may be
reproduced without prior permission from the
copyright holder.

For information write to
Markus Wiener Publishing,
225 Lafayette Street, New York, NY 10012

Library of Congress Cataloging-in-Publication Data

Film history.

    (Selected reading lists and course outlines from American colleges and universities)
    Bibliography: p.
    Contents: v. 1. Introductory courses, interdisciplinary courses, courses about directors, and about film and literature -- v. 2. Film history, film genres, and foreign films.
    1. Motion pictures -- Study and teaching. 2. Motion pictures--Bibliography. I. Lunde, Erik S. (Eric Sheldon) II. Noverr, Douglas A. III. Series.
PN1993.7.F5 1988   791.43'01'5   88-17395
ISBN 1-55876-002-4 (v. 2)

Printed in America

FILM HISTORY:
SELECTED COURSE OUTLINES AND READING LISTS

ERIK S. LUNDE
DOUGLAS A. NOVERR

TABLE OF CONTENTS

I. The Evolution Of Film Studies

1. ERIK S. LUNDE and DOUGLAS A. NOVERR, Michigan State University
   Introduction and Overview 3
2. BARRY K. GRANT, Brock University
   "Film Study in the Undergraduate Curriculum: An Overview" 7

II. Film History

1. JIM CASH, Michigan State University
   The History of Motion Pictures 23
2. JACK C. ELLIS, Northwestern University
   The History of Film (1, 2, 3) 26
3. LOUIS GIANNETTI, Case Western Reserve University
   History of Cinema to 1940 39
   American Cinema Since 1940
4. DOUGLAS GOMERY, The University of Maryland
   The History of the American Film Industry (bibliography) 42
5. BARRY K. GRANT, Brock University
   The Documentary Film (historical essay and course syllabus) 56
6. MIRIAM HANSEN, Rutgers University
   American Silent Film: History and Theory 78
   American Cinema (1, 2)
7. E. ANN KAPLAN, State University of New York at Stony Brook
   History and Criticism of Film 85
8. BRUCE KAWIN, University of Colorado at Boulder
   Silent and Early Sound Film 90
   Film History 2
9. DANIEL J. LEAB, Seton Hall University
   Film and History: the 1930s 97
10. JACK NACHBAR, Bowling Green State University
    The American Silent Cinema 101
    American Films of the 1930s
    American Films of the 1940s
    American Films of the 1950s
11. JIMMIE REEVES, The University of Michigan
    Film History 115

12. ADAM REILLY, University of Colorado at Denver
    Early Foreign Cinema 121
    Before Talkies: Early American Film
13. DAVID H. SHEPARD, University of Southern California
    International Silent Cinema 138
14. ROBERT SKLAR, New York University
    American Film, 1945-1960 145
    Film Historiography (1, 2)
15. THOMAS SOBCHACK, University of Utah
    Introduction to American Film 151
16. VIVIAN SOBCHACK, University of California, Santa Cruz
    Silent Film History:
    German Expressionist and Soviet Cinemas 152
    American and French Silent Cinemas
    Sound Film History: Film and Historiography
    Sound Film History: Film and Ideology
    Documentary Film

III. Film Genres

1. LEO BRAUDY, University of Southern California
   Genre Theory 175
2. EDWARD D.C. CAMPBELL, JR., Virginia State Library and Archives
   The Southern: A Regionalist Approach to Film 178
3. GEOFFREY COCKS and PAUL LOUKIDES, Albion College
   "Teaching Film Images of World War II" (essay) 187
   Film Images of World War II
4. EDWARD C. MAPP, Borough of Manhattan Community College, The City University of New York
   Images of Blacks in Motion Pictures 199
5. JACK NACHBAR, Bowling Green State University
   The Western Film 209
6. DOUGLAS A. NOVERR, Michigan State University
   The Sports Film 214
7. VIVIAN SOBCHACK, University of California, Santa Cruz
   The American Science Fiction Film (1, 2) 219
8. JON TUSKA, Portland State University
   Images of the American West 225
9. GREGORY A. WALLER, University of Kentucky
   Genre Criticism and the American Horror Film 229
10. WILLIAM VINCENT, Michigan State University
    The Hollywood Musical 231

to the rapt enthusiasm of Pauline Kael.

At the same time, a number of scholars began to devote their attention to the popular media. An important teacher of media education and former scholar of medieval literature, Professor Gerald O'Grady of the State University of New York at Buffalo, embraced the utopianism of Buckminster Fuller and the "expanded cinema" approach of Gene Youngblood, proclaiming that in his research activity he had dropped the "eval" in order to emphasize the "media". The popularization of Marshall McLuhan's ideas in particular helped cultivate a new awareness of film and other forms of popular culture as media with their own distinctive properties.

Students were of the first television generation, and the swelling of enrollments in film courses testified to their clear interest in the subject. Consequently, film courses sprang into being in colleges across North America. With stable enrollments, healthy budgets, and active student interest in all the humanities, many institutions experienced little difficulty in establishing courses in film, even though such courses may entail considerable expense (film rentals, projection equipment, and staff fees) and administrative problems (timetabling, adequate screening facilities).

Thus film culture was thriving by the late 1960s. But the study of film did not completely fulfill its promise to become the darling discipline of the 70s. Of course this was in part the result of the steady decline in humanities enrollments employing his own comic persona, the film was nevertheless listed in the opening credits as "A Herbert Ross film," since Ross directed it. And if, as now seems clear, classical auteurism had its serious limitations in both theory and practice, it should be remembered that it was ultimately responsible as well for shifting critical concern from overt theme to mise-en-scene -- that is to say, from the social importance of subject to the felicities of style. As well, it was none other than Sarris who suggested that an auteur may be discovered by locating "the tension between a director's personality and his material"[4] -- an attitude that has led to the subsequent ideological deconstruction of classic Hollywood films, a critical activity that has characterized much recent significant writing on the cinema.

The 1960s also witnessed both the crumbling of the Hollywood studio system and the critical and commercial success of a number of bold, exciting films by independent feature filmmakers that seemed to connect with the concerns of the nation's young people more seriously than the youth exploitation movies that preceded them. As a result of these developments, American film, for so long dismissed as mere entertainment, began to be viewed with a new critical attentiveness. And, too, European "art" films, such as those of Ingmar Bergman, Jean-Luc Godard, Federico Fellini, and Michelangelo Antonioni, began appearing more often (at least in large cities) on American screens. The distaste for the movies voiced by established critics like H.L. Mencken and Edmund Wilson -- even by highbrow film critics like Dwight Macdonald and John Simon -- seemed now crusty and outdated compared

The Village Voice) generated a new intellectual curiosity among Americans seriously interested in film. The so-called "Hitchcocko-Hawksians" of la nouvelle vague praised the work of many Hollywood directors in wildly enthusiastic terms, and if some of the more excessive writing verged on the mystical, it presaged a new way of talking about the cinema that demanded informed response. British critics, writing in such newer journals as Movie, rebelled against the conservative, content-oriented criticism of the established periodicals and adopted approaches similar to what Richard Roud in Sight and Sound called "The French Line."[3] And then Robin Wood, a frequent contributor to Movie, in his influential work Hitchcock's Films (1965) asserted -- a claim that for many amounted to nothing less than heresy -- that the films of the Master of Suspense were as complex as the plays of the Bard of Avon and that they required an equally elaborate exegesis.

By this time auteurism was enshrined as the privileged critical methodology in film studies, since it claimed to base its approach on both the economic (acknowledgement of the studio system) and aesthetic (mise-en-scene) properties of the medium. Auteurism was largely responsible for redeeming much of Hollywood cinema from the trash bins of disposable popular entertainment to which most of it had previously been consigned. As a measure of the extent to which auteurism took hold of the Hollywood sensibility itself as a way of legitimizing its own activity, one need only consider the case of Play it Again, Sam (1972): written by and starring Woody Allen, based on his own stage play, and clearly

"FILM STUDY IN THE UNDERGRADUATE CURRICULUM: AN OVERVIEW"

by Barry Keith Grant

Less than a century old, film history begins in 1895 with the first public showing of the Lumiere brothers' films in Le Grand Cafe in Paris. Thus the academic study of film, in comparison to, say, that of literature or painting, has not had adequate time to acquire a firm sense of tradition. From the 1920s through the 1950s, the occasional college course in film was offered -- Dudley Andrew points out that the University of Iowa offered film courses during World War 1^1 -- but these scattered few were of necessity tentative in approach. By the 1940s five universities had established film departments (USC, UCLA, CCNY, NYU, and Boston University), and by the 50s a number of other universities were offering individual courses in film. Yet it has been estimated that at this time there were still less than 100 persons in the United States engaged in film teaching, and for most of them it was regarded as a secondary field of interest.^{2}

In the history of film theory, it was not until Andre Bazin's writings in the late 1940s that the narrow formative aesthetics of Sergei Eisenstein, Rudolf Arnheim, Bela Belazs, and others was challenged to any significant extent. In the 1950s, the enthusiasm of *Cahiers du Cinema* and other journals for American auteurs, followed by Andrew Sarris's pioneering articles in English beginning in 1963 (and his long-running weekly column in

(1925). In many ways, Orson Welles' Citizen Kane (1941) is a majestic compilation of sequences derived from a host of superior films dating back to the silent era. Alfred Hitchcock's Psycho (1960) owes part of its special brilliance to Hitchcock's fascination with such silent films as Robert Wiene's The Cabinet of Dr. Caligari (1919).

In his famous paper on the significance of the American frontier, delivered at the American Historical Association meeting in Chicago in 1893, Frederick Jackson Turner invited his audience to consider a new approach to American history through a careful study of Western development. In acknowledging the end of America's physical frontier, Turner called for a new kind of pioneer in an innovative field of academic endeavor. And it is significant that just ten years after Turner's address, Edwin S. Porter's The Great Train Robbery (1903), drawing on the mythology of the Western story and creating a new tradition, would be released and so help inaugurate the development of narrative film as a pioneering art form.

So too the contributors to this volume have been pioneers. Drawing on their expertise in literature, history, sociology, the film arts, as well as film, they are fashioning innovative courses which study the film heritage both the Lumières and Porter launched.

Recognizing that a study of the history of the popular media can also lend insight to a national culture, these scholars and teachers have stimulated students to ask new questions about their assumptions concerning one of the most prominent sources of that culture's aspirations and doubts. In this way, these historians have aided in preserving films, in reassessing films, and in rediscovering films. Drawing on their research in film and manuscript archives, they have uncovered new details and insights about major films and their makers; they have helped keep film rental agencies functioning and have influenced the growth of videotape reproductions of seminal films. Under their guidance, "old" films become "new" films to generations never exposed to them. Students become "active" spectators rather than passive receptors of moving imagery. They come to realize that great films of the past are not just ephemeral illusions in black and white, but rather cerebral and timeless commentaries on the human condition. And they learn that a history of major ideas is incomplete without studying how these ideas were expressed in film.

Relying on rather than rejecting the pattern of students' extensive viewing behavior, film scholars are encouraging students to step back and analyze what the role of "spectator" is. They are integrating both the print and non-print media. They are developing an essential dimension in the instructional mission of all enterprising colleges and universities.

We are honored that we can offer the instructional materials of so many creative and resourceful individuals. Through their research and teaching they have expanded our knowledge of film history and served to recover the rich heritage of film that is one of our culture's significant contributions to world culture. As well, we would like to acknowledge our publisher, Dr. Markus Wiener, whose unending support has allowed us to compile this volume and a companion book, Film Studies: Selected Course Outlines and Reading Lists.

Hopefully, by the 1990s and beyond, undergraduate and graduate students will be able to select rewarding film courses such as those listed here at whatever institutions they attend. If this volume enhances this possibility in any way, we shall be satisfied.

Erik S. Lunde	Michigan State University
Douglas A. Noverr	East Lansing, Michigan

1987. A review of Douglas Gomery's bibliography in the second section of this volume illustrates the impressive and comprehensive nature of film history literature. Furthermore, these syllabi point the way to new areas of research for the potential scholar.

These courses present both standard and innovative methodologies scholars use in approaching film history. Many of these syllabi begin with the silent film era, recognizing that by the time of the introduction of "talkies" in the late 1920s, film as a visual medium, what critic Robert Warshow called the "immediate" experience," was already a mature art form. By the 1920s, early filmmakers had fully developed a wide range of techniques in terms of visual imagery, intertitling, and musical accompaniment. They had mastered the power of camera movement, editing, special effects, shot-making, transitions like the dissolve and iris-in and iris-out, set decoration, the close-up, and comic pantomime. They had elevated filmmaking to a solid professional level. Furthermore, the silent film era launched the Hollywood studio system, the movie palaces, and improved photographic and projection equipment. Contained in these syllabi are other "signposts" central to an understanding of the cinematic past: the influence of German expressionism and Soviet "montage" in the 1920s; the dominance of the studio system in the 1930s; the effect of major wars like World War I, World War II, Korea, Vietnam; the "film noir" style of the 1940s; the Supreme Court decision of 1948 directing studios to divest themselves of their theatre chains; the impact of the second Red Scare in the late 1940s and early 1950s; the challenge of television to marketing strategies in the 1950s; the demise of the Hollywood Production Code in the 1960s and the subsequent rise of independent film productions; the Hollywood Renaissance of the 1970s and 1980s. Film history is so rich and complex because it so closely and immediately responds to history and its currents.

Many of these syllabi illustrate the vitality of the documentary tradition, traced so effectively by Barry K. Grant in his essay in the second section. As Grant demonstrates, films began as documentaries with the Lumières, and, to this day, even the most imaginative narrative fantasies often incorporate "realistic" sequences, a tribute to the documentary heritage.

Further, the syllabi in the film genre section suggest how essential an historical approach has become to understanding film genres. For instance, a full study of the Western film must include an appreciation of silent film classics like William S. Hart's Hell's Hinges (1916) and Tom Mix's The Great K and A Train Robbery (1926). Any study of the gangster film must begin with D.W. Griffith's Musketeers of Pig Alley (1912). At least six of the contributors here have been major figures in defining film genres: Jack Nachbar and Jon Tuska for the "Western," Edward D.C. Campbell for the "Southern," Edward C. Mapp for the Black Film, and Vivian C. Sobchack and Gregory A. Waller in the Science Fiction Film.

By introducing students to major films of the past, film historians give their classes major reference points for better appreciating contemporary filmmakers. Many current directors utilize allusions to vintage films: in his The Last Picture Show (1971), Peter Bogdanovich, himself a film historian, includes sequences from Vincent Minnelli's Father of the Bride (1950) and Howard Hawks' Red River (1948); in his Bonnie and Clyde (1967), Arthur Penn introduces a sequence in a migrant camp, a direct homage to John Ford's The Grapes of Wrath (1940); in his The Untouchables (1987), Brian de Palma creates an action scene on the interior stairway of a railway station, clearly inspired by Sergei Eisenstein's celebrated "Odessa Steps" sequence in The Battleship Potemkin

terms of its historical reality and its mythology.

These course materials also demonstrate how often film history courses offer the only occasion where films of master "auteurs" like D.W. Griffith, Charlie Chaplin, John Ford or Alfred Hitchcock are originally screened. Given the financial difficulties "revival" theatres face in the United States, partially caused by the videotape revolution, universities and colleges have increasingly provided the central forum where classic films are properly shown and studied. Clearly, the survival of films as films, rather than just as videotape reproductions, depends on institutions of higher education.

For our major divisions of the contents of this volume, we have begun with a collection of course materials treating film history directly. Of the thirty-one course syllabi offered here, seven of them concentrate on the silent film era. Also, two syllabi treat the documentary heritage; four deal with specific decades; and several incorporate the European cinematic tradition.

In the section on film genres, at least seven different kinds of genre are covered, including two of the most recently defined genres, the "Southern" and the "Sports film." The last section presents courses dealing with film as an international medium.

These course materials underline the rich and various directions film history as a field is taking. In these courses, there is an emphasis on the origins, development and change in film as a collaborative art form, with the recognition that some of the earliest feature films remain vivid works of creative energy and imagination. There is also a stress on how technological advances in such areas as sound equipment, color photography and screen size have shaped film in terms of art, production and exhibition. Film history as part of the process of business and industrial development is also featured. Another central theme is how films are "period" pieces or cultural documents which reflect and express the hopes and anxieties of so many individuals who lived through the eras in which they were made. The initiate in this field soon realizes that a study of the history of American film is really another rewarding way to explore recent social American history as a whole. For instance, no one can fully understand the implications of the Depression without studying classic gangster films like Little Caesar, (1931), The Public Enemy, (1931) or Scarface (1932).

These curricular materials demonstrate as well how film history offers a genuine interdisciplinary approach in higher education. By examining the nature of how films were made and distributed, the instructor and student draw on a whole variety of disciplines, from "straight" history to economics to sociology to geography to political science to literature to philosophy. Also, film history opens a passage into an exploration of the history of all the arts, since films have derived so many of their artistic ideas and strategies from diverse crafts like still photography, novels, dance choreography, painting, sculpture, music, theatre, among others. Also, some of these courses concern film historiography, a relatively new field defined brilliantly in Robert Allen's and Douglas Gomery's recent book, Film History: Theory and Practice (1985).

The reading assignments in these courses reveal how far research and writing in film history have progressed since such seminal books as David Ramsaye's A Million and One Nights and Lewis Jacobs' The Rise of the American Film were first published in 1926 and 1939 respectively. While these pioneering works still remain essential sources for all film history students, there currently exists on most major library shelves a multiplicity of excellent texts, some of them written by this volume's contributors, like Gerald Mast, Jack Ellis, Louis Giannetti, Douglas Gomery, Annette Insdorf, Robert Sklar, Thomas Sobchack, and Vivian Sobchack. A new journal entitled Film History was first issued in

INTRODUCTION AND OVERVIEW

As the centennial of the first screening of the Lumière Picture Show in 1895 draws near, so too will the decade of the 1990s mark the full emergence of film studies as a legitimate field of academic inquiry. As Barry K. Grant states in the subsequent essay, film studies since the 1960s has gradually found a place at most major North American colleges and universities. At such institutions, partially because of the enthusiasm of their immediate predecessors for film, students can choose from a rich array of film courses offered by a wide variety of academic units. Many of these courses treat directly or indirectly one of the most researched areas within film studies, the history of film itself.

Because of the expansion of film studies programs, we decided that this was an opportune time to assess the status of film history by soliciting syllabi from more than one hundred film scholars. Drawing on standard sources like the National Faculty Directory and the Directory of American Scholars, we devised a list of potential contributors and sent out a general solicitation letter to them. We not only hoped to "target" film historians with established reputations, but also junior scholars in the formative stages of their careers. Some of our respondents were most helpful in steering us to other scholars not on our original list. Our publisher, Dr. Markus Wiener, also aided us immensely in this task by making contacts in the New York City universities. At our invitation, twenty-nine individuals, representing twenty-three institutions, set in submissions.

We have compiled this volume in the faith that any community of scholars would benefit by sharing finely tuned, carefully crafted course materials. In the future development and enhancement of their own courses, specialists could learn from the experience of others.

Even the most cursory survey of the contents of this volume suggests the richness of film history as an appropriate vehicle to study cultural history. What is instantly impressive about these syllabi are the length and breadth of the reading and screening lists. These course materials are exceptionally detailed and instructive. They also reveal how many film courses defy the popular and inappropriate adage that such presentations involve solely viewing "fun" films, and little more. Indeed, the courses represented in this volume require extensive and substantial reading in addition to solid viewing schedules; much writing in examination and out-of-class paper formats; attendance at lecture and active involvement in class discussions. Course materials often reveal the character of the presenter, who must make difficult choices in terms of what films to select and analyze within the time constraints of the course being offered. Since so many of the contributors have themselves produced excellent histories and specialized studies of film, their course syllabi are particularly useful in informing others about the kinds of decisions such scholars have made.

These syllabi also demonstrate how their authors often "connect" with students. Any college instructor who has had the good fortune to offer a film course knows the special excitement such an experience can engender. The opportunity to screen vintage films for a receptive student audience and then to share one'e perceptions, complemented with the sharp insights students can contribute, renders moments just as exciting as the more magical film sequences. The chance to introduce students to a new language, the visual language of film, and to instruct students on how to "read" a film is special indeed. And in film history courses, one often "discovers" a new way to explore the past, both in

I. THE EVOLUTION OF FILM STUDIES

IV. European and World Film

1. ANNETTE INSDORF, Columbia University
   Latin American Cinema 241
2. RICHARD McCORMICK, University of Minnesota, Twin Cities
   The New German Cinema 242
3. ROBERT STAM, New York University
   Third World Cinema 249
4. ANNETTE INSDORF, Columbia University
   French Cinema from the 1930s 261
5. JARED M. BECKER, Columbia University
   Italian Film from 1945 to the Present 267

About the Contributors 275

About the Editors 280

during that decade, with the marked shift of students in an increasingly difficult economy toward more job-oriented programs in business and the sciences. Yet there are additional factors with which the serious study of cinema has had to contend. The unfortunate associations of commercialism and cheap (aesthetically as well as economically) entertainment that often characterized the medium in its early days as vaudeville and peep-show attraction continue to do so for some. "Movies" are still regarded by most people more as a social event and emotional diversion than as an intellectual experience. This attitude informs the use of film in the classroom by so many heedless, if not simply bored, elementary and high school teachers. Until quite recently teachers at these levels had not undertaken any study of film and used the medium merely as a substitute for books and lectures. Since film (with the exception, perhaps, of so many of those awful "educational" documentaries with their pompous "voice-of-God" narration) provides an inherent visual interest, many teachers look to movies to do their jobs for them. Movies instead of teaching, I have discovered in my own screen education classes for teachers, is the way teachers think all too often. It is no coincidence that film use in the public schools increases on Fridays and just before holidays, times when both teachers and students begin thinking more about what will happen after class than of what is going on in it.

Students, in turn, are glad when a film is shown in class because it is, first of all, something different; also, they can assume an easy, passive relation to a movie just as they do in the theater or at home when watching television. Nothing in their experience has taught them how to -- indeed, that they must -- look critically at a visual text. When these students enter college, they often consider a course in film as "Mickey Mouse" (itself a cinematic term of reference not without its implications), that is, as an easy subject of study. However, with the greater number of film courses now offered at the college level and with the recent development at some schools of programs in screen education for teachers, this unproductive state of affairs already has begun to change.

Such an uncritical attitude toward film seems even more distressing when one considers the enormous implications of serious film study. We live in a media-saturated culture -- a "wired nation" that continues to colonize the "global village" -- in which film and television play a large and important role. Studies have shown that many young children spend a large percentage of their time watching television and that by the time they reach high school most young people have devoted more hours to television than they have spent in the classroom. As a result, children are socialized to a large extent through the visual media and do not realize the degree to which their values and behavior patterns have been shaped by the images these media generate. Children in our schools are taught to read but almost never to look. As teachers we owe it to our students to show them how the visual media shape one's perceptions of the world, so that they may think more independently; as concerned individuals we owe it to ourselves to help open the media to the possibility of alternative ideological points of view. These are, to be sure, ethical and political arguments, but they are essential to a serious consideration of what the teaching of film involves and to the informing philosophy of a liberal arts education.

The refusal to take film seriously as a mass medium and as a valid field of critical inquiry is not restricted to the public schools. The common notion among actors in the early part of the century that film acting was a debasement of their art may have disappeared with the rise of Hollywood and the star system, with the lure of fame and fortune, but this view remains essentially that of many elitist intellectuals. It is true (for reasons too complex to discuss here) that film adaptations of great novels have most often produced inferior works of cinema, and for many academics trained in literary analysis this has been sufficient proof of the medium's inherent inability to achieve aesthetic complexity. Forgetting that great films have been made from mediocre fiction, they consign the study of film to what they consider the more appropriate yet distinctly inferior area of popular culture (if, indeed, they consider that vague, questionable field worthy of serious study).

As a result of this attitude, and because film incorporates aspects of so many other disciplines (history, psychology, art, architecture, sociology, philosophy, politics, drama, photography), the question of where in the conventional departmental structure of higher education film might or should be taught has become particularly problematic. In the anthology of essays on the teaching of film which I edited for the Modern Language Association in 1983, Film Study in the Undergraduate Curriculum, at least five of the seventeen contributors considered this issue of paramount importance in describing their efforts to mount a program of film study.[5] The interdisciplinary nature of many university film programs suggest that in many cases either administrations have not been particularly eager to adequately fund these programs, or that the field of study has not been deemed worthy enough to require full departmental status. Nevertheless, many film scholars have adopted an interdisciplinary model for their programs simply to get the subject into the curriculum, although some do prefer it for the greater flexibility it offers.[6]

Two related issues also emerge as major considerations in the serious teaching of film. The first is the question of the text. Because of the nature of the medium, it is impossible without access to special equipment (analytic projectors, moviolas) to engage in a close analysis of a film. Without such equipment, the text remains ephemeral and elusive; the class must rely on memory -- so often extremely unreliable, as anyone who has ever taught film can attest. Moreover, while poems, for example, can be re-read many times before a class discussion, students will likely have seen the film to be discussed only once. Under such circumstances, classroom seminars may seem doomed to degenerate into a series of impressionistic, subjective assertions. Thus the teaching of film is seriously suspect for those who value rigorous textual analysis.

However, there are ways around this problem. Students can purchase published screenplays, for example; and while this is not an ideal solution, since they do not detail camera movements, sound effects and other textual elements, it can be enormously helpful. Generally, though, any serious program in film study must have the necessary financial support to allow for the purchase of analytical equipment and the support staff to supervise and maintain it. The introduction of relatively inexpensive, widespread video technology in recent years, and the large number of classic films now available in video format, offers still another possible direction for film programs. And while video viewing should not be practised as a substitute for the experience of the large screen, it is perfectly suited to the task of close analysis which may follow a regular 16mm screening.

The second issue is the relation between theory and practice, film analysis and filmmaking, academic and professional training. While the university context, in my view, should not be geared toward the training of Hollywood professionals, the two areas cannot in fact be so easily separated. Just as teachers of literature (English) programs consider writing (whether analytical or creative, itself a problematic distinction) integral to their activity, so the production of images has enormous value in gaining a critical understanding of them. Most teachers of film criticism, theory, and history agree on the importance of "hands-on" experience and that it can be managed satisfactorily with a minimum of equipment. Lev Kuleshov's post-revolutionary Soviet film workshops even operated without film stock! From a pragmatic point of view, it should be remembered that many students first enter academic programs with vague but optimistic hopes of becoming movie directors; and rather than crush these dreams we can present a more sober, realistic picture of the industry even while encouraging students to devote more time to thinking about the kinds of images they want to make.

By now the study of the cinema has clearly proved itself academically respectable and worthy of administrative support. It is those who resist this who should be on the defensive. Much of the ground-breaking work of the newer critical theories and methods -- structuralism, feminism, semiology, and Marxism -- has taken place in film criticism, often with exciting and productive results. While the expectations for film studies in the 1960s may have failed to materialize fully, the subject nevertheless has found a place -- even if it remains precariously and vaguely defined -- in the post secondary curriculum, and enrollment in film studies has managed, if not to increase, at least to hold its own. Acccording to the American Film

Institute's Guide to College Courses in Film and Television, published in 1978, courses in film and/or television are offered at no fewer than 1,067 colleges and universities in the United States alone.[7] The Guide lists a total of 9,228 courses in film and television, of which 7,015 are at the undergraduate level and 2,133 at the graduate level (the remainder are available for either undergraduate or graduate credit) under the auspices of a wide range of departments (eleven). Taking into account that the AFI's survey was far from comprehensive, these statistics are quite impressive.

There are as well other indications of a new academic respect toward film study. Publishing in the field has increased dramatically in recent years. There are many new scholarly journals dealing exclusively or primarily with film, and a number of publishers, including some major university presses, have been actively developing a film book market. Annual film conferences, where scholarly papers are read and ideas exchanged, are supported by a number of universities (Purdue, University of Wisconsin at Milwaukee, Ohio). Professional societies in the field have become firmly established. The Society for Cinema Studies, for example, has consistently grown since its inception (as the Society of Cinematologists) in 1959 from under 25 to over 600 members in 1987. The organization accordingly has reached a more mature, self-reflexive stage in its development where it now engages in such activites as establishing procedural guidelines for refereed journals and for promotion and tenure review.

Undoubtedly, some will view these developments as an unfortunate co-optation of cinema study by the educational system. The burgeoning shelves of academic publications on cinema, for example, indicate not only a greater intensity of scholarly activity, but is also the result of the academic "publish or perish" syndrome. However, in my view this increase in film-related activity indicates a more healthy film culture generally; and given the pervasiveness of the visual media in contemporary life, and our society's encouragement of the popular view that everyone is a film critic, it can only prove beneficial in the end.

The rapid growth and maturation of film study in the last three decades is startling, especially when one considers that until recently most teachers of film came to the discipline (and some still do) out of personal interest but trained in other fields (most often, literature). The teaching of film had tended, therefore, to define itself under fire rather than to be recollected in tranquility. Still, again until recently, the infrequent literature that has appeard on film pedagogy has rarely risen above the cant of McLuhanesque "open classroom" optimism. But this situation is now changing, largely because academic positions in film are being filled more frequently by young Ph.D.s of graduate film programs. The more experienced teachers, meanwhile, have now had time to reflect upon what it is they do. The collection of writings in which this article appears is itself testimony to the continuing development of film study as a distinct field of scholarly activity and pedagogical reflection, perhaps one of the most significant for a liberal arts education in the latter part of the Twentieth Century.

NOTES

[1] Dudley Andrew, "An Open Approach to Film Study and the Situation at Iowa," in Film Study in the Undergraduate Curriulum, ed. Barry Keith Grant (New York: Modern Language Association, 1983), p. 45.

[2] Ramona Curry, "Twenty Five Years of SCS: A Socio-Political History," Journal of Film and Video, Vol. 38, no. 2 (Spring 1986), p. 44.

[3] Richard Roud, "The French Line," Sight and Sound, Vol. 29, no. 4 (Autumn 1969), pp. 166-171.

[4] Andrew Sarris, "Notes on the Auteur Theory in 1962," Film Culture, No. 27 (Winter 1962/63), p. 7.

[5] See the essays by Dudley Andrew, James Michael Welsh, Jerry Wood, Gerald Mast, and Jack Nachbar.

[6] This is the position taken by Andrew, for example. Op. Cit.

[7] The American Film Institute Guide to College Courses in Film and Television, ed. Dennis R. Bohnenkamp and Sam L. Grogg, Jr. (Princeton: Peterson's Guides, 1978).

II. FILM HISTORY

```
TELECOMMUNICATIONS 280
THE HISTORY OF MOTION PICTURES
FALL - 1987

JIM CASH
201 MORRILL HALL

TEXTBOOK: "A SHORT HISTORY OF THE MOVIES" by Gerald Mast.
Chapters 2, 3, 5, 6, 9, and 11.
```

1.	FRIDAY, SEPTEMBER 25 Introduction to course The Beginnings of Film	"THE TOY THAT GREW UP" "BIOGRAPHY OF THE CAMERA"
2.	MONDAY, SEPTEMBER 28 The Early Pioneers Film Narrative	"KINETOSCOPE SHORTS" "THE MAGIC LANTERN" "A TRIP TO THE MOON" "RESCUED BY ROVER" "THE GREAT TRAIN ROBBERY" "THE LONELY VILLA"
3.	WEDNESDAY, SEPTEMBER 30 Silent Comedy	"WHEN COMEDY WAS KING"
4.	FRIDAY, OCTOBER 2 Charlie Chaplin	"THE GOLD RUSH"
5.	MONDAY, OCTOBER 5 Chaplin's Masterpiece	"MODERN TIMES"
6.	WEDNESDAY, OCTOBER 7 The Coming of Sound	"FOX SHORT: G. B. SHAW" "THE JAZZ SINGER" "THE SEX LIFE OF THE POLYP" "STEAMBOAT WILLIE"
7.	FRIDAY, OCTOBER 9 The Problems of Sound	"SINGIN' IN THE RAIN"
8.	MONDAY, OCTOBER 12 Warner Brothers Social Realism	"THE PUBLIC ENEMY"
9.	WEDNESDAY, OCTOBER 14 Backstage Musicals Busby Berkeley	"FORTY-SECOND STREET"
10.	FRIDAY, OCTOBER 16 Columbia Frank Capra Screwball Comedy	"IT HAPPENED ONE NIGHT"

11.	MONDAY, OCTOBER 19 Color in Hollywood Movies for Kids	"THE ADVENTURES OF ROBIN HOOD"
12.	WEDNESDAY, OCTOBER 21 MGM	"THE PHILADELPHIA STORY"
13.	FRIDAY, OCTOBER 23 RKO Orson Welles	"CITIZEN KANE"
14.	MONDAY, OCTOBER 26 Prelude to War	"FOREIGN CORRESPONDENT"
15.	WEDNESDAY, OCTOBER 28 From Stage to Screen	"THE MAN WHO CAME TO DINNER"
16.	FRIDAY, OCTOBER 30 Howard Hawks	"HIS GIRL FRIDAY"
17.	MONDAY, NOVEMBER 2 Hollywood at War Women at War	"SO PROUDLY WE HAIL"
18.	WEDNESDAY, NOVEMBER 4 The Accidental Masterpiece	"CASABLANCA"
19.	FRIDAY, NOVEMBER 6 EXAM EXAM EXAM	EXAM EXAM EXAM
20.	MONDAY, NOVEMBER 9 From Novel to Screen	"FROM HERE TO ETERNITY"
21.	WEDNESDAY, NOVEMBER 11 Billy Wilder Paramount	"STALAG 17"
22.	FRIDAY, NOVEMBER 13 Hollywood Biography	"THE GLENN MILLER STORY"
23.	MONDAY, NOVEMBER 16 Post War Changes: Women Tracy and Hepburn	"ADAM'S RIB"
24.	WEDNESDAY, NOVEMBER 18 Science Fiction Allegory Post War Changes: Survival	"THE DAY THE EARTH STOOD STILL"
25.	FRIDAY, NOVEMBER 20 Post War Changes: Youth	"REBEL WITHOUT A CAUSE"
26.	MONDAY, NOVEMBER 23 Alfred Hitchcock	"REAR WINDOW"

27.	WEDNESDAY, NOVEMBER 25 Twentieth Century Fox Westerns	"BUTCH CASSIDY AND THE SUNDANCE KID"
28.	FRIDAY, NOVEMBER 27 Holiday -- No Class	
29.	MONDAY, NOVEMBER 30 Mike Nichols	"THE GRADUATE"
30.	WEDNESDAY, DECEMBER 2 Universal George Lucas	"AMERICAN GRAFFITI"
31.	FRIDAY, DECEMBER 4 Capra's Masterpiece	"IT'S A WONDERFUL LIFE"

FINAL EXAM: THURSDAY, DECEMBER 10
12:45 - 2:45

615 C12-1   THE HISTORY OF FILM: COURSE OUTLINE & ASSIGNMENTS

M 2:00-4:00
TWTh 2:00-2:50
Annie May Swift 325

TEXT: Jack C. Ellis,
A History of Film, Englewood
Cliffs, N.J.: Prentice-Hall.
1985 (2nd ed.), 447 pp.

Bibliography: compiled by
Chris List, available from
Kinko's

Instructor
Jack Ellis
AMS 209
Office hours:
TW 3:00-4:00

Teaching Assistant
Donna Kennedy

Both of the above
have mail boxes in
AMS 212

I. Developments prior to 1895 that led to the motion picture
    READING: pp. 1-30. (All page numbers refer to the
    text above. Reading the assignments before Monday's
    class.)
    M Screening: see Screening Schedule for film titles
    T Lecture: course activities and requirements; goals of
      course in relation to film history
    W Discussion: Monday's films
    Th Discussion: remaining questions and mechanics of course

II. International childhood of a new medium and art, 1895-
    1914
        READING: pp. 31-51
    M Screening
    T Discussion: Monday's films
    W Conferences on panels and papers
    Th Conferences on panels and papers

III. Rise of the American Film, 1914-1919
        READING: pp. 52-76
    M Screening
    T Discussion: Monday's films
    W Research panel
    Th Conferences on panels and papers

IV. Scandinavian film, 1917-1924
        READING: pp. 77-85
    M Screening
    T Discussion: Monday's film
    W Research panel
    Th Conference on panels and papers

C12 History, Professor Ellis, Fall '86

- V. Great German silents, 1919-1925
  READING: pp. 86-103
  M Screening
  T Discussion: Monday's films
  W Research panel
  Th Conferences on panels and papers

- VI. Great German silents. 1919-1925 (concl.)
  M Screening
  T Discussion: Monday's film
  W Research panel
  Th Conferences on panels and papers

- VII. Art and dialectic in the Soviet film, 1925-1929
  READING: pp. 104-122
  M Screening
  T Discussion: Monday's film
  W Research panel
  Th Conferences on panels and papers

- VIII. Art and dialectic in the Soviet film, 1925-1929 (concl.)
  M Screening
  T Discussion: Monday's film
  W Research panel
  Th Conferences on panels and papers

- IX. French Impressionists and the avant-garde, 1919-1929
  READING: pp. 123-131
  M Screening
  T Discussion: Monday's films
  W Research panel
  Th Conferences on panels and papers

- X. Hollywood in the twenties, 1919-1929
  READING: pp. 132-149
  M Screening
  T Discussion: Monday's film
  W Research panel
  Th Conferences on panels and papers

- XI. Hollywood in the twenties, 1919-1929 (concl.)
  M Screening
  T Discussion: Monday's film
  W Research panel
  Th Discussion: the course and film history

C12 History, Professor Ellis, Fall'86

ASSIGNMENTS:

Research panel. Each student will give a ten-minute oral presentation based on library research on one of the nine feature films from the third week on. Films are to be selected in the first week.

Written reports. Each student will write three brief (about 4 pages) research reports based on library research and/or supplemental screening. They are to be about one small topic, or aspect, of three of the eight assigned chapters of the text (pp. 1-149) Papers are not to be on individual directors or individual films. A limited topic and the consulting of numerous sources, especially primary and contemporary ones, will make for the best papers.
 The three papers are to be on periods other than the one your research panel film is in. Show the relationship of each paper to the text--you should provide additions or corrections or alternative interpretations to the text.
 You must obtain the instructor's approval of the topic for each paper. Papers are due at the end of the week devoted to the national period with which they deal; no papers will be accepted after those dates.

GRADES:

The research panel comprises two-fifths of the course grade; the three written reports one-fifth each. Your presence in class and participation in discussion are expected; a minus will be added to your grade for excessive absences, plus for especially valuable contributions to class discussions.
 No incompletes will be given. Missing assignments will receive an F and be averaged into the course grade.

615 C12-1   THE HISTORY OF FILM: SCREENING SCHEDULE   Fall '86

Mondays 2:00-4:00 p.m.   Annie May Swift Room 325

September 22   Animated Cartoons: The Toy that Grew Up
                  France, 1946, Roger Leenhardt
               Biography of the Motion Picture Camera
                  France, 1946, Roger Leenhardt
               Early Edison Shorts
                  U.S., 1893-1901, Edison Company
               Lumiere Program
                  France, 1895-1908, Louis Lumiere

September 29   A Trip to the Moon
                  France, 1902, George Melies
               The Great Train Robbery
                  U.S., 1903, Edwin S. Porter
               Dante's Inferno
                  Italy, 1911, Cines Studio
               The New York Hat
                  U.S., 1912, David Wark Griffith

October 6   Teddy at the Throttle
                  U.S., 1917, Mack Sennett
               Broken Blossoms
                  U.S., 1919, D.W. Griffith

October 13   The Story of Gosta Berling
                  Sweden, 1924, Mauritz Stiller

October 20   Dr. Mabuse, the Gambler (Part I)
                  Germany, 1922, Fritz Lang

October 27   Faust
                  Germany, 1926, F.W. Murnau

November 3   Fragment of an Empire
                  U.S.S.R., 1929, Friedrich Ermler

November 10   The End of St. Petersburg
                  U.S.S.R., 1927, V.I. Pudovkin

November 17   Fievre
                  France, 1921, Louis Delluc
               Paris qui dort (The Crazy Ray)
                  France, 1924, Rene Clair

November 24   The Marriage Circle
                  U.S., 1924 Ernst Lubitsch

December 1   Easy Street
                  U.S., 1917, Charles Chaplin
               Our Hospitality
                  U.S., 1923, Buster Keaton

Professor Jack C. Ellis

615 C12-2 THE HISTORY OF FILM:

COURSE OUTLINE AND ASSIGNMENTS

I. Sound comes to America, 1927-1935
Reading: pp. 160-175 (all page numbers refer to text listed below)

    M Screening
    T Course activities and requirements; goals of course in relation to film history
    Th Discussion of films screened
    F Remaining questions about mechanics of course

II. Golden Age of French Cinema, 1935-1939
Reading: pp. 176-91

    M Screening
    T Discussion of film screened
    Th Research panel
    F Conferences on panels and papers

III. Hollywood in the thirties, 1929-1939
Reading: pp. 192-222

    M Screening
    T Discussion of film screened
    Th Research panel
    F Conferences on panels and papers

IV. British wartime semi-documentaries, 1939-1945
Reading: pp. 223-236

    M Screening
    T Discussion of films screened
    Th Research panel
    F Conferences on panels and papers

V. British postwar comedies, 1947-1955
Reading: pp. 236-239, 249-250

    M Screening
    T Discussion of film screened
    Th Research panel
    F Conferences on panels and papers

VI. Hollywood in the forties, 1940-1952
Reading: pp. 239-240, 249, 250-251, 252-256

    M Screening
    T Discussion of film screened
    Th Research panel
    F Conferences on panels and papers

VII. Hollywood in the forties, 1940-1952
      Reading: pp. 256-269
               M   Screening
               T   Discussion of film screened
               Th Research panel
               F   Conferences on panels and papers

VIII. Italian neorealism, 1945-1952
      Reading: pp. 241-243, 249-250, 251
               M   Screening
               T   Discussion of film screened
               Th Research panel
               F   Conferences on panels and papers

IX.   Asian film, 1951-
      Reading: pp. 270-291
               M   Screening
               T   Discussion of film screened
               Th Research panel
               F   Discussion of course and of film history

TEXT: Ellis, Jack C., A History of Film.
      Englewood Cliffs, N.J. Prentice-Hall,
      1979. 452 pp.

BOOKS ON RESERVE (2 hour plus overnight):

    Anderson, Joseph L., and Donald
       Richie, The Japanese Film:
       Art and Industry (Expanded Edition).
       Princeton, N.J.: Princeton University
       Press, 1982. 500 pp.

    Armes, Roy, A Critical History of British Cinema.
       New York: Oxford University Press, 1978.
       374 pp.

    Balio, Tino, ed., The American Film Industry. Madison:
       University of Wisconsin Press, 1976. 499 pp.

    Bernouw, Erik, and S. Krishnaswamy. Indian Film.
       New York: Oxford University Press, 1980. 327 pp.

    Barr, Charles, Ealing Studios. London: Cameron
       and Tayleur in association with David and Charles, 1977. 198 pp.

    Baxter, John, Sixty Years of Hollywood. Cranbury, N.J.: A.S.
       Barnes, 1973. 284 pp.

    Bondanella, Peter, Italian Cinema: From Neorealism to the Present.
       New York: Frederick Ungar, 1983. 440 pp.

    Kindem, Gorham, ed., The American Movie Industry: The Business of
       Motion Pictures. Carbondale and Edwardsville: Southern
       Illinois University Press, 1982. 448 pp.

Sklar, Robert, Movie-Made America: A Social History of American Movies. New York: Random House, 1975. 340 pp.

Walker, Alexander, The Shattered Silents: How the Talkies Came to Stay. London: Elm Tree Books, 1978.

ASSIGNMENTS:

Research Panel. Each student will give a ten-minute oral presentation based on library research on one of the eight feature films from the second week on. Films are to be selected in the first week.

Written reports. Each student will write three brief (about four pages) research reports based on library research and/or supplemental screening. They are to be about one small topic, or aspect, of three of the seven assigned chapters of the text (pp. 160-291).

Papers are not to be on individual directors or individual films. A limited topic and the consulting of numerous sources, especially primary and contemporary ones, will make for the best papers.

The three papers are to be periods other than the one your research panel film is in. Show the relationship of each paper to the text--you should provide additions or corrections or alternative interpretations to the text.

You must obtain the instructor's approval of the topic for each paper. Papers are due at the end of the week(s) devoted to the national period with which they deal; no papers will be accepted after those dates.

GRADES:

The research panel comprises one-third of the course grade; the written reports two-thirds. Your presence in class and participation in discussion are expected; a minus will be added to your grade for excessive absences, a plus for especially valuable contributions to class discussions.

No incompletes will be given. Missing assignments will receive an F and be averaged into the course grade.

Professor Jack C. Ellis

615 C94-2 THE HISTORY OF FILM: WINTER 1984 SCREENING SCHEDULE

Mondays
10:00 a.m. - 12:00 noon

Annie May Swift
Room 325

January 4
: Shaw Talks for Movietone
U.S., 1927, Fox Movietone News

  The Jazz Singer (excerpts)
  U.S., 1927, Alan Crosland

  The Lights of New York
  U.S., 1928, Brian Foy

  Steamboat Willie
  U.S., 1928, Walt Disney

  The Sex Life of the Polyp
  U.S., 1928, Robert Benchley

January 9
: The Crime of Monsieur Linge
France, 1936, Jean Renoir

January 16
: Swingtime
U.S., 1936, George Stevens

January 23
: In Which We Serve
U.K., 1942, David Lean and Noel Coward

January 30
: A Run for Your Money
U.K., 1949, Charles Frend

February 6
: Paisan
Italy, 1946, Roberto Rosellini

February 13
: Double Indemnity
U.S., 1944, Billy Wilder

February 20
: The Best Years of Our Lives
U.S., 1946, William Wyler

February 27
: Princess Yaug Kwei Fei
Japan, 1955, Kenji Mizoguchi

March 5
: Pather Panchali
India, 1955, Satyajit Ray

VISITORS WELCOME

Professor Jack C. Ellis

615 C12-2 THE HISTORY OF FILM: WINTER 1985

SCREENING SCHEDULE

Mondays
12:00 - 2:00

Annie May Swift
Room 325

January 7
The Jazz Singer (excerpts)
U.S., 1927, Alan Crosland
Shaw Talks to Movietone
U.S., 1927, Fox Movietone News
The Sex Life of the Polyp
U.S., 1928, Robert Benchley
Steamboat Willie
U.S., 1928, Walt Disney
The Lights of New York
U.S., 1928, Brian Foy

January 14
Cesar
France, 1936, Marcel Pagnol

January 21
Top Hat
U.S., 1935, Mark Sandrich

January 28
Target for Tonight
U.K., 1941, Harry Watt
Diary for Timothy
U.K., 1945, Humphrey Jennings

February 4
Tawny Pipit
U.K., 1944, Charles Saunders and Bernard Miles

February 11
The Spiral Staircase
U.S., 1945, Robert Siodmak

February 18
My Son John
U.S., 1952, Leo McCarey

February 25
Shoeshine
Italy, 1946, Vittorio de Sica

March 4
Tokyo Story
Japan, 1953, Yasujiro Ozu

VISITORS WELCOME

Professor Jack C. Ellis

615 C12-3 THE HISTORY OF FILM: COURSE OUTLINE AND ASSIGNMENTS

I. The film of the auteur, 1954 –
Reading: pp. 300-311 (all page numbers refer to text listed below.)

   M Screening
   T Course activities and requirements; goals of course in relation to film history
   W Discussion of film screened
   Th Remaining questions about mechanics of course

II. The French New Wave, 1959 –
Reading: pp. 311-326

   M Screening
   T Discussion of film screened
   W Research panel
   Th Conferences on panels and papers

III. The new Italians, 1960 –
Reading: pp. 327-342

   M Screening
   T Discussion of film screened
   W Research panel
   Th Conferences on panels and papers

IV. Eastern European Cinema, 1954 –
Reading: pp. 343-361

   M Screening
   T Discussion of film screened
   W Research panel
   Th Conferences on panel and papers

V. British film, 1956 –
Reading: pp. 362-381

   M Screening
   T Discussion of film screened
   W Research panel
   Th Conferences on panels and papers

VI. American reevaluation, 1963 –
Reading: pp. 382-394

   M Screening
   T Discussion of film screened
   W Research panel
   Th Conferences on panels and papers

VII. American reemergence, 1963-1977
Reading: pp. 394-405

   M Screening
   T Discussion of film screened
   W Research panel
   Th Conferences on panels and papers

VIII. Third World Cinema, 1959 -
Reading: pp. 406-412

    M Screening
    T Discussion of film screened
    W Research panel
    Th Conferences on panels and papers

X. Here and now: U.S., 1977 -
Reading: pp. 412-420

    M Screening
    T Discussion of film screened
    W Research panel
    Th Discussion of the course and of film history

ASSINGMENTS:

Research panel. Each student will give a ten-minute oral presentation based on library research on one of the nine feature films from the second week on. Films are to be selected in the first week.

Written reports. Each student will write three brief (about four pages) research reports based on library research and/or supplemental screening. They are to be about one small topic, or aspect, of three of the seven assigned chapters of the text (pp. 300-431).

Papers are not to be on individual directors or individual films. A limited topic and the consulting of numerous sources, especially primary and contemporary ones, will make for the best papers.

The three papers are to be on periods other than the one your research panel film is in. Show the relationship of each paper to the text--you should provide additions or corrections or alternative interpretations to the text.

You must obtain the instructor's approval of the topic for each paper. Papers are due at the end of the week devoted to the national period with which they deal; no papers will be accepted after those dates.

GRADES:

The research panel comprises one-third of the course grade; the written reports two-thirds. Your presence in class and participation in discussion are expected; a minus will be added to your grade for excessive absences, plus for especially valuable contributions to class discussions.

No incompletes will be given. Missing assignments will receive an F and be averaged into the course grade.

Professor Jack C. Ellis

615 C12-3   THE HISTORY OF FILM   SPRING 1985   SCREENING SCHEDULE

Mondays (except May 27)   Annie May Swift
10:00 - 12:00   Room 325

Date	Film
March 25	Wild Strawberries Sweden, 1958, Ingmar Bergman
April 1	Hiroshima, mon amour France, 1959, Alain Resnais
April 8	L'Avventura Italy, 1960, Michelangelo Antonioni
April 15	Ashes and Diamonds Poland, 1958, Andrzej Wajda
April 22	O Dreamland U.K., 1954, Lindsay Anderson Saturday Night and Sunday Morning U.K., 1960, Karel Reisz
April 29	Rebel Without a Cause U.S., 1955, Nicholas Ray
May 6	Bonnie and Clyde U.S., 1967, Arthur Penn
May 13	The Marriage of Maria Braun Germany, 1979, Rainer Werner Fassbinder
May 20	Picnic at Hanging Rock Australia, 1975, Peter Weir
May 29	Annie Hall U.S., 1977, Woody Allen

VISITORS WELCOME

Professor Jack C. Ellis

615 C12-3 THE HISTORY OF FILM: SCREENING SCHEDULE
SPRING 1986

Mondays (except May 26)   Annie May Swift
10:00 - 12:00   Room 325

March 24   The Dove (Die Duve)
                 U.S., 1968, George Coe and Anthony Lover

               Persona
                 Sweden, 1966, Ingmar Bergman

March 31   The Mischief Makers
                 France, 1957, Francois Truffaut

               Breathless
                 France, 1960, Jean-Luc Godard

April 7   La Dolce Vita
                 Italy, 1960, Federico Fellini

April 14   Kanal
                 Poland, 1956, Andrezej Wajda

April 21   A Kind of Loving
                 U.K., 1962, John Schlesinger

April 28   China Gate
                 U.S., 1957, Samuel Fuller

May 5   Thieves Like Us
                 U.S., 1974, Robert Altman

May 12   The American Friend
                 West Germany, 1977, Wim Wenders

May 19   The Last Wave
                 Australia, 1977, Peter Weir

May 27   Manhattan
                 U.S., 1980, Woody Allen

VISITORS WELCOME

HISTORY OF CINEMA TO 1940 Eng. 368 M. Fall, 1987. Professor Louis Giannetti

Course has a $15 lab fee to help defray costs of film rentals. Payable at Cashier's Office in Adelbert Main. Return receipt to instructor. Nonpayment of lab fee will result in a grade of I.

COURSE OBJECTIVES: To understand the history of movies from their inception to the advent of World War II, with particular emphasis on the cinemas of the USA, France, Great Britain, Germany, and the USSR. Films will be examined from a variety of perspectives, including author, genre, style, industry, period, and ideology.

COURSE REQUIREMENTS: Responsible attendance, occasional quizzes, midterm, final, term paper (8-10 typed pages). Late papers will be penalized. Excessive absences will result in a lowered grade: 5 unexcused absences lower your grade one full level.

REQUIRED TEXT: Flashback, A Brief History of Film, by Louis Giannetti and Scott Eyman (Prentice-Hall, 1986), in paper. Recommended text: Masters of the American Cinema, by Louis Giannetti (Prentice-Hall, 1981), in paper. This book will also be placed on closed reserve for required readings, including the chapters on D.W. Griffith, Charles Chaplin, Buster Keaton, Ernst Lubitsch, Frank Capra, John Ford, Fritz Lang, and Alfred Hitchcock. These chapters must be read before film is shown.

REQUIRED FILMS: All shown in Hatch Auditorium (Baker Bldg.) on Thursday evenings 7-9 p.m. unless otherwise (*) noted.

*Tues. Aug. 25.	Top Hat (USA, 1935), Mark Sandrich.	CWRU Film Soc.
Thurs. Aug. 27.	The Gold Rush (USA, 1925), Charles Chaplin.	
Thurs. Sept. 3.	The Hunchback of Notre Dame (USA, 1923), Wallace Worsley.	
Thurs. Sept. 10.	The General (USA, 1926), Buster Keaton and Clyde Bruckman.	
*Sun. Sept. 13.	The Philadelphia Story (USA, 1940), George Cukor.	CWRU F.S.
Thurs. Sept. 17.	Hot Water and Safety Last (USA, 1923), Fred Newmeyer/Sam Taylor.	
Thurs. Sept. 24.	Thirty Years of Fun. Compilation film of American silent comedy.	
Thurs. Oct. 1.	The End of St. Petersburg (USSR, 1927), V.I. Pudovkin.	
Thurs. Oct. 8.	The Blue Angel (Germany, 1929), Josef von Sternberg.	
Thurs. Oct. 15.	M (Germany, 1930), Fritz Lang.	
*Sun. Oct. 18.	You Can't Take It With You (USA, 1938), Frank Capra.	CWRU F.S.
Thurs. Oct. 22.	Trouble in Paradise (USA, 1932), Ernst Lubitsch.	
Thurs. Oct. 29.	Of Human Bondage (USA, 1934), John Cromwell.	
*Sun. Nov. 1.	Mr. Smith Goes to Washington (USA, 1939), Frank Capra.	CWRU F.S.
Thurs. Nov. 5.	Camille (USA, 1936), George Cukor.	
Thurs. Nov. 12.	The 39 Steps (Great Britain, 1935), Alfred Hitchcock.	
Thurs. Nov. 19.	Grand Illusion (France, 1937), Jean Renoir.	
Thurs. Dec. 3.	The Grapes of Wrath, (USA, 1940), John Ford.	

CLASSROOM FILMS (Guilford 232   1:30-2:20)

Mon. Aug. 31.	The Great Director (D.W. Griffith).
Wed. Sept. 16.	The Eternal Tramp (Charles Chaplin).
Mon. Sept. 21.	The Cabinet of Dr. Caligari (Germany, 1919), Robert Wiene.
Mon. Sept. 28.	Abel Gance, documentary by Kevin Brownlow.
Wed. Sept. 30.	Potemkin (USSR, 1925), Sergei Eisenstein.
Mon. Oct. 5.	Two Tars (USA, 1928) Laurel & Hardy short.
	It's a Gift (USA, 1934), W.C. Fields excerpt
Wed. Oct. 21.	The Twenties, and the Movies Learn to Talk (two documentaries)
Mon. Oct. 26.	The Art of the Film: The Love Goddess (docu)
Wed. Nov. 4.	The Dentist (USA, 1932) W.C. Fields short
	Horsefeathers (USA, 1932) excerpt from Marx Brothers comedy
Mon. Nov. 9.	The Movies March On (1903-1939). Docu.
	The Barber Shop (USA, 1933), W.C. Fields short
Mon. Nov. 16.	The Music Box (USA, 1932), Laurel & Hardy short.
Mon. Nov. 23.	Life in the 1930s. Docu.
Mon. Nov. 30.	The Golden Age of Hollywood, Part I. Docu.

AMERICAN CINEMA SINCE 1940. English 368 C. Spring, 1987. Prof. Louis Giannetti

Course has a $15 LAB FEE to help defray costs of film rentals. Payable at Cashier's Office in Adelbert Main. Return receipt to instructor. Nonpayment of lab fee will result in a grade of I.

COURSE OBJECTIVES: A)To understand how the 26 films of the course fit into the evolutionary development of the American cinema; B)To allow the student to evaluate any post-war American film and place it in its aesthetic and social context.

COURSE REQUIREMENTS: Responsible attendance, occasional quizzes, midterm, final, term paper (8-10 typed pages--Graduate students 20 pages). Late papers will be penalized. Grade will be lowered one full level for each 6 unexcused absences.

REQUIRED TEXT: Masters of the American Cinema, by Louis Giannetti (Prentice-Hall, 1981), in paper. Recommended text: Flashback: A Brief History of Film, by Louis Giannetti and Scott Eyman. (Prentice-Hall, 1986), paperback.

REQUIRED FILMS. All Monday evening movies* will be shown in Hatch Auditorium in Baker Building. The remainder will be shown by CWRU Film Society in Strosacker.

*Jan. 12.   The Maltese Falcon. 1941. Directed by John Huston.
Jan. 13.   My Fair Lady. 1964. George Cukor.
*Jan. 19.   Casablanca. 1943. Michael Curtiz.
Jan. 24.   Baby It's You. 1983. John Sayles.
*Jan. 26.   Citizen Kane. 1941. Orson Welles.
Jan. 27.   Mean Streets. 1973. Martin Scorsese.
Feb. 1.   Sunday. Downhill Racer. 1969. Michael Ritchie.
*Feb. 2.   Scarlet Street. 1945. Fritz Lang.
*Feb. 9.   Strangers on a Train. 1951. Alfred Hitchcock.
Feb. 10.   David and Lisa. 1963. Frank Perry.
*Feb. 16.   The Member of the Wedding. 1953. Fred Zinnemann.
Feb. 21.   Blue Velvet. 1986. David Lynch.
*Feb. 23.   On the Waterfront. 1954. Elia Kazan.
*Mar. 2.   Singin' in the Rain. 1952. Gene Kelly and Stanley Donen.
*Mar. 16.   Some Like It Hot. 1959. Billy Wilder.
*Mar. 23.   Dr. Strangelove. 1963. Stanley Kubrick.
Mar. 24.   Shadow of a Doubt. 1943. Alfred Hitchcock.
*Mar. 30.   The Graduate. 1967. Mike Nichols.
Apr. 5   Sunday. Raging Bull. 1980. Martin Scorsese.
*Apr. 6.   Straw Dogs. 1971. Sam Peckinpah.
Apr. 7.   The King and I. 1956. Walter Lang.
*Apr. 13.   California Split. 1974. Robert Altman.
Apr. 19.   Sunday. Breaking Away. 1979. Peter Yates.
*Apr. 20.   Play It Again, Sam. 1972. Herbert Ross/Woody Allen.
Apr. 25.   East of Eden. 1955. Elia Kazan.
*Apr. 27.   Rocky. 1976. John Avildsen.

Douglas Gomery
University of Maryland
4817 Drummond Avenue
Chevy Chase, MD 20815

Reading List:

"The History of the American Film Industry"

This reading list is meant to be a selected guide to the growing literature concerned with the history of the American film industry. It is confined to scholarship available in English.

Several anthologies are frequently cited and are thus abbreviated as follows:

AUSTIN = Austin, Bruce A., Current Research in Film, Volume 2 (Norwood, New Jersey: Ablex, 1986). [Note there is a volume 1 and 3 also listed in this series.]

BALIO = Balio, Tino, The American Film Industry: An Anthology of Readings Revised Edition (Madison: University of Wisconsin Press, 1985).

KERR = Kerr, Paul, The Hollywood Film Industry: A Reader (London: Routledge & Kegan Paul, 1986).

KINDEM = Kindem, Gorham A., American Film Industry: A Case Studies Approach (Carbondale: Southern Illinois University Press, 1982).

I. Film Historiography

Allen, Robert C. and Douglas Gomery, Film History: Theory and Practice (New York: Alfred A. Knopf, 1985)

Altman, Charles F., "Toward a Historiography of American Film," *Cinema Journal*, Volume 16, Number 1 (Spring, 1977), pages 1 - 25.

Branigan, Edward, "Color and Cinema: Problems in Writing of History," *Film Reader IV* (1979), pages 16 - 34, reprinted in KERR, pages 120 - 147.

Buscombe, Edward, "Bread and Circuses: Economics and the Cinema," in Patricia Mellencamp and Philip Rosen (eds.), *Cinema Histories, Cinema Practices* (Frederick, Maryland: University Publications of America, 1984), pages 3 - 16.

Buscombe, Edward, "Thinking It Differently: Television and the Film Industry," *Quarterly Review of Film Studies*, Volume 9, Number 3 (Summer, 1984), pages 196 - 203.

Gomery, Douglas, "Movie Audiences, Urban Geography, and the History of the American Film," *The Velvet Light Trap*, Number 19 (Spring, 1982), pages 23 - 29.

Gomery, Douglas, "Film and Business History: The Development of an American Entertainment Industry," *Journal of Contemporary History*, Volume 19, Number 1 (January, 1984), pages 89 - 103.

II. The Early Years: 1895 - 1909

Allen, Robert C.,"Contra the Chaser Theory," *Wide Angle*, Volume 3, Number 1 (Spring, 1979), pages 4 - 11.

Allen, Robert C., "Motion Picture Exhibition in Manhattan: 1906 - 1912," *Cinema Journal*, Volume 18, Number 2 (Spring, 1979), pages 2 - 15, reprinted in KINDEM, pages 12 - 24.

Allen, Robert C., "The Movies in Vaudeville: Historical Context of the Movies as Popular Entertainment," in BALIO, pages 57 - 82.

Allen, Robert C., *Vaudeville and Film: 1985 - 1915 : A Study in Media Interaction* (New York: Arno Press, 1980).

Allen. Robert C.," Vitascope/Cinematographe: Initial Patterns of American Film Industrial Practice," *Journal of the University Film Association*, Volume 31, Number 2 (Spring, 1979), pages 13 - 18, reprinted in KINDEM, pages 3 - 11.

Anderson, Robert, "The Motion Pictures Patents Company: A Reevaluation," in BALIO, pages 133 - 152.

Anderson, Robert, "The Role of the Western Film Genre in Industry Competition, 1907 - 1911," Journal of the University Film Association, Volume 31, Number 2 (Spring, 1979), pages 19-27.

Cassady, Ralph, Jr., "Monopoly in Motion Picture Production and Distribution: 1908 - 1915," Southern California Law Review, Volume 32, Number 4 (Summer, 1959), pages 325 - 390, reprinted in KINDEM, pages 25 - 67.

Hampton, Benjamin B., A History of the Movies (New York: Covici-Friede, 1931).

Hendricks, Gordon, The Edison Motion Picture Myth (Berkeley: University of California Press, 1961).

Jobs, Gertrude, Motion Picture Empire (Hamden, Connecticut: Archon Books, 1966).

Musser, Charles, "American Vitagraph, 1897 - 1901," Cinema Journal, Volume 22, Number 3 (Spring, 1983), pages 4 - 46.

Norden, Martin F., "The Pathé Frères Company During the Trust Era," Journal of the University Film Association, Volume 33, Number 3 (Summer, 1981), pages 15 - 32.

Pryluck, Calvin, "Industrialization of Entertainment in the United States," in AUSTIN, pages 117 -135.

Pryluck, Calvin, "The Itinerant Movie Show and the Development of the Film Industry," Journal of the University Film and Video Association, Volume 35, Number 4 (Fall, 1983), pages 11 - 22.

Ramsaye, Terry A Million and One Nights Two volumes (New York: Simon and Schuster, 1926).

Staiger, Janet, "Combination and Litigation: Structures of U.S. Film Distribution, 1891 - 1917," Cinema Journal, Volume 23, Number 2 (Winter, 1984), pages 41 - 72.

Staiger, Janet, "Seeing Stars," The Velvet Light Trap, Number 20, (Summer, 1983), pages 10 - 14.

III. The Teens

DeBauche, Leslie M., "Advertising and the Movies: 1908-1915," Film Reader VI (1986), pages 115 - 124.

Gunning, Tom, "Weaving a Narrative: Style and Economic Background in Griffith's Biograph Films, " Quarterly Review of Film Studies, Volume 6, Number 1 (Winter, 1981), pages 11 - 26.

Hampton, Benjamin B., A History of the Movies (New York: Covici-Friede, 1931).

Jenkins, Reese V., Images and Enterprise (Baltimore: Johns Hopkins University Press, 1975).

Jobs, Gertrude, Motion Picture Empire (Hamden, Connecticut: Archon Books, 1966).

Lahaue, Kalton C., Dreams for Sales: The Rise and Fall of the Triangle Film Company (New York: A.S. Barnes, 1971).

Merritt, Russell, "Nickelodeon Theatres, 1905 - 1914," in BALIO, pages 83 - 102.

Ramsaye, Terry A Million and One Nights Two volumes (New York: Simon and Schuster, 1926).

Slide, Anthony, The Kindergarten of the Movies: A History of the Fine Arts Company (Metuchen, New Jersey: Scarecrow Press, 1980).

Staiger, Janet, "Blueprints for Feature Films: Hollywood's Continuity Scripts," in BALIO, pages 173 - 194.

Staiger, Janet, "Dividing Labor for Production Control: Thomas Ince and the Rise of the Studio System," Cinema Journal, Volume 18, Number 2 (Spring, 1979), pages 16 - 25, reprinted in KINDEM, pages 94 - 103.

Staiger, Janet, "Mass Produced Photoplays: Economic and Signifying Practices in the First Years of Hollywood," Wide Angle, Volume 4, Number 3 (1980), pages 12 - 24, reprinted in KERR, pages 97 - 119.

Wasko, Janet, "D.W. Griffith and the Banks: A Case Study in Film Financing," Journal of the University Film Association, Volume 30, Number 1 (Winter, 1978), pages 15 - 20, reprinted in KERR, pages 31 - 42.

IV. The 1920s

Balio, Tino, United Artists: The Company Built By the Stars (Madison: University of Wisconsin Press, 1976).

Beardsley, Charles, Hollywood's Master Showman: The Legendary Sid Grauman (New York: Cornwall Books, 1983).

Crowther, Bosley, The Lion's Share: The Story of an Entertainment Empire (New York: E. P. Dutton, 1957).

Gomery, Douglas, "The Growth of Movie Monopolies: The Case of Balaban & Katz," Wide Angle, Volume III, Number 1 (1979), pages 54 - 63.

Gomery, Douglas, "The Movies Become Big Business: Publix Theatres and the Chain Store Strategy," Cinema Journal, Volume XVIII, Number 2 (Spring, 1979), pages 26 - 40, reprinted in KINDEM, pages 104 - 115.

Gomery, Douglas, "The Picture Palace: Economic Sense or Hollywood Nonsense," The Quarterly Review of Film Studies, Volume II, Number 1 (Winter, 1978), pages 23 - 36, reprinted in KERR, pages 204 - 219.

Gomery, Douglas, "U.S. Film Exhibition: The Formulation of a Big Business," in BALIO, pages 218 - 228.

Hall, Ben M., The Best Remaining Seats: The Story of the Golden Age of the Movie Place (New York: Bramhall, 1961).

Hampton, Benjamin B., A History of the Movies (New York: Covici-Friede, 1931).

Jobs, Gertrude, Motion Picture Empire (Hamden, Connecticut: Archon Books, 1966).

Kennedy, Joseph P., The Story of the Films (Chicago: A. W. Shaw, 1927).

Lewis, Howard T., The Motion Picture Industry (New York: Van Nostrand, 1933).

Sobel, Robert, "Marcus Loew: An Artist in Spite of Himself," in Robert Sobel, The Entrepreneurs: Explorations Within the American Business Tradition (New York: Weybright and Talley, 1974), pages 247 - 288.

V. The Coming of Sound

Gomery, Douglas, "The Coming of Sound: Technological Change in the American Film Industry," in BALIO, pages 229 - 251.

Gomery, Douglas, "Failure and Success: Vocafilm and RCA Innovate Sound," Film Reader II (1977), pages 213 - 221.

Gomery, Douglas, "Hollywood Converts to Sound: Chaos or Order?," in Evan William Cameron (ed.), Sound and the Cinema (Pleasantville, New York: Redgrave, 1980), pages 24 - 37.

Gomery, Douglas, "Problems in Film History: How Fox Innovated Sound," in Peter Rollins (ed.), Hollywood as Historian: American Film in a Cultural Context (Lexington: University of Kentucky Press, 1983), pages 20 -31.

Gomery, Douglas, "Warner Bros. Innovates Sound: A Business History," in Gerald Mast, The Movies in Our Midst (Chicago: University of Chicago Press, 1982), pages 267 - 282.

Gomery, Douglas, "The Warner-Vitaphone Peril: The American Film Industry Reacts to the Innovation of Sound," Journal of the University Film Association, Volume 28, Number 1 (Winter, 1976), pages 11 - 19, reprinted in KINDEM, pages 119 - 132.

Gomery, Douglas, "Writing the History of the American Film Industry," Screen, Volume 17, Number 1 (Spring, 1976), pages 40 53, reprinted in Bill Nichols (ed.), Movies and Methods, Volume II (Berkeley: University of California Press, 1985), pages 109- 120.

Greenwald, William I., "The Impact of Sound Upon the Film Industry: A Case Study in Innovation," Explorations in Entrepreneurial History, Volume 4 (May, 1952), pages 178 - 192.

Hampton, Benjamin B., A History of the Movies (New York: Covici-Friede, 1931).

Jobs, Gertrude, Motion Picture Empire (Hamden, Connecticut: Archon Books, 1966).

Wasko, Janet, Movies and Money (Norwood, New Jersey: Ablex, 1982).

VI. Hollywood's Golden Age: 1930 - 1949

Allvine, Glendon, The Greatest Fox of Them All (New York: Lyle Stuart, 1969).

Behlmer, Rudy (ed.) Inside Warner Brothers: 1935 - 1951 (New York: Viking, 1985).

Behlmer, Rudy (ed.) Memo From David O. Selznick (New York: Viking, 1972).

Carey, Gary, All the Stars in Heaven: Louis B. Mayer's MGM (New York: E. P. Dutton, 1981.)

Dawson, Anthony, "Hollywood's Labor Troubles," Industrial and Labor Relations Review, Volume 1, Number 4 (July, 1948), pages 638 - 647.

Dawson, Anthony, "Motion Picture Economics," Hollywood Quarterly, Volume 3, Number 3 (Spring, 1948), pages 217 - 239.

Gomery, Douglas, "Film Culture and Industry: Recent Formulations in Economic History," Iris , Volume II, Number 2 (Spring, 1985), pages 17 - 29.

Gomery, Douglas, The Hollywood Studio System (New York: St. Martins, 1986).

Gomery, Douglas, "Movie-Going During Hollywood's Golden Age," North Dakota Quarterly Volume 51, Number 3 (Summer, 1983), pages 36 - 45.

Gomery, Douglas, "Popularity of Filmgoing in the U.S., 1930 - 1950," in Colin MacCabe (ed.), High Theory/Low Culture: Analysing Popular Film and Television (Manchester: Manchester University Press, 1986), pages 71 - 79.

Gomery, Douglas, "Rethinking American Film History: The Depression Decade and Monopoly Capital," Film and History, Volume X, Number 2 (May, 1980), pages 32 - 38.

Gussow, Mel, Darryl F. Zanuck: Don't Say Yes Until I Finish Talking (New York: Doubleday, 1971).

Handel, Leo, Hollywood Looks at Its Audience (Urbana: University of Illinois Press, 1950).

Harmetz, Aljean, The Making of the Wizard of Oz (New York: Alfred A. Knopf, 1982).

Haralovich, Mary Beth, "Sherlock Holmes: Genre and Industrial Practice," Journal of the University Film Association, Volume 31, Number 2 (Spring, 1979), pages 53 - 57.

Hurst, Richard M., Republic Studios: between Poverty Row and the Majors, (Metuchen, New Jersey: Scarecrow Press, 1979).

Jeter, Ida, "The Collapse of the Federated Motion Picture Crafts: A Case of Class Collaboration," The Journal of the University Film Association, Volume 31, Number 2 (Spring, 1979), pages 37 - 46, reprinted in KERR, pages 78 - 96.

Jewell, Richard B., The RKO Story (New York: Arlington House, 1982).

Jobs, Gertrude, Motion Picture Empire (Hamden, Connecticut: Archon Books, 1966).

Kindem, Gorham, "Hollywood's Movie Star System During the Studio Era," Film Reader VI (1986), pages 13 - 26.

Klapert, Cathy, "The Star as Market Strategy: Bette Davis in Another Light," in BALIO, pages 351 - 376.

"Loew's, Inc.'" in BALIO, pages 334 - 350.

"Metro-Goldwyn-Mayer," in BALIO, pages 311 - 333.

McLaughlin, Robert, Broadway and Hollywood: A History of Economic Interaction (New York: Arno Press, 1974).

Mayer, Arthur, Merely Colossal (New York: Simon and Schuster, 1953).

Onosko, Tim, "Monogram: Its Rise and Fall in the Forties," The Velvet Light Trap, Number 5 (Fall, 1973), pages 2 - 4.

Nielson, Mike, "Towards a Worker's History of the U.S. Film Industry," in Vincent Mosco and Janet Wasko (eds.), The Critical Communications Review: Volume I: Labor, The Working Class, and the Media (Norwood, New Jersey: Ablex, 1983), pages 47 - 84.

Roddick, Nick, A New Deal in Entertainment: Warner Brothers in the 1930s (London: British Film Institute, 1983).

Ross, Murray, Stars and Strikes: Unionization of Hollywood (New York: Columbia University Press, 1941).

Selznick, Irene Mayer, A Private View (New York: Alfred A. Knopf, 1983).

Schary, Dore, Case History of a Movie (New York: Random House, 1950).

Schary, Dore Heyday (Boston: Little Brown, 1979).

Schwartz, Nancy Lynn, The Hollywood Writer's Wars (New York: Alfred A. Knopf, 1982).

Thomas, Bob, King Cohn (New York: G. P. Putnam's, 1967).

Watkins, Gordon S., "The Motion Picture Industry," The Annals of the American Academy of Political and Social Science, Volume 254 (November, 1947).

VII. The Paramount Case

Bertrand, Daniel, Duane Evans, and Blanchard, E.L., "Investigation of Concentration of Economic Power," Study Made for the Temporary National Economic Committee, Monograph 43, The Motion Picture Industry -- A Pattern of Control (Washington, DC: United States GPO, 1941).

Cassady, Ralph Jr, "Impact of the Paramount Decision on Motion Picture Distribution and Price Making," Southern California Law Review, Volume 32, Number 4 (Summer, 1959), pages 325 - 390.

Conant, Michael, Antitrust in the Motion Picture Industry (Berkeley: University of California Press, 1960).

Conant, Michael, "The Paramount Decrees Reconsidered," Law and Contemporary Problems, Volume 44 (Autumn, 1981), pages 79-107, reprinted in BALIO, pages 537 - 573.

Crandall, Robert W., "The Postwar Performance of the Motion Picture Industry," The Antitrust Bulletin, Volume 20, Number 1 (Spring, 1975), pages 49 - 88.

Gomery, Douglas, "Hollywood, the National Recovery Administration, and the Question of Monopoly Power," Journal of the University Film Association, Volume 31, Number 2 (Spring, 1979), pages 47 - 52, reprinted in KINDEM, pages 205 - 213.

Edgerton, Gary and Cathy Pratt, "The Influence of the Paramount Decision on Network Television in America," Quarterly Review of Film Studies, Volume 8, Number 3 (Summer, 1983), pages 9 - 24.

Hellmuth, William F., "The Motion Picture Industry," in Walter Adams (ed.), The Structure of American Industry: Some Case Studies Third Edition (New York: Macmillan, 1961), pages 393-429.

Huettig, Mae, Economic Control of the Motion Picture Industry (Philadelphia: University of Pennsylvania Press, 1944).

Nizer, Louis, <u>New Courts of Industry: Self Regulation Under the Motion Picture Code</u> (New York: Longacre, 1935).

Schwichtenberg, Cathy, "A Case Study of Film Antitrust Legislation: R. D. Goldberg v. Tri-States Theatre Corporation, " in AUSTIN, pages 238 - 248.

Whitney, Simon N., <u>Antitrust Policies</u> (New York: The Twentieth Century Fund, 1958), reprinted in KINDEM, pages 161-204.

VIII. The 1950s and 1960s

Austin, Bruce A., "The Development and Decline of the Drive-In Movie Theatre," in Bruce A. Austin (ed.), <u>Current Research in Film</u>, Volume 1 (Norwood, New Jersey: Ablex Publishing, 1985), pages 59 - 92.

Belton, John, "CinemaScope: The Economics of Technology," <u>The Velvet Light Trap</u>, Number 21 (Summer, 1985), pages 35 - 43.

Doherty, Thomas, "American Teenagers and Teenpics, 1955-1957: A Study of Exploitation Filmmaking," in AUSTIN, pages 47-61.

Dunne, John Gregory, <u>The Studio</u> (New York: Farrar, Straus & Giroux, 1968).

Erffmeyer, Thomas, "20th Century-Fox Introduces CinemaScope: A Study of Technological and Organizational Innovation," <u>Film Reader VI</u> (1986), pages 27 - 32.

Guback, Thomas H., <u>The International Film Industry</u> (Bloomington: Indiana University Press, 1969).

Higham, Charles, <u>Hollywood at Sunset: The Decline and Fall of the Most Colorful Empire Since Rome</u> (New York: Saturday Review Press, 1972).

Hincha, Richard, "Selling CinemaScope: 1953 - 1956," <u>The Velvet Light Trap</u>, Number 21 (Summer, 1985), pages 44 - 53.

Knox, Donald, <u>The Magic Factory: How MGM Made An American in Paris</u> (New York: Praeger, 1973).

Moldea, Dan E., *Dark Victory: Ronald Reagan, MCA, and the Mob* (New York: Viking, 1986).

Ross, Lillian, *Picture* (New York: Rinehart & Company, 1952).

Smith, Richard Austin, *Corporations in Crisis* (New York: Doubleday, 1966).

Staiger, Janet, "Individualism Verses Collectivisim," *Screen*, Volume 24, Numbers 4 - 5 (July - October, 1983), pages 68 - 79.

IX. Hollywood and Television

Boddy, William, "The Studios Move Into Prime Time: Hollywood and the Television Industry in the 1950s," *Cinema Journal*, Volume 24, Number 4 (Summer, 1985), pages 23 - 37.

Gomery, Douglas, "The Coming of Television and the 'Lost' Motion Picture Audience," *Journal of Film and Video*, Volume 37, Number 3 (Summer, 1985), pages 5 - 11.

Gomery, Douglas, "Failed Opportunities: The Integration of the U.S. Motion Picture and Television Industries," *Quarterly Review of Film Studies*, Volume X, Number 2 (Summer, 1984), pages 219 - 228.

Gomery, Douglas, "Television, Hollywood, and the Development of Movies Made-for-Television," in E. Ann Kaplan, *Perspectives on Television* (Frederick, Maryland: University Publications of America, 1983), pages 120 - 129.

Gomery, Douglas, "Television, Hollywood, and the Evolution of the Made-for-Television Motion Picture," in John E. O'Connor (ed.), *American History/American Television* (New York: Frederick Ungar Publishers, 1983), pages 208 - 231, reprinted in Horace Newcomb, *Television: The Critical Edition* Fourth Edition (New York: Oxford University Press, 1987), pages 197 - 220.

Gomery, Douglas, "Theatre Television: The 'Missing Link' of Technical Change in the U.S. Motion Picture Industry," *The Velvet Light Trap*, Number 21 (Summer, 1985), pages 54 - 61.

Gomery, Douglas, "Vertical Integration, Horizontal Regulation -- The Growth of Rupert Murdoch's US Media Empire," *Screen*, Volume 24, Number 3-4 (May - August, 1986), pages 78-87.

Guback, Thomas H. and Dennis J. Dombrowski, "Television and Hollywood: Economic Relations in the 1970s," <u>Journal of Broadcasting</u>, Volume 20, Number 4 (Fall, 1976), pages 511 - 527.

Lardner, James, <u>Fast Forward: Hollywood, the Japanese, and the VCR Wars</u> (New York: W. W. Norton, 1987).

Litman, Barry, "Decision-Making in the Film Industry: The Influence of the TV Market," <u>Journal of Communication</u>, Volume 32, Number 3 (Summer, 1982), pages 33 - 52.

Litman, Barry, "The Economics of the Television Market for Theatrical Movies," <u>Journal of Communication</u>, Volume 29, Number 4 (Autumn, 1979), pages 20 -33, reprinted in KINDEM, pages 308-321.

Thomas, Bob, <u>Walt Disney: An American Original</u> (New York: Simon and Schuster, 1976).

Vianello, Robert, "The Rise of the Telefilm and the Network's Hegemony Over the Motion Picture Industry," <u>Quarterly Review of Film Studies</u>, Volume 9, Number 3 (Summer, 1984), pages 204 - 218.

X. The Contemporary Film Industry: 1970s and 1980s

Austin, Bruce A., "The Film Industry, Its Audience, and New Communications Technologies," in AUSTIN, pages 80 - 116.

Bach, Steven, <u>Final Cut: Dreams and Disaster in the Making of "Heaven's Gate"</u> (New York: William Morrow, 1985).

Daly, David A., <u>A Comparison of Exhibition and Distribution Patterns in Three Recent Feature Motion Pictures</u> (New York: Arno Press, 1980).

Earnest, Olen J., "Star Wars: A Case Study of Motion Picture Marketing," in Bruce A. Austin (ed.), <u>Current Research in Film</u>, Volume 1 (Norwood, New Jersey: Ablex, 1985), pages 1 - 18.

Edgerton, Gary, <u>American Film Exhibition and An Analysis of the Motion Picture Industry's Market Structure, 1963 - 1980</u> (New York: Garland, 1983).

Edgerton, Gary, "The Film Bureau Phenomenon in America: State and Municipal Advocacy of Contemporary Motion Picture and Television Production," in AUSTIN, pages 204 - 224.

Gomery, Douglas, "The American Film Industry of the 1970s: Stasis in the 'New Hollywood,'" Wide Angle, Volume 5, Number 4 (Winter, 1983), pages 52 - 59.

Gomery, Douglas, "Competition and Concentration in the Contemporary Film Industry," in William S. Hendon, Nancy K. Grant, and Douglas V. Shaw (eds.), The Economics of Cultural Industries (Akron, Ohio: Association for Cultural Economics, 1985), pages 135 - 140.

Gomery, Douglas, "Corporate Ownership and Control in the Contemporary US Film Industry," Screen Volume 25, Numbers 4 - 5 (July - October 1984), pages 60 - 69.

Gomery, Douglas, "Economic Structure and Conduct in the US Film Industry of the 1980s," On Film, Number 13 (Fall, 1984), pages 4 - 13.

Gomery, Douglas, "Hollywood's Business," The Wilson Quarterly, Volume X, Number 3 (Summer, 1986), pages 43 - 57.

Guback, Thomas H., "Government Financial Support to the Film Industry in the United States," in Bruce A. Austin (ed.), Current Research in Film, Volume 3 (Norwood, New Jersey: Ablex, 1987), pages 88 - 105.

Guback, Thomas, "Ownership and Control in the Motion Picture Industry," The Journal of Film and Video, Volume 38, Number 1 (Winter, 1986), pages 7 - 20.

Guback, Thomas H.,"The Theatrical Film," in Benjamin M. Compaign (ed.), Who Owns the Media? Second Edition (White Plains: Knowledge Industry Publications, 1982), pages 199 - 298.

Harmetz, Aljean, Rolling Breaks and Other Movie Business (New York: Alfred A. Knopf, 1983).

Lazarus, Paul N. III, The Movie Producer (New York: Barnes & Noble, 1985).

Lees, David and Stan Berkowitz, The Movie Business (New York: Vintage, 1981).

Litwak, Mark, Reel Power: The Struggle for Influence and Success in the New Hollywood (New York: William Morrow, 1986).

McClintick, David, Indecent Exposure: A True Story of Hollywood and Wall Street (New York: William Morrow, 1982).

Mayer, Michael, The Film Industries, Second Edition (New York: Hastings House, 1978).

Mathews, Jack, The Battle of Brazil (New York: Crown, 1987).

Obst, Lynda, "The Ontology of the Pitch," The Best of California (Santa Barbara: Capra Press, 1986), pages 105 - 113.

Phillips, Joseph D., "Film Conglomerate Blockbusters: International Appeal and Product Homogenization," Journal of Communication, Volume 25 (Spring, 1975), pages 171 - 181, reprinted in KINDEM, pages 325 - 335.

Simonet, Thomas, "Conglomerates and Content: Remakes, Sequels, and Series in the New Hollywood," in Bruce A. Austin (ed.), Current Research in Film, Volume 3 (Norwood, New Jersey: Ablex, 1987), pagers 154 - 162.

Squire, Jason (ed.), The Movie Business Book (Englewood Cliffs, New Jersey: Prentice Hall, 1983).

Sutak, Ken, The Great Motion Picture Soundtrack Robbery: An Analysis of Copyright Protection, (Hamden, Connecticut: Archon, 1976).

Taylor, John, Storming the Magic Kingdom (New York: Alfred A. Knopf, 1987).

Vogel, Harold L., Entertainment Industry Economics, (New York: Cambridge University Press, 1986).

Wasko, Janet, Movies and Money (Norwood, New Jersey: Ablex, 1982).

Teaching Documentary Film at the Undergraduate Level

by Barry Keith Grant

Teaching the documentary film, whether as a unit in a film course or as the subject of the entire course, presents some unique pedagogical problems. These difficulties are a result of both student preconceptions and the inherent complexity of the documentary form itself. In this essay, I want to explore briefly the nature of these problems, and to suggest some strategies for successfully dealing with them.

The most immediate difficulty is one of definition. While there is relative agreement, for example, about what a Howard Hawks film is, or a "Howard Hawks" film, or even a Western, critics are still stumbling over definitions of documentary. As Bill Nichols has pointed out, the standard definitions that we have are woefully inadequate. As he summarizes them: "Truth as reified possession, reality as something that can be mechanically reproduced upon a screen, and a noncommercial purpose: one lame stab at intentions and two gross epistemological naiveties scarcely constitute an adequate model."[1] To demonstrate the extent of the problem, Nichols refers to Richard Meran Barsam's Nonfiction Film: A Critical History, one of the very few books that aspires to present a comprehensive history of the documentary, but which nonetheless gets tangled in its opening chapter on definitions by reiterating previous questionable ones and compounding the problem by even specifying running times as well.[2] A more flexible definition is clearly needed, but descriptions such as John Grierson's famous "the creative treatment of actuality" are so vague as to be practically useless. Given the generality of this kind of statement, Andrew Sarris once puckishly suggested that all films are to some degree documentary since they necessarily document the filmmaker's perceptions or the cultural zeitgeist. The term is indeed problematic, yet it has remained the most commonly used. Grierson himself said that "Documentary is a clumsy description, but let it stand."[3]

In this essay, my approach is to include as documentary any film that derives its visual and/or aural material from actual events or situations. Such a definition allows for the inclusion of films that manipulate actual events to a significant degree (eg., the reverse motion of Standish Lawder's Necrology) or that reconstruct historical events (eg., Peter Watkins' Colloden). This definition inevitably raises problems of its own. But it has the necessary flexibility to prevent the prescriptive exclusion of films that do partake of the documentary impulse, however remotely. Thus, one of the difficulties that this definition raises is the very multiplicity that it permits.

This problem becomes apparent when considered in the context of the undergraduate film course. Undergraduate courses tend to be organized within a clearly defined category: the historically significant and/or representative (the typical introductory overview), genre (for example, the Western), auteur (the films of Alfred Hitchcock), or nationalist (the New German cinema). More advanced undergraduate courses are sometimes structured by theoretical issues or methodological approaches, such as "Film Theory," "Film and Philosophy," or Authorship in the Cinema" (a somewhat different focus than the applied auteurist criticism of a course like the one on Hitchcock's films). Documentary film, however, is an area of film study of such sweep that it may be seen to overlap all the others. Any study of the documentary that aims to be comprehensive must cut across nationalist boundaries, as well as span the entire history of film, from its beginning, the first public screening of the Lumiere actualites in 1895, right up to the present. There is an impressive variety of documentary styles (cinema verite, the compilation film) and genres (the city symphony, the "rockumentary"). And the history of documentary includes the work of many auteurs (Frederick Wiseman, Michael Rubbo), some of whom, like Robert Flaherty, have attained "pantheon" status for Sarris and other director-oriented critics. In short, then, it could be claimed that unlike most other film courses, a course in the documentary must proceed with an absence of clear paradigms.

As well, undergraduate students commonly enter a course on documentary with decided, even if unacknowledged, preconceptions or expectations about films labelled documentary. Much of this will depend, of course, upon both the individual student's critical sophistication and his or her previous coursework. Students in such a course typically will have been exposed to documentary only in a first-year introductory film course; but for many this brief encounter is insufficient to make them fully aware that documentaries, like fiction films, are constructions and not windows on an unmediated world. Or, some students may obstinately cling to the naive moral position that documentaries must be understood and assessed according to the degree of fidelity to the pro-filmic event. Then, too, they are likely to be less familiar with the films screened in a documentary course than in any fiction film course, since there are so few screening venues for documentaries. And finally, because documentary courses are often cross-listed with other disciplines, like Sociology or History, there is the additional problem of teaching the material to students with widely divergent experience and ability in film theory and analysis.

Thus, a variety of obstacles immediately present themselves when documentary film is taught at the undergraduate level. However, this is not necessarily an insurmountable disadvantage, nor even a disadvantage at all, for real learning can occur when students are particularly challenged. It is possible to contextualize a course on documentary by initially presenting the variety of definitions that have been offered, systematically suggesting the different limitations of each through screenings and discussion, and then starting from zero with the class. Such a procedure in fact may become the organizing focus of the course, and as a group, the students can be encouraged to articulate basic principles of documentary style(s) as the course progresses. Since no single definition of documentary is really adequate to account for the variety of film practices conventionally placed within that label, it is logical, therefore, to incorporate screenings in the course of all possible approaches to the form. Such heterogeneity may stretch to the breaking point inadequate concepts of documentary and stimulate further reflection on the part of the students. Thus the sample syllabus presented below is deliberately wide-ranging, seeking to encompass all the significant developments in the history of documentary film.

Sample Syllabus

First, some explanatory remarks. It should be noted that the organization of material suggested here is clearly not the only one possible. One previously published model syllabus, for example, arranged documentary history into different units than those offered below, beginning with Flaherty and the American Romantic Tradition, then moving on to the Kino-Eye in Revolutionary Russia in the Thirties, and ending with Propaganda and War Films.[4] Another, taught by documentary filmmaker James Blue at SUNY/Buffalo in the early 'Seventies, began with Pare Lorentz in the Thirties, then continued with Joris Ivens and Helen von Dongen, American and British documentaries during the war years, British Free Cinema, Canadian cinema verite', American direct cinema, the films of Frederick Wiseman, ethnographic cinema, and concluded with contemporary politically engaged documentary.

Secondly, since the syllabus below was taught at a Canadian university, it follows the norm for undergraduate courses in the Canadian post-secondary system in that it is two semesters in length. Both of the other courses mentioned above were one semester affairs, and so neither pretended to offer a complete overview of the history of documentary. Hence the first course concentrates on the earlier history, the second on the more recent.

Obviously, the syllabus below is not subject to this constraint to the same degree; however, there are omissions, nonetheless. Glaringly absent, for example, are films on gay or feminist issues and films on Central America--subjects which have been emphasized in the documentaries of recent years. Such choices, though, do not reflect my personal political views, but my judgment concerning their relative unimportance in terms of stylistic or structural innovation as opposed to new subject matter.[5] No syllabus is likely to be comprehensive and satisfy everyone's critical and political priorities. Substitutions can of course be made. And while many will not have the luxury of teaching the documentary with the kind of depth a two-semester system allows, the model syllabus can be approached as a basic structure that may be abridged, condensed or otherwise altered as deemed necessary.

Term 1

The Documentary Impulse

week 1   The photographic image and reality
week 2   Lumiere and Melies films
week 3   NANOOK OF THE NORTH (Robert Flaherty, 1922)
           MAN OF ARAN (Flaherty, 1934)

The Documentary and Political Engagement

week 4   THE MAN WITH THE MOVIE CAMERA (Dziga Vertov, 1929)
           BATTLESHIP POTEMKIN (Sergei Eisenstein, 1925)
week 5   DRIFTERS (John Grierson, 1929)

INDUSTRIAL BRITAIN (Flaherty/Grierson, 1932)

HOUSING PROBLEMS (Edgar Anstey/Arthur Elton, 1935)

NIGHT MAIL (Basil Wright/Harry Watt, 1936)

week 6   TRIUMPH OF THE WILL (Leni Riefenstahl, 1936)

week 7   THE PLOW THAT BROKE THE PLAINS (Pare Lorentz, 1936)

THE RIVER (Lorentz, 1937)

THE SPANISH EARTH (Joris Ivens, 1937)

week 8   PRELUDE TO WAR (WHY WE FIGHT series) (Frank Capra, 1942)

THE BATTLE OF SAN PIETRO (John Huston, 1945)

A DIARY FOR TIMOTHY (Humphrey Jennings, 1945)

The Documentary as Poetry: The "City Symphony"

week 9   BERLIN: THE SYMPHONY OF A CITY (Walter Ruttmann, 1927)

THE BRIDGE (Ivens, 1928)

A PROPOS DE NICE (Jean Vigo, 1930)

THE CITY (Willard Van Dyke/Ralph Steiner, 1939)

Free Cinema, Direct Cinema, Cinema Verite

week 10   O DREAMLAND (Lindsay Anderson, 1953)

NICE TIME (Claude Goretta/Alain Tanner, 1957)

WE ARE THE LAMBETH BOYS (Karel Reisz, 1959)

week 11   PAUL TOMKAWICZ: STREET RAILWAY SWITCHMAN (Roman Kroiter, 1954)

LES RAQUETTEURS (Gilles Groulx/Michel Brault, 1958)

BACK BREAKING LEAF (Terence McCartney-Filgate, 1959)

LONELY BOY (Kroiter/Wolf Koenig, 1961)

week 12   PRIMARY (Drew Associates, 1960)

HAPPY MOTHER'S DAY (Richard Leacock, 1964)

CHRONICLE OF A SUMMER (Jean Rouch/Edgar Morin, 1961)

A MARRIED COUPLE (Alan King, 1969)

Term II

week 1   SALESMAN (Maysles Brother, 1969)

week 2   GIMME SHELTER (Maysles Brothers, 1970)

Ethnographic Cinema

week 3   LAND WITHOUT BREAD (Luis Bunuel, 1932)

           DEAD BIRDS (Robert Gardner, 1963)

Documentary Auteurs

week 4   SAD SONG OF YELLOW SKIN (Michael Rubbo, 1970)

           WAITING FOR FIDEL (Rubbo, 1974)

           SOLZHENITSEN'S CHILDREN (Rubbo, 1978)

week 5   HIGH SCHOOL (Frederick Wiseman, 1968)

week 6   PRIMATE (Wiseman, 1974)

week 7   MEAT (Wiseman, 1974)

week 8   MODEL (Wiseman, 1982)

Experimental Documentary

week 9   VERY NICE, VERY NICE (Arthur Lipsett, 1961)

           FREE FALL (Lipsett, 1965)

           A TRIP DOWN MEMORY LANE (Lipsett, 1965)

           WINDOW WATER BABY MOVING (Stan Brakhage, 1959)

           THE ACT OF SEEING WITH ONE'S OWN EYES (Brakhage, 1971)

           REPORT (Bruce Conner, 1967)

           DANGLING PARTICIPLE (Standish Lawder, 1970)

           NECROLOGY (Lawder, 1970)

week 10   COLLODEN (Peter Watkins, 1964)

           THE WAR GAME (Watkins, 1966)

Docudrama

week 11   IN THE KING OF PRUSSIA (Emile de Antonio, 1982)

week 12   THE DAY AFTER (Nicholas Meyer, 1984)
New Personal Documentary
week 13   SHERMAN'S MARCH (Ross McElwee, 1986)

The course begins by addressing "the documentary impulse," the ability of the camera to capture (or, as Siegfried Kracauer puts it, to redeem) physical reality. Such issues as realism in the cinema, the ontological nature of the photographic image, and the nature of visual metaphor (in the case of cinema verite and direct cinema, "found" metaphor) are introduced here--topics that will likely remain central as the course progresses. Beginning with still photography is a good idea, since these issues can be broached free of the complications of motion and duration. Work by such photographers as Matthew Brady, Edward Muybridge, Walker Evans, and Diane Arbus seem to work well in this context. The Lumiere films are then considered as the beginnings of documentary film and, in contrast to the work of George Melies, are viewed in terms of the conventional distinction between realism and expressionism in the cinema. Next, two films by Robert Flaherty are screened. The first, Nanook of the North, serves an historical function (the first feature-length documentary) and, in conjunction with the second, Man of Aran, raises issues of pro-filmic manipulation (the shark hunting sequence, for example). The Flaherty films also set the groundwork for the later, more intensive consideration of auteurism, as well as raise issues of documentary method (Flaherty's immersion in the cultures he filmed), which will become important to the later discussions of ethnographic cinema.

Finally, Flaherty's notion of the ability of documentary to get at a deeper, perhaps more spiritual truth beneath the surface physical reality is a good introduction to the philosophical implications of the documentary and its relation to truth and the real.

The second section, "Documentary, Society and Politics," covers those films from the silent period through World War II and includes a variety of films made in different countries with diverse political ideologies. Included here are Dziga Vertov's Soviet The Man With a Movie Camera, the work of John Grierson's film unit sponsored by the British government, Leni Riefenstahl's celebration of German National Socialism, Triumph of the Will, Pare Lorentz's agrarian New Deal Films, Joris Ivens' film on the Spanish Civil War, and World War II films by Hollywood directors working for the American armed forces. Although different in style and ideology, these films together demonstrate the propaganda value of the documentary and how it has been exploited by various governments. Of particular interest in this context is the adroit use of footage from Riefenstahl's fascist spectacle in Capra's jingoistic Prelude to War, for the latter virtually reverses the meanings of these images as offered in the former. Vertov's film also raises the issue of self-reflexivity in the documentary, a concern that is central to the documentary work of such later filmmakers as Michael Rubbo, Stan Brakhage and Ross McElwee.

The "Documentary as Poetry" section marks a radical shift in approach. Focusing on the "city symphony" form, examples from different countries demonstrate the possibilities of the plastic

manipulation of pro-filmic subjects in the cinema. The old
Griersonian debate about poetry versus propaganda, introduced
in the discussion of Flaherty's work, is considered here in greater
depth.

The next unit is the largest, for it includes the British
Free Cinema movement, cinema verite, and direct cinema. The
relation between documentary form and technology is examined,
since these kinds of films became possible only with the introduction of new, lightweight portable cameras, tape recorders and
sync units in the late Fifties. The Heisenbergian principle of
the altering of the pro-filmic event by the very presence of the
camera also becomes central to the analysis of these films. This
concern easily carries over into the brief unit on ethnographic
cinema. Bunuel's Land Without Bread and Robert Gardner's Dead
Birds both present views of remote cultures and employ voice-over
narration, but the two films are widely different in tone and
meaning.

The section on "Documentary Auteurs" introduces the concept
of authorship and a sustained personal vision over a number of
films in the documentary. This approach will have been applied
to some extent in the earlier discussions of, for example, Flaherty,
Lorentz, Huston, and Capra. Here, though, authorship is considered
more deeply in three films by Michael Rubbo and four by Frederick
Wiseman. Rubbo unabashedly places himself at the center of the
pro-filmic events he documents, while Wiseman in this sense is
completely absent from his films (in Bill Nichols' terms, their
work employs the modes of direct and indirect address, respectively):[6]

but both have distinct styles and, to use the hoary phrase of classic auteurism, they "stamp their personalities" on their work.

The grouping of experimental films contains a variety of short works by filmmakers usually considered as working within the experimental rather than documentary tradition. But in different ways all of these films make use of documentary material, from the found footage constructions of Arthur Lipset and Bruce Connor to Stan Lawder's humourous meditations to Brakhage's personal essays on seeing. Peter Watkins applies direct cinema techniques to the distant past and the hypothetical future with considerable skill and to powerful effect in Colloden and The War Game, respectively.

Watkins' work also provides a convenient transition to docudrama, that hybrid form that has been so popular in recent years, particularly on television. Nichols Meyer's The Day After, when originally telecast, was one of the most popular instances of the genre, and it also serves as a useful contrast to The War Game, in that both deal with nuclear attack. Meyer's film, by focusing on a few specific individuals, reveals the melodramatic influence on the docudrama form.

The course finishes with an examination of Ross McElwee's Sherman's March, a film that addresses a number of issues, including nuclear attack, but is primarily a documentary of the filmmaker's own life. This film provides an apt conclusion to the course, as it returns the class to the issues of subjectivity and spiritual truth with which it began.

Texts

Choosing the best text(s) is frequently a problem in film courses, since material on the cinema tends to go out of print rather quickly or, surprisingly often, is simply non-existent. The documentary is no exception. There are, for example, few books which attempt anything like a comprehensive history of the documentary and, to my knowledge, two of the three are out of print.[7] Most of the few books on the documentary, if they are indeed available cover only a particular period or aspect of the form: Thomas Waugh's anthology, "Show Us Life": Toward a History and Aesthetics of the Committed Documentary and William Alexander's Film on the Left: American Documentary Film from 1931 to 1942 are two examples. These books are certainly valuable as resource material, but their focus is too narrow for them to serve as basic texts for a documentary course.

The one history that is still in print and which has proven useful in the classroom is Erik Barnouw's Documentary: A History of the Non-Fiction Film (New York: Oxford, 1974). This book covers the history of the documentary until the mid-Seventies, including the Vietnam period. Given its publication date, it is now somewhat dated, but it would not be very difficult to identify a few additional readings on more recent developments in documentary filmmaking. Barnouw organizes his discussions of the documentary by descriptive categories (prophet, explorer, reporter, painter, and so on, through observer, catalyst, and guerilla) that are particularly helpful for students wading through the many names of films and filmmakers, since these categories provide them with a conceptual organization of the history. Moreover, the book's structure dovetails nicely with the syllabus above.

Lewis Jacobs' anthology, The Documentary Tradition (second edition, New York: Norton, 1979), reinforces Barnouw's history by providing a well-chosen selection of contemporary reviews of most of the films listed in the syllabus. While Jacobs' selections for the most part do not offer great critical insight, they do allow students to understand how thinking about the documentary film (many of the pieces in the book are written by the filmmakers themselves) evolved along with the history. Neither book may be wholly satisfactory, but until the ideal text appears, these two are highly recommended because they work extremely well together. Of course, these primary texts can be supplemented with some further readings that discuss trends in documentary and/or provide detailed analyses of specific films or issues that unite a group of films in the syllabus.

Conclusion

The study of the documentary film requires the consideration of certain aesthetic and theoretical issues and concepts. Theories of realism and the cinema, for example, are central to any serious understanding of the documentary. The functions of metaphor, the soundtrack (especially voice-over narration) and the institution of the cinema (for example, the marginalization of the documentary in the structures of exhibition) all need to be examined. Inevitably, the nature of propaganda is significant for class discussion of films like *Triumph of the Will* and *Prelude to War*, but might very well arise at any point in the course, from Flaherty to Wiseman. Thus an analysis of cultural theories of ideology is also necessary.

But here, as in most other film courses (with the exception of those advanced courses that are primarily theoretical in orientation), class discussion and analysis should return to the primary texts themselves. Students must examine closely the films' approach to their material--in this case, the organization and treatment of the pro-filmic events which constitute their subjects. The use of iconography and camera movement in *Triumph of the Will*; formal composition in the city symphony films; the relation of sound to image in *Dead Birds* or *Dangling Participle*; editing in Wiseman's films; devices of classical cinema in the work of Flaherty; and so on: the formal strategies of documentary films are as complex as those of fiction films. This is to say, finally, that there is little difference between the aims and procedures of a course on documentary and other film courses. To perceive the ways in which the cinema constructs meaning from the world it photographs, and the position of the spectator in relation to it, is, after all, what film study is all about.

NOTES

[1] Bill Nichols, Ideology and the Image (Bloomington: Indiana University Press, 1981), p. 173.

[2] Richard Meran Barsam, Nonfiction Film: A Critical History (New York: Dutton, 1973), p. 4.

[3] John Grierson, "First Principles of Documentary," in Richard Meran Barsam, ed., Nonfiction film: Theory and Criticism (New York: Dutton, 1976), p. 19.

[4] Dennis Bohnenkamp, "Course File," American Film Institute Education Newsletter, Vol. 2, No. 5 (May/June 1979), unpaginated.

[5] I find the arguments for a distinctly feminist aesthetic of documentary to be unconvincing. See, for example, Julia Lesage, "Feminist Documentary: Aesthetics and Politics," in "Show Us Life": Toward a History and Aesthetics of the Committed Documentary, ed., Thomas Waugh (Metuchen, N.J.: Scarecrow Press, 1984), p.223-251.

[6] Nichols, op. cit., Chap. 6.

[7] The two out of print books are Barsam, op. cit., and Paul Rotha, Documentary Film (New York: Hastings, 1952).

Course Outline: FILM/COMM/SOCI: 254: The Documentary Film   1986/87

Instructor: Barry Grant

Seminars, lectures: Tuesday, 12:30 - 1:30
                    Thursday, 12:30 - 2:30

Labs: Tuesdays, 7:30 - 9:30 All Screenings are in The Studio and begin at 7:30 a.m. sharp (except where noted*)

TERM I

The documentary impulse
    Sept 9   The photographic image and reality
         16   Lumiere and Melies programs (*Note: screening begins at 5:00 p.m.)
         23   NANOOK OF THE NORTH (Robert Flaherty, 1922)
              MAN OF ARAN (Flaherty, 1934)

The documentary, society and politics
    Sept 30   THE MAN WITH A MOVIE CAMERA (Dziga Vertov, 1929)
              KINO PRAVDA (Vertov)

    Oct 7   BATTLESHIP POTEMKIN (Sergei Eisenstein, 1925)* 5:00 p.m.
              DRIFTERS (John Grierson, 1929)* 7:00 p.m.
              NIGHTMAIL (Basil Wright/Harry Watt, 1936)
              HOUSING PROBLEMS (Edgar Anstey and Arthur Elton, 1935)
              INDUSTRIAL BRITAIN (Flaherty/Grierson, 1932)
         14   TRIUMPH OF THE WILL (Leni Riefenstahl, 1936)* 7:00 p.m.
              OLYMPIA (Riefenstahl, 1938) (diving and marathon sequences)
         21   THE PLOW THAT BROKE THE PLAINS (Pare Lorentz, 1936)
              THE RIVER (Lorentz, 1937)
              SPANISH EARTH (Joris Ivens, 1937)
         28   WHY WE FIGHT (Prelude to War) (Frank Capra, 1942-1945)
              THE BATTLE OF SAN PIETRO (John Huston, 1945)
              LET THERE BE LIGHT (Huston, 1946)

Documentary as poetry: the "city symphony"
    Nov 4   BERLIN: THE SYMPHONY OF A CITY (Walter Ruttmann, 1927)
              THE BRIDGE (Ivens, 1928)
              A PROPOS DE NICE (Jean Vigo, 1930)
              THE CITY (Willard VanDyke/Ralph Steiner, 1939)

Free cinema, direct cinema, cinema verite
    Nov 11   A DIARY FOR TIMOTHY (Humphrey Jennings, 1945)
              NICE TIME (Claude Goretta/Alain Tanner, 1957)
              WE ARE THE LAMBETH BOYS (Karel Reisz, 1959)
    Nov 18   PAUL TOMKAWICZ: STREET RAILWAY SWITCHMAN (Kroiter, 1954)
              LES RAQUETTEURS (Gilles Groulx/Michel Brault, 1958)
              BACK BREAKING LEAF (Terence McCartney - Filgate, 1959)
              LONELY BOY (Kroiter/Wolf Koenig, 1961)
    Nov 25   PRIMARY (Drew Associates, 1960)
              HAPPY MOTHER'S DAY (D.A. Pennebaker, 1963)
              DAY AFTER DAY (Clemont Perron, 1962)
    Dec 2   A MARRIED COUPLE (Alan King, 1969)

TERM II

Cinema verite (continued)
    Jan 6   SALESMAN (Maysles Brothers, 1969)
        13   GIMME SHELTER (Maysles Brothers, 1970)

Ethnographic cinema
    Jan 20   LAND WITHOUT BREAD (Luis Bunuel, 1932)
             DEAD BIRDS (Robert Gardner, 1963)

Documentary Auteurs
    Jan 27   SAD SONGS OF YELLOW SKIN (Michael Rubbo, 1970)
             WAITING FOR FIDEL (Michael Rubbo, 1974)
             SOLZHENITSEN'S CHILDREN (Rubbo, 1978)
    Feb 3   HIGH SCHOOL (Frederick Wiseman, 1968)
        10   PRIMATE (Wiseman, 1974)
        17   MEAT (Wiseman, 1975)
    Mar 3   MODEL (Wiseman, 1982)

Experimental documentary
    Mar 10   COLLOCEN (Peter Watkins, 1964)
             THE WAR GAME (Watkins, 1966)
        17   VERY NICE, VERY NICE (Arthur Lipsett, 1961)
             FREE FALL (Lipsett, 1964)
             TRIP DOWN MEMORY LANE (Lipsett, 1965)
             WINDOW WATER BABY MOVING (Stan Brakhage, 1959)
             THE ACT OF SEEING WITH ONE'S OWN EYES (Brakhage, 1971)
             REPORT (Bruce Conner, 1967)
             DANGLING PARTICIPLE (Standish Lawder, 1970)
             NECROLOGY (Lawder, 1970)

Docudrama and television
    Mar 24
    Mar 31   Threads
    Apr 7   tba

Required texts:

1. Barnouw, Eric   Documentary: A History of the Non-Fiction Film (New York: Oxford, 1974)

2. Jacobs, Lewis   The Documentary Tradition, 2nd ed. (New York: Norton, 1979)

Reserve material:

	Grierson on Documentary
Beveridge, James	John Grierson, Film Master
Evans, Gary	John Grierson and the National Film Board
Sussex, Elizabeth	Rise and Fall of British Documentary
Jacobs, Lewis	The Documentary Tradition
Rosenthal, Alan	The New Documentary in Action
Rotha, Paul	Documentary Film
Levin, G. Roy	Documentary Exploration: 15 Interviews With Filmmakers
Stott, William	Documentary Expression and Thirties America

READINGS:

Nov. 4 Documentary Tradition:
Chapman, "Two Aspects of the City"
Kracauer, "Cross-Section Films"
Ivens, "The Making of Rain"
Kaufman, "Jean Vigo's A Propos de Nice"
Winsten, "The City goes to the Fair"
Meyers & Leyda, "Joris Ivens: Artist in Documentary"
Documentary:
Barnouw, "Painter"

Nov. 11 Documentary Tradition:
Anderson, "Some Aspects of the Work of Humphrey Jennings"
Barry, "A Diary for Timothy"
Clurman, "Flaherty's Louisiana Story"
Miller, "Progress in Documentary"
Tyler, "Documentary Technique in Film Fiction"
Jacobs, "New Trends in British Documentary: Free Cinema"
Documentary:
Barnouw, pp. 139-148; 185-198

Nov. 18 Documentary Tradition:
Rosenblum, "The Quiet One: A Milestone"
Jacobs, "The Turn Toward Conservatism"
Benjamin, "The Documentary Heritage"
Sufrin, "Filming Skid Row"
Lee, "Canada Carries On"

Nov. 25 Documentary Tradition:
Jacobs, "Documentary Becomes Engaged and Verite"
Schlesinger, "The Fiction of Fact -- The Fact of Fiction"
Swallow, "The Current Affairs Documentary"
Hazam, "Documentary and Dollars"
Blue, "One Man's Truth"
Freyer, "Chronicle of a Summer"
Documentary:
Barnouw, "Promoter," pp. 231-245

Dec. 2 Documentary Tradition:
Kauffmann, "Alan King's Warrendale"
Blumer, "King's A Married Couple"
Haskell, "Three Documentaries"
Rosenthal, New Documentary in Action, Chap. 1 (RESERVE)

Jan. 6 Documentary Tradition:
Reynolds, "Focus on Al Maysles"
Simon, "A Variety of Hells"
Rosenthal, New Documentary in Action, Chap. 3 (RESERVE)
Levin, Documentary Explorations, interview w/ Maysles (RESERVE)

READINGS:
(Note that readings should be completed by the date indicated)

Sept. 16 Jacobs, "Precursors and Prototypes", Documentary Tradition
          Barnouw, Documentary, Part 1

Sept. 23 Documentary Tradition:
          Jacobs, "The Feel of a New Genre"
          Sherwood, "Robert Flaherty's Nanook of the North"
          Canudo, "Another View of Nanook"
          Grierson, "Flaherty's Poetic Moana"
          Flaherty, "Filming Real People"

          Documentary:
          Barnouw, "Explorer"

Sept. 30 Documentary Tradition:
          "Symposium on Soviet Documentary"
          Blakeston, "Two Vertov Films"
          Vaughan, "The Man With the Movie Camera"
          Documentary:
          Barnouw, "Reporter"

Oct. 7   Documentary Tradition:
          Potamkin, "Grierson's Drifters"
          Hurwitz, "The Revolutionary Film -- Next Step"
          Gerstein, "English Documentary Films"
          Documentary:
          Barnouw, pp. 85-100

Oct. 14   Documentary Tradition:
          Jacobs, "From Innovation to Involvement"
          Tyler, "Leni Riefenstahl's Olympia"
          Everson, "The Triumph of the Will"
          Documentary:
          Barnouw, pp. 100-111

Oct. 21   Documentary Tradition:
          Seldes, "Pare Lorentz's The River"
          Winge, "Some New American Documentaries"
          Belitt, "The Camera Reconnoiters"
          Wright, "Land Without Bread and Spanish Earth"
          Documentary:
          Barnouw, pp. 111-139

Oct. 28   Documentary Tradition:
          Elson, "DeRochemont's The March of Time"
          Bryan, "War is, Was, and Always Will be Hell"
          Jacobs, "The Military Experience and After"
          Lorentz, "The Ramparts We Watch"
          Hardy, "British Documentaries in the War"
          MacCann, "World War II: Armed Forces Documentary
          Documentary:
          Barnouw, pp. 155-164

READINGS:

Jan. 13 Documentary Tradition:
         MacDonald, "Woodstock: One for the Money"
         Barron, "Toward New Goals in Documentary"

Jan. 20 Documentary Tradition:
         Gardner, "A Chronicle of the Human Experience"
         Barnouw, "Chronicler" and "Catalyst", Documentary

Jan. 27 Jacobs, "From Political Activism to Women's Consciousness"
         DT Handleman, "The Selling of the Pentagon"

Feb. 3   Rosenthal, New Documentary in Action, Chap. 2 (RESERVE)

Feb. 10 Documentary Tradition:
         Schickel, "Sorriest Spectacle: Titticut Follies"
         Denby, "Documenting America"
         Atkins, "Frederick Wiseman's America"
         Barnouw, Documentary, pp. 244-248
         Levin, Documentary Explorations, interview W. Wiseman (RESERVE)

     17 Documentary Tradition:
         Arnold, "The Present State of the Documentary"

Mar. 10 Documentary Tradition:
         Biskind, "Hearts and Minds"
         Barnouw, "Guerilla", Documentary
         Rosenthal, New Documentary in Action, Chap. 8 (RESERVE)

Mar. 24 Documentary Tradition:
         McCormick, "Women's Liberation Cinema"

Mar. 31 Documentary Tradition:
         Davidson, "TV's Historical Dramas: Fact or Fiction?"

ASSIGNMENTS

1. First Term Essay: An in-depth analysis of any one film screened during first term. Your analysis should demonstrate a clear awareness of the strategies the film has employed to construct and express a "creative treatment of actuality."

Length: 8-10 pp. (typed)
Deadline for registering topic: Tuesday, Nov. 4
Essay Due Date: Thursday, Nov. 27, 1986

2. Second Term Essay: A discussion of an issue central to documentary cinema which employs extended consideration of at least two films (only one of these films need be from among those screened for the course). Acceptable topics include: analysis of a particular movement or style of documentary (eg. Free Cinema, cinema verite); the work of a particular filmmaker; documentary and its relation to a social issue (e.g. feminism, nuclear power, education); and so on. Topics of your own choosing may also be acceptable.

Second Term Essay (cont'd)

Length: 10-15 pp (typed)
Deadline for registering topic: Tuesday, March 10, 1987
Essay Due Date: Thursday, March 26, 1987

**NOTE: All essays must be typed. Essays submitted after due date will be graded on a pass/fail basis and not annotated. Essays submitted after the last day of classes will not be accepted. Essays must follow proper essay style (see Fine Arts Dept. student handbook, Turabian essay manual or MLA style sheet) or marks will be deducted. No exceptions to any of the above.

Seminars: In addition to regular seminar participation, you will lead a one-half hour (approximately) discussion on a topic related to the film(s) screened for the course that week. Seminars will be done either in groups or individually, depending upon class size. Topics and further details will be presented in class.

Grading scheme:

1st Term Essay - 20%
2nd Term Essay - 25%
Seminar Participation - 20%
Seminar Presentation - 15%

FILM SERIES FEE: Required of all students registered in film courses above the first year level. This fee covers discounted admission to the public film series (programmed for your academic enrichment), screened in The Studio.

Students may choose one of two special packages:

Package 1: International Film Series: discount, 7 films for $14.00. (regular cost: $19.25). (You'll have to choose Thursday or Friday night for this series and register the night with the instructor).
Package 2: International Film Series AND Bob Fosse Series*: Discount, 11 films for $22.00 (regular cost: $31.25)

NOTE: Students may not choose to attend only the Fosse Series. *The Fosse Series is on Friday nights: Sept. 26, Oct. 3, 10, 30.

The International Series is on Thursdays, Sept. 18, Oct. 16, Nov. 20, Dec. 4, Jan. 15, Feb. 12, Mar. 26
or
Fridays, Sept. 19, Oct. 17, Nov. 21, Dec. 5, Jan. 16, Feb. 13, Mar. 27

Registration for Package 1 or 2 will occur at the first class, Wednesday, Sept. 10. Series tickets will be picked up from Joyce De Forest (Rm. 134, Fine Arts Dept.) on September 17. You will pay her directly on that date (in time for the first film that week).

AMERICAN SILENT FILM: HISTORY AND THEORY   Miriam Hansen
Freshman Seminar   Fall 1985

Seminar Meetings: Tu, 3:00-5:00 pm; 401D, Sever Hall
Screenings: Mo, 7:00-9:00 pm; B 04, Carpenter Center
Office Hours: Mo, 4:00-5:00 pm; 61 Kirkland St. (5-0729)

Readings: John L. Fell, ed., Film before Griffith
                   Robert Sklar, Movie-Made America
                   Robert Allen & Douglas Gomery, Film History (optional)
                   + xeroxes on reserve at Lamont Library
                   Recommended: Bordwell/Thompson, Film Art: An Introduction
                                Bordwell/Staiger/Thompson, The Classical Hollywood Cinema

Requirements: Attendance at screenings and active participation in class; two
                   short papers (2-3pp.) and one longer paper (10-12pp.). Students
                   will also be asked to take turns writing up a brief summary of
                   classroom discussion for the following meeting.

Sept. 24:   INTRODUCTION; FILM/CINEMA; APPARATUS, SOCIAL INSTITUTION

            Edwin S. Porter, Uncle Josh at the Moving Picture Show (1902)

            Reading: Plato, parable of the cave (handout)
                     Fell, 1-66
                     Heath, "The Cinematic Apparatus" (res.)

Sept. 30   PROBLEMS OF FILM HISTORY / THE "NOVELTY" PERIOD
/Oct. 1:
            Edison kinetoscope films (1894-98)
            Lumière films (1895-98)
            A Trip to the Moon (Georges Méliès, 1902)
            Before the Nickelodeon (Charles Musser, 1982; 60 min.)

            Reading: Fell, 101-116; 144-161; 244-257; 299-310
                     Sklar, 3-17
                     Allen/Gomery, 25-64, 143-152 (opt.)

Oct. 7/8:   THE RISE OF NARRATIVE: CONTINUITY, MOTIVATION, ALTERNATION / EDITING (1)

            Uncle Tom's Cabin (Porter, 1903)
            Life of an American Fireman (Porter, 1903)
            The Great Train Robbery (1903)
            The Kleptomaniac (1905)
            Rescued by Rover (Cecil Hepworth, 1904; 6 min.)
            The Lonely Villa (D. W. Griffith, 1909)
            The Lonedale Operator (Griffith, 1911; 14 min.)
            A Corner in Wheat (Griffith, 1909)

            Reading: Allen, "Film History: The Narrow Discourse" (res.)
                     Musser, "The Nickelodeon Era Begins" (res.)
                     Musser, "Another Look at the 'Chaser Theory'" (res.)
                     Fell, 272-283, 311-338
                     Burch, "Porter, or Ambivalence" (res.)
                     Gunning, "Weaving a Narrative" (res.)

Oct.9/15: THE SPECTATOR-IN-THE-FILM: VISION, DESIRE, IDENTIFICATION / EDITING (2)

        Grandpa's Reading Glass (1902)
        The Gay Shoe Clerk (Porter, 1903)
        The Teddy Bears (Porter, 1907)
        A Drunkard's Reformation (Griffith, 1909) ½VHS--in class½
        The Girl and Her Trust (Griffith, 1913; 14 min.)

        Correction Please (Noel Burch, 1979; 60 min.)

        Reading: Burch, "Narrative/Diegesis - Thresholds, Limits" (res.)
                Brewster, "A Scene at the °Movies'" (res.)
                Branigan, "Formal Permutations of the Point-of-View Shot"
                Munsterberg, part I of The Photoplay: A Psychological
                    Study (1916) (opt./res.)

Oct. 14: Columbus Day--screening on Oct. 9

Oct. 21/22: HISTORY AND NARRATIVE; IDENTIFICATION AND IDEOLOGY

        The Birth of a Nation (1915; 167 min.)

        Sklar, 48-64
        Rogin, "°The Sword Became a Flaming Vision'" (opt./res.)
        Heath, "On Screen, in Frame: Film and Ideology" (res.)
        Baudry, "Ideological Effects of the Basic Cinematographic
            Apparatus" (opt./res.)

Oct. 28/29: BABEL TO BABYLON: UNIVERSAL LANGUAGE, MONTAGE, MODERNISM

        Intolerance (Griffith, 1916; 170 min.)

        Eisenstein, "Dickens, Griffith and the Film Today," Film Form (res.)

Nov. 4/5: IMMIGRANTS AND SPECTATORS: SOCIOLOGY AND MYTH

        The Musketeers of Pig Alley (Griffith, 1912; 15 mins.)
        The Immigrant (Chaplin, 1917; 23 min.)
        Easy Street (Chaplin, 1917; 20 min.)
        Sherlock Jr. (Keaton, 1924; 56 min.)

        Merritt, "Nickelodeon Theaters, 1905-1914" (res.)
        Sklar, 18-47 (opt.)
        Fell, 162-175; 196-206
        Mayne, "Immigrants and Spectators" (res.)

Nov.6/11: COMEDY: ANARCHY, SERIALITY, MATERIALISM, SEXUALITY

        Cops (Keaton, 1922; 20 min.)
        Max Linder Learns to Skate (1905; 6 min.)
        The Knock-Out (Mack Sennett/Chaplin/Arbuckle, 1914; 30 min.)
        Tillie's Punctured Romance (Normand/Chaplin/Dressler, 1914; 42 min.)

        Reading: Sklar, 104-121

Nov. 11: Veteran's Day--screening on Nov. 6

Nov. 18/19: SPECTATORS AND CONSUMERS; PROJECTING THE OTHER

The Cheat (Cecil B.DeMille, 1915; 50 min.)
A Fool There Was (Frank Powell, 1914; 82 min.)

Reading: Fell, 339-354
Ewen, "City Lights: Immigrant Women and the Rise of the Movies" (res.)
Sklar, 67-85
Bordwell/Thompson, 163-172, 296 (opt./res.)

Nov. 25/26: WOMEN: SPECTATORS AND DIRECTORS

A House Divided (Alice Guy Blaché, 1915; 13 min.)
Too Wise Wives (Lois Weber, 1921, 74 min.)

Reading: Blaché, handout
Rudman, "Lois Weber's Sacred Duty" (res.)
Ryan, "The Projection of a New Womanhood" (res.)

Dec. 2/3: MARKETING THE CRISIS: CINEMATIC AMBIGUITY AND THE DOUBLE STANDARD

Foolish Wives (Erich von Stroheim, 1921; 118 min.)

Reading: Sklar, 86-103, 122-140
Allen/Gomery, 153-172

Dec. 9/10: STARS: IDENTIFICATION, PERVERSION, EXOTICISM

Sparrows (Mary Pickford, 1926; 70 min.)
The Son of the Sheik (Rudolph Valentino, 1926; 75 min.)

Reading: Allen/Gomery, 143-152, 172-186

Dec. 16/17: MARKETING FILM AS ART: GERMAN EXPRESSIONISM AND HOLLYWOOD

Sunrise (F. W. Murnau, 1927; 95 min.)

Reading: Allen/Gomery, 86-104; 115-124
Andrew, "The Gravity of Sunrise" (xerox)
Sklar, 141-157 (opt.)

Jan. 6: FINAL PAPER DUE

Jan. 6/7: THE COMING OF SOUND; MASS CULTURE AND THE FAILURE OF THE AMERICAN DREAM

The Crowd (King Vidor, 1928; 121 min.)

Reading: Allen/Gomery, 109-130 (opt.)

AMERICAN CINEMA Miriam Hansen
01: 354: 315 (CAC) Office: Murray Hall 047
Fall 1984 Tel.: 932-7332

Lectures: M2, Th2, Murray 309
Screenings: Th7-8-9, Van Dyck 211
Readings: Robert Sklar, Movie-Made America
 Thomas Schatz, Hollywood Genres
 Xeroxes on reserve at Alexander Library
Requirements: 1. ATTENDANCE. Class attendance and student participation are considered very important for this course. Keep in mind that screenings cannot be repeated (since a number of films have to be rented from commercial distributors) and that the quality of your written work will crucially depend upon first-hand knowledge of each film. Films preceded by an * may not be discussed extensively in the lectures but are also required. Students who miss more than <u>five</u> classes will fail the course, unless a note from the Dean's Office can explain the cause of absence.
 2. READINGS. Students are expected to have completed the readings before the meetings for which they were assigned.
 3. PAPERS. One short paper (3-4pp.), due on Oct. 8, and one longer paper (7-8pp.), due on Nov. 26. Late papers will be penalized and cannot be accepted without prior consultation.
 4. EXAMS. A midterm (Oct. 15) and a

Sept. 6: Introduction: American cinema as social institution and symbolic form

 The Life of an American Fireman (E.S. Porter, 1903; 6 min.)
 The Great Train Robbery (Porter, 1903; 10 min.)
 The Musketeers of Pig Alley (D.W. Griffith, 1912; 12 min.)
 Easy Street (Ch. Chaplin, 1917; 20 min.)
 The Immigrant (Chaplin, 1917; 21 min.)--in class

 Reading: Sklar, v-vi, 3-64, 104-116

Sept.10/13: Variations on some basic themes: violence/law, class structure/social mobility, sexuality/romance/nuclear family

 Bonnie and Clyde (Arthur Penn, 1967; 111 min.)
 *You Only Live Once (Fritz Lang, 1937; 85 min.)

 Reading: Sklar, 286-304
 Pauline Kael, "Crime and Poetry" (reserve)
 Arthur Penn, selected interviews (reserve)

Sept.17/20: The concept of genre; genre and myth; the western

 *Hell's Hinges (Thomas Ince, 1916; 59 min.)
 My Darling Clementine (John Ford, 1946; 97 min.)

 Reading: Schatz, 4-41, 261-271, 45-80

Sept.24/27: The myth of the self-made man (I): the gangster film

 *The Public Enemy (William Wellman, 1931; 84 min.)
 Scarface (Howard Hawks, 1932; 99 min.)

 Reading: Schatz, 81-110; Sklar, 141-181

Oct. 1/4: The myth of the self-made man (II): mass society, consumerism, and individual experience

 Excerpts from The Cheat (Cecil B. DeMille, 1915)--in class
 The Crowd (King Vidor, 1928; 90 min.)

 Reading: Sklar, 86-103, 228-43

AMERICAN CINEMA (354: 315)   Miriam Hansen

Oct. 8:   FIRST PAPER DUE
Oct.8/11:   Demolishing the American Dream: comedy (I)

            Cops (Buster Keaton, 1922; 18 min.)--in class
            Liberty (Stan Laurel/Oliver Hardy, 1929; 20 min.)
            Duck Soup (Marx Brothers, 1933; 68 min.)
            Easy Living (Mitchell Leisen, 1937; 91 min.)

            Reading: Sklar, 116-121, 175-194

Oct.15:   MIDTERM
Oct.15/18: Restoring the Fantasy: comedy (II)

            Bringing up Baby (Hawks, 1938; 90 min.)
            *Christopher Strong (Dorothy Arzner, 1933; 77 min.)

            Reading: Schatz, 150-172; Sklar, 187-188, 195-197

Oct.22/25: Constructing an American past: myth, narrative and ideology

            Young Mr. Lincoln (Ford, 1939; 100 min.)

            Reading: Cahiers du Cinema, editors, "John Ford's Young Mr.Lincoln" (res.)

Oct.29/   Hollywood magic, or, Whatever happened to Miss Gulch: self-reflexivity
Nov. 1:   and the musical

            The Wizard of Oz (Mervyn LeRoy, 1939; 102 min.)

            Reading: Schatz, 187-220

Nov.5/8:   Inversions of the nuclear family (I): film noir and the myth of the
            powerful woman

            Mildred Pierce (Michael Curtiz, 1945; 113 min.)

            Reading: Sylvia Harvey, "Woman's Place: The Absent Family of Film Noir"(res.)
                     Christine Gledhill, excerpt from "Klute: Pt. 1" (reserve)
                     Schatz, 111-116

Nov.12/15: Anxiety, alienation, and the crisis of male identity

            It's A Wonderful Life (Frank Capra, 1946; 129 min.)

            Reading: Sklar, 205-214; Schatz, 170-185

Nov. 19:   Review (I): genre, narrative, and other formal aspects of the classical
            text; the 'spectator-in-the-text'; movements of desire, manipulations of
            sexual difference

Nov. 22:   No class, no screening (Thanksgiving)--make-up class Dec. 11

Nov. 26:   SECOND PAPER DUE

Nov.26/29: Inversions of the nuclear family (II): melodrama (style, excess, ironic
            distancing); contradictions of sex, race, and class

            Imitation of Life (Douglas Sirk, 1959; 124 min.)

            Reading: Schatz, 221-260

Dec.3/6:   American landmarks, oedipal itinerary: psychoanalyzing the spectator

            North by Northwest (Alfred Hitchcock, 1959; 136 min.)

            Reading: Kari Hanet, "Bellour on North by Northwest" (reserve)

Dec.10/11: Review (II); make-up screenings.

AMERICAN CINEMA (01: 354: 316: 01)
Miriam Hansen / Spring 1988
Office Hours: T 1:00-2:00, Th 11:30-12:30, 43 Mine Street, Tel.: 932-7355

LECTURES: T,Th5; Murray 219 (CAC)
SCREENINGS: T8,9; Van Dyck 211
READINGS: Thomas Schatz, Hollywood Genres
Books and xeroxes on reserve at Alexander Library

REQUIREMENTS: 1. Attendance at both lectures and screenings is mandatory. Students who miss more than five (5) classes will fail (F) the course unless a note from the Dean's Office can satisfactorily explain the cause of absence. Keep in mind that screenings cannot be repeated outside the time scheduled for them and that the quality of your written work will crucially depend upon first-hand knowledge of each film. Use of video tapes is encouraged (insofar as the films are available on tape), but VCR-viewing cannot become a substitute for main screenings.
2. Readings. You are expected to have completed the readings before the meetings for which they were assigned.
3. Papers. One short paper (2-3pp.), due February 16, and one slightly longer paper (5-7pp.), due April 19. Late papers will be penalized and cannot be accepted without prior consultation.
4. Exams. A midterm (March 15) and a 3-hr. final (May 10).

Jan. 26/28: STUDIO ERA; ECONOMY, SOCIAL INSTITUTION AND SYMBOLIC FORM
Reading: Schatz, 3-13,
Maltby, "The Political Economy of Hollywood"

Stagecoach (John Ford, 1939; 99 min.)

Febr. 2/4: THE WESTERN: HISTORY, RITUAL, MYTH, IDEOLOGY, PARODY
Reading: Schatz, 45-80

Blazing Saddles (Mel Brooks, 1974; 93 min.)

Febr. 9/11: THE CONCEPT OF GENRE; STARS, GENRE-CROSSING, SELF-REFLEXIVITY
Reading: Schatz, 14-41, 261-267
Altman, "A Semantic/Syntactic Approach to Film Genre"

Destry Rides Again (George Marshall, 1939; 94 min.)

Febr. 16: FIRST PAPER DUE

Febr. 16/18: THE GANGSTER FILM: VIOLENCE, CONSUMERISM AND SEXUAL IDENTITY
Reading: Schatz, 81-110
Kuhn, "Sexual Disguise and Cinema"

Some Like It Hot (Billy Wilder, 1959; 122 min.)

Febr. 18: (in class) Scarface (Howard Hawks, 1932; excerpt)

Febr. 23/25: THE MATERNAL MELODRAMA: SOCIAL MOBILITY, GENDER AND SACRIFICE
Reading: Viviani, "Who Is Without Sin?"
Kaplan, "The Case of the Missing Mother"

Stella Dallas (King Vidor, 1937; 106 min.)

March 1/3: WOMAN'S PLACE: SPECTATORSHIP AND PARANOIA
Reading: Haskell, "The Woman's Film"

The Spiral Staircase (Siodmak, 1945; 83 min.)

March 8/10: AUTEUR IN EXILE; MEDIA, CENSORSHIP AND THE POLITICS OF LYNCHING
Reading: Demonsablon, "The Imperious Dialectic of Fritz Lang"
Ferguson, "Hollywood's Half a Loaf" (1936)
"The Motion Picture Production Code of 1930"
Melling, "The Mind of the Mob" (opt.)

Fury (Fritz Lang, 1936; 94 min.)

March 15: MIDTERM

March 15/17: STYLES OF COMEDY; PERFORMANCE, THEATRICALITY, POLITICS
Reading: Schatz, 150-172

To Be or Not to Be (Ernst Lubitsch, 1942; 99 min.)

March 29/31: WHATEVER HAPPENED TO MISS GULCH: HOLLYWOOD MAGIC; THE MUSICAL
Reading: Schatz, 186-220
Neale, "Color and Film Aesthetics"

The Wizard of Oz (Mervyn LeRoy, 1939; 102 min.)

April 5/7: INVERSIONS OF THE NUCLEAR FAMILY: FILM NOIR AND THE THREAT OF THE SELF-MADE WOMAN
Reading: Place, "Women in Film Noir"
Harvey, "Woman's Place: The Absent Family of Film Noir"
Schatz, 111-149

Mildred Pierce (Michael Curtiz, 1945; 113 min.)

April 12/14: PATCHING UP THE AMERICAN DREAM: A RESPONSE TO FILM NOIR
Reading: Schatz, 170-185

It's A Wonderful Life (Frank Capra, 1946; 129 min.)

April 19: SECOND PAPER DUE

April 19/21: MASCULINITY IN CRISIS: THE FAMILY MELODRAMA (I)
Reading: Schatz, 221-245

Bigger than Life (Nicholas Ray, 1956; 95 min.)

April 26/28: FAMILY MELODRAMA (II): CONTRADICTIONS OF RACE, SEX, AND CLASS; STYLISTIC EXCESS AND IM/POSSIBILITIES OF VIEWER IDENTIFICATION
Reading: Schatz, 245-260
Elsaesser, "Tales of Sound and Fury" (excerpt)

Imitation of Life (Douglas Sirk, 1959; 124 min.)

May 3/5: IDENTIFICATION AS MASQUERADE: TAKING THE SPECTATOR FOR A RIDE
Reading: Hanet, "Bellour on North by Northwest"

North by Northwest (Alfred Hitchcock, 1959; 136 min.)

May 10: FINAL

E. Ann Kaplan
Office: 43 Mine St.
Hours: Mon/Thu
2.0-3.0, and by appt.
Extension: 7355 or 8209

SYLLABUS
HISTORY AND CRITICISM OF FILM

The purpose of this course is two-fold: on the one hand, we will briefly survey the major movements in film history from the "Primitive" era to the present; on the other, we will examine developments in film criticism and theory from their beginnings to the contemporary scene. Each study is itself complex because "facts" cannot so easily be distinguished from "discourse:" film history, for example, involves the problem of how various film scholars have constructed historical film discourses and called the results "facts"; in the study of film theory, we need to distinguish critical discourses that emerged in a particular historical period from recent theoretical discourses which position the same text differently.

The course has four parts: In Part I, on Early Cinema, we look at some examples of films from 1895-1906 in the context of current debates about film historiography and the cinematic apparatus. These early film reels, spliced together later with explanatory narrative form a marked contrast to a recent Noel Burch film, Correction Please, which combines old footage with reconstructions in order to foreground the way the cinematic apparatus functions.

Part II focusses on developments in four major national cinemas--the American, Soviet, German and French--and on the critical schools that emerged in connection with each one. Our discussions of the films will thus take a double-barreled form: a) studying the degree to which the film does/does not embody technical devices and theoretical concepts evident in the text assigned; and b) developing analyses that emerge out of our own so-called "reading formations" (of which more in the class).

In Part III, we look at recent film theory and at the key Hollywood films to which theory has been applied. Contemporary film criticism, as is well-known, draws on Russian formalism, Brecht, psychoanalysis, semiotics, structuralism and post-structuralism, at least; we will of necessity read excerpts from work of some theorists on whom theorists draw most heavily (Lacan, Foucault, Althusser).

Finally, in Part IV, we look at the contemporary "art" and "avant-garde" film theorized as "counter" to the classical Hollywood text. Feminist theories and practices that have done much to advance our understanding of alternate cinemas will naturally be considered here.

FILMS, READINGS, ASSIGNMENTS

WEEK   DATE

PART I: THE EARLY CINEMA

1   1/22   Introduction to the Course
           Films: The Great Primitives (In class)
           Melies/Lumiere Films (Evening)
           READINGS: Rosen, pp. 507-534

2   1/29   TOPIC: HISTORIOGRAPHY AND THE CINEMATIC APPARATUS
           READINGS: Noel Burch "Spatial and Temporal Articulations"

           Noel Burch, "Institutional Mode of Film"
           Noel Burch "Correction Please"
           FILMS: Noel Burch Correction Please, USA, 1979 (Extracts in class)
           D. W. Griffith Way Down East, USA, 1920

           PART II: CLASSICAL FILM THEORY: USA, USSR, GERMANY, FRANCE

3   2/05(a) TOPIC: GRIFFITH AND THE USA: EARLY MELODRAMA
           READINGS: Rosen, pp. 483-506 (Noel Burch)
           E. Ann Kaplan, "Theories of Melodrama"
           FF, pp. 195-255 (1944) (Eisenstein)
           FILM: Charlie Chaplin Modern Times, USA, 1925

4   2/12   TOPIC: CHAPLIN & SUBVERSIVE COMEDY?
           READINGS: Rosen, pp. 17-34 (David Bordwell)
           In-class student presentations on Griffith and Chaplin films
           FILMS: Weine Caligari, Germany, 1920
           Fritz Lang Metropolis, Germany, 1927

5   2/19(b) TOPIC: GERMAN CINEMA AND THEORY: EXPRESSIONISM
           READING: Sigfried Kracauer, From Caligari to Hitler
           Brecht, "Modernism and the Theatre"
           Thomas Elsaesser, "Social Mobility . . .,"
           FILM: Sergei Eisenstein Strike, USSR, 1925

6   2/26   TOPIC: SOVIET CINEMA I: EISENSTEIN AND RUSSIAN FORMALISM
           READING: Sergei Eisenstein, Film Form (essays from 1929 to 1944)
           Rosen, pp. 172-178 (Barthes on Eisenstein)
           FILM: Vertov Man With A Movie Camera, USSR, 1929

7   3/05   TOPIC: SOVIET CINEMA II: VERTOV'S KINO-EYE
           READINGS: Vertov's Papers
           Vertov, "Film Directors: A Revolution"
           FILMS: Bunuel Un Chien Andalou, France, 1929
           Dulac Seashell and the Clergyman, France
           Entre Acte

| 8 | 3/12 | TOPIC: FRENCH CINEMA I: SURREALIST CINEMA: THE FREUDIAN IMPETUS
READINGS: Rosen, pp. 286-318
    Freud, "Creative Writing and Day Dreaming" and "The Family Romance"
In-class student reports
FILM: Jean Renoir Le Crime du Monsieur Lange, France, 1932 |

| 9 | 3/19 | VACATION |

| 10 | 3/26 | TOPIC: FRENCH CINEMA II: THEORIES OF REALISM
READINGS: Andre Bazin, What is Cinema?, Vol. 1
In-class student report
VIDEO: Douglas Sirk, All That Heaven Allows, USA, 1957 |

PART III: CONTEMPORARY THEORY AND THE CLASSICAL HOLLYWOOD FILM

| 11 | 4/02 | a) Psychoanalysis and Melodrama
READINGS: Lacan "The Mirror Stage"
    Rosen, pp. 198-209 (Mulvey)
    Mulvey, "Notes on Sirk and Melodrama"
    Rosen, pp. 379-420 (Heath)
    Rosen, pp. 335-348 (Mary Ann Doane)
FILM: John Ford Young Mr. Lincoln, USA, 1939 |

| 12 | 4/09 | b) Structuralism and Theories of the "Progressive Text".
READINGS: Rosen, pp. 444-482 (Cashiers du Cinema, eds.)
    Rosen, pp. 179-197
    Althusser, "Ideological State Apparatuses"
FILM: Orson Welles Touch of Evil, USA, 1958 |

| 12 | 4/16 | c) Semiotics of the Cinema
READINGS: Rosen, pp. 35-101 (Metz and Bellour)
    Rosen, pp. 421-443 (Comolli)
    Heath, Excerpts from "Film Analysis"
    Rosen, pp. 244-280 (Metz, "Imaginary Signifier")
FILM: Godard La Chinoise, France, 1966 |

PART IV: COUNTER-CINEMA, FEMINISM AND THE AVANT-GARDE

| 13 | 4/23 | a) The Theory of Counter-Cinema
READINGS: Rosen, pp. 120-129 (Wollen)
    Rosen, pp. 210-218 (Willemen)
    Foucault, "The Order of Discourse"
In-class Student Presentations
FILM: Ingmar Bergman Persona, Sweden, 1970
VIDEO: Lizzie Borden Born in Flames, USA, 1983 |

| 15 | 4/30 | TOPIC: FEMINIST FILM THEORY: AN INTRODUCTION
READINGS: Kaplan, Women and Film (1983)
    Rosen, pp. 360-372 (De Lauretis)
FILM: McCabe, et al Sigmund Freud's Dora, USA, 1979
    Sally Potter Thriller, Britain, 1979 |

E.A. Kaplan

HISTORY AND CRITICISM OF FILM

Class Tests and Requirements

You should buy the following required texts:

Sergei Eisenstein. Film Form: Essays in Film Theory. Ed. and Trans. Jay Leyda, New York: Harcourt, Brace, 1949.
Siegfried Kracauer. From Caligari to Hitler: A Psychological Study of the German Film. Princeton, N.J.: The Princeton University Press, 1947.
Andre Bazin. What is Cinema? Vol. I. Ed. Hugh Gray, Berkeley, CA: The University of California Press, 1967.
E. Ann Kaplan. Women and Film: Both Sides of the Camera. London and New York, 1983.
Philip Rosen, ed. Narrative, Apparatus, Ideology: A Film Theory Reader. New York: Columbia University Press, 1986.

Recommended (as a reliable study of the basic elements of film form and the filmic instruction):

David Bordwell and Kristin Thompson, Film Art. (New edition)

and for an introduction to methods in film history:

Robert C. Allen and Douglas Gomery. Film History: Theory and Practice. New York: Alfred Knopf, 1985.

REQUIREMENTS:

1. Ability to attend the Thursday night screenings is a condition for being in the class. Lecture/discussion session at 43 Mine St.; film showings, 309 Murray (not Van Dyke!)

2. Please bring copies of assigned readings to class for in-depth analysis and discussion.

3. Students will be expected to participate in class discussion and performance here and in an in-class report on a film will make up one-third of the final grade; two-thirds will be based on a 20 page research paper. A word about each of the projects:

a) In-class report: One of the difficulties with the course is making links between theoretical/historical material and in-depth analysis of the films shown. Part of the problem is simply time: much of the course period has to be devoted to understanding the theoretical materials and to tracing a series of intellectual developments; on the other hand, students need to learn a critical discourse to apply to analysing films.

The distinction between these two activities is in a sense a false one: most of the reading materials provide evidence of a particular theoretical approach applied to a film we will see; the problems seem to emerge when students are asked to write their research papers and feel that there has not been sufficient practice in developing their own discourse about film. It is for this reason that I am asking people to do an in-class presentation on a film (no more than ten minutes) so as to permit discussion of this discourse. There are basically three discourses that people usually resort to in talking about a film:

1) a personal, subjective, often anecdotal discourse that has to do with people's gut responses to a film; which in turn has to do with what Bennett calls "reading formations."

2) an implicitly literary, aesthetic discourse (such as the standard film critics--Pauline Kael, John Simon often use) that emerges from fairly conventional literary methods;

3) A self-conscious theoretical film discourse that a student can only have access to through study of the history and practice of film theory. Students will be given examples of different kinds of theoretical discourse on individual films that represent recent developments and hopefully will be interested either in confronting a particular theory or in developing further a direction that a scholar has initiated. The in-class assignment should aim to help a student think closely and self-consciously about critical method.

b) The research paper:

The topic should be chosen from among those covered in the course or have been stimulated by work in the course. You should demonstrate that you have mastered theories covering the class, but that you are also able to critique or further develop these theories. You might want to compare and contrast the dominant theoretical paradigm in the course with other critical paradigms. You should be self-conscious about methodology, and show how a particular theory may be used to illuminate meanings of specific films. It is preferable to write about films not seen and discussed in class, but this is something that individual students can consult with me about.

It is important to start thinking about the final paper as soon as possible; I am happy to talk with you about possibilities at any time. I will ask for a tentative topic and preliminary explanatory paragraph on March 5; this means that students will be able to work on topics during the break, if so desired. I will look over outlines or even first drafts if students would like to submit them around April 9th. Final papers are due no later than May 5th. I cannot accept incompletes in this class.

Hum 305/Film Studies 305   Bruce Kawin
Fine Arts North 141   Office: Dennison 146A
TuTh 2-5:30 pm   TuTh 12:30-1:30, ext. 6471

            Film History I: Silent and Early Sound Film

Readings:
David Cook, A HISTORY OF NARRATIVE FILM (Norton). You should read this
     at your own pace; by the end of the term, you will be responsible for
     pp. 1-350.
Frank Norris, MCTEAGUE. Have this read before the showing of GREED.

Exams and grades:
There will be three closed-book quizzes, each counting toward 20% of the final
grade, and a final exam, counting 40%. Your grade can be modified by class
participation. Regular attendance is mandatory, and there will be no special
screenings arranged for people who miss scheduled films. Except in the case of
a documented medical emergency, there will be no exams repeated and no grades
of Incomplete given. In this class, the films are the primary texts, and every
effort has been made to secure the best and most complete available prints; for
every film shown, there are 20 others that ought to have been included, so be
sure to see every one of the films shown in class. Some films (and lectures)
may run overtime--several of the films are 3 hours or more--so it would be a
good idea not to make firm plans for the evening until 6 pm. The quizzes will
test recall of the films and memorization of production data (names, dates, etc.);
the final, which will include an objective section, will also give you a chance
to write an essay and demonstrate your skill at handling ideas.

Showing, by class meeting:
 1. Th Sep 6--no film; syllabus passed out. Over the weekend, start reading Cook.
 2. Tu Sep 11: NANOOK OF THE NORTH;MENILMONTANT;HIROSHIMA/NAGASAKI FOOTAGE.
 3. Th Sep 13: EDISON REEL; LUMIERE REEL; FILMS OF THE 1890's; BEGINNINGS OF
               BRITISH FILM.
 4. Tu Sep 18: MELIES REELS; MELIES PROGRAM; RITUAL IN TRANSFIGURED TIME; MESHES
               OF THE AFTERNOON; STUDY IN CHOREOGRAPHY FOR CAMERA.
 5. Th Sep 20: PORTER PROGRAM; A PAGE OF MADNESS.
 6. TU Sep 25: GRIFFITH BIOGRAPH PROGRAM.
 7. Th Sep 27: THE BIRTH OF A NATION.
 8. Tu Oct 02: INTOLERANCE.
 9. Th Oct 04: BROKEN BLOSSOMS, Quiz #1. UNKNOWN CHAPLIN.
10. Tu Oct 09: GREED.
11. Th Oct 11: THE GOLD RUSH; SHERLOCK JR.
12. Tu Oct 16: A SHORT HISTORY OF ANIMATION; REVENGE OF THE KINEMATOGRAPH
               CAMERMAN; RETURN TO REASON; SYMPHONIE DIAGONALE; MOTHLIGHT.
13. Th Oct 18: THE FALL OF THE HOUSE OF USHER (2 versions); UN CHIEN ANDALOU;
               RHYTHMUS 21; GHOSTS BEFORE BREAKFAST; OLYMPIA DIVING SEQUENCE.
14. Tu Oct 23: ABLE GANCE, YESTERDAY AND TOMORROW; first half of LA ROUE.
15. Th Oct 25: LA ROUE, completed.
16. Tu Oct 30: THE CABINET OF DR. CALIGARI; THE PHANTOM CHARIOT.
17. Th Nov 01: THE LAST LAUGH. Quiz #2
18. Tu Nov 06: METROPOLIS.
19. Th Nov 08: THE LOVE OF JEANNE NEY.
20. Tu Nov 13: STRIKE
21. Th Nov 15: MOTHER.
22. Tu Nov 20: BATTLESHIP POTEMKIN   (Th Nov 22: Holiday.)
23. Tu Nov 27: OCTOBER.
24. Th Nov 29: THE MAN WITH A MOVIE CAMERA.
25. Tu Dec 04: THE PASSION OF JOAN OF ARC. Quiz #3.
26. Th Dec 06: SUNRISE.
27. Tu Dec 11: THE COMING OF SOUND; LAND WITHOUT BREAD.
28. Th Dec 13: SNOW WHITE AND THE SEVEN DWARFS; COMPOSITION IN BLUE. Review.

Film History I, Dec 85, Kawin: FINAL EXAM

Note: Use one or more bluebooks; do not answer on this exam sheet. Make sure your name is on the front cover and first inside page of each bluebook.
This exam is worth a maximum of 200 points, with no extra credit. Spelling counts 50%. Give last name where a name is called for; titles and dates must be complete and exact, whether in English or in the original language.

I. Objective Section. Each question is worth 2 points. Answer all.
1. Name the cinematographer on Battleship Potemkin.
2. How long, in reels, is Potemkin?
3. True or fales: Potemkin was expanded from a single page of the script for The Year 1905. Grigori Alexandrov, who played the mustached officer Gilyarovsky in Potemkin, was the co-director of October.
4. Name the play Eisenstein staged in a real Moscow gas factory in 1924.
5. The Mozhukhin Experiment and "creative geography" were devised and explored by _____, whose work had varying degrees of influence on that of Eisenstein, Vertov, and especially Pudovkin.
6. Name the Head of the Provisional Government (Feb-Oct 1917).
7. Give the British release title of October.
8. Under the regime of [name] _____, many Soviet artists, notably Eisenstein, were persecuted for "formalism".
9. Potemkin and Mother were both made for the 20th anniversary of the ____ Revolution (give year).
10. Give the release date of Man With a Movie Camera.
11. How do you say "cinema verite" in Russian?
12. Name one "city symphony".
13. True or false: Yelizaveta Svilova, who edited many of Vertov's films, was married to Denis Kaufman.
14. What film shown in class ends with a reference to the Marquis de Sade's 120 Days of Sodom?
15. Name the producer of Sunrise.
16. Who won the first Oscar for cinematography?
17. True or false: Both Napoleon and The Passion of Joan of Arc were released by the Societe Generale de Films.
18. Name the Director of Ordet.
19. Name the actress who played Joan in The Passion of Joan of Arc.
20. Name the man who served as chief or co-art director on The Cabinet of Dr. Caligari and The Passion of Joan of Arc.
21. Name Warner Brothers' sound-on disk process.
22. Name Fox's optical sound process (Their trade name for it).
23. Name Lee DeForest's optical sound process (his name for it).
24. Give the trade name under which RCA marketed an improved version of DeForest's optical process (also associated with RKO, as #22 was with Fox).
25. True or false: In 35mm, Dolby Stereo is a 4-channel, 2-track optical sound format.
26. Name the director of Don Juan and The Jazz Singer.
27. Who lectured on The Sex Life of the Polyp in the 1928 short?
28. Who starred in The Jazz Singer?
29. Give the release date of Intolerance.
30. True or false: The following is the correct release order of these films: Rescued by Rover, The Lonely Villa, The Lonedale Operator, Broken Blossoms, The Last Laugh, Sunrise, Citizen Kane, Ivan the Terrible Part II.
31. Name the star of Gance's Au secours! (Help!).
32. How does Marcus precipitate Mac and Trina's financial disaster, and what animal is he compared to (if Mac and Trina are lovebirds in a cage)?
33. What is the fate of "Brown Eyes" in Intolerance?

Kawin, Film Final,

I, cont'd:)

34. Name the cinematographer who worked most often with Griffith.
35. Name the actress who starred in many of Chaplin's early comedies, notably The Cure and The Immigrant.
36. Name the director who was known as "the human mop" in his parents' vaudeville act and who was recruited into the movies by Roscoe ("Fatty") Arbuckle.
37. Name the author of Film Technique and Film Acting.
38. Name the author of Film Form and The Film Sense.
39. Name the film shown in class that was shot in 1919, released by Ufa in 1920, produced by Decla-Bioscop, and employed the talents of several actors trained by Max Reinhardt (Lil Dagover, for instance, was a Reinhardt actress, but Friedrich Feher, who has a major role in this film, clearly was not).
40. Name the man who reconstructed Napoleon and co-produced the Unknown Chaplin series.

II. This essay is worth a maximum of 40 points.
  On the next pages you will find four frame enlargements, all taken from Intolerance. 1A is the last frame of its shot, and 1B is the first frame of the next shot; this is a straight cut from the strike sequence in the Modern Story. 2A and 2B, likewise, are sequential frames--another straight cut from the trial scene in the Modern Story. You are to write on both of these cuts.
  Begin by identifying the actors and giving the names of the characters. Then examine significant aspects of the mise-en-scene--costumes, lighting, interior vs. exterior, masks, etc. Go on to analyze the use (position, angle, etc.) of the camera in each of the four shots. What purposes do all of these techniques serve (explain re. the narrative, the aesthetic structure of the whole, or whatever else you consider significant)? Finally, and most significantly, analyze both of these as cuts. What is the reason for isolating subjects of interest in 2A and 2B, or the logic of their being put together? How is the cut from 2A to 2B different from that from 1A to 1B? What does each of these cuts mean, and what does each cut reveal about the nature of cinematic language in general and of Griffith's practice in particular?
  This is an exercise in looking closely at frame enlargements (full-frame blowups from the film as released), seeing how much you can learn from them. It is also an opportunity to write about edtiing with clear examples in front of you, and to build up critical generalizations from very specific texts. To organize all this material, focus on what 1B adds to 1A, what the two mean together, and also on what 2B adds to 2A and what they mean together.
  You might wish to go on to consider which of these major devices--the camera (which includes camera position, movement, choice of lens, and lighting) or the editing--is most effective, most responsible for making Griffith's points, and (in your view) the richest resource for the cinema in general.

[Parts III and IV follow the frame enlargement pages.]

III. Write on any <u>one</u> of the following topics (essay worth maximum of 40 points):

1. Discuss the relative merits of silent and sound film.
2. Compare the use of intertitles in <u>The Birth of a Nation</u>, <u>Intolerance</u>, <u>The Last Laugh</u>, <u>Sherlock Jr.</u>, and <u>The Passion of Joan of Arc</u>.
3. Choose any film shown in class and relate it to the differences between Lumiere and Melies.
4. Compare and contrast the uses and relative merits of hand-painting (frame-by-frame coloring), tinting and toning, and color photography.
5. Using at least two of the following films, plus any others you might wish to discuss (whether shown in class or not), compare and contrast the relative merits of documentary and the narrative (fiction) film in constructing a political or social argument and then in convincing an audience to agree with that position: <u>Broken Blossoms</u>, <u>Nanook of the North</u>, <u>October</u>, <u>Potemkin</u>, <u>The Birth of a Nation</u>, <u>Intolerance</u>, <u>Hiroshima-Nagasaki August 1945</u>, <u>L'Age d'or</u>, <u>Man with a Movie Camera</u>, <u>City Lights</u>.

IV. Write on any <u>one</u> of the following topics (essay worth maximum of 40 points):

1. Compare and contrast the achievements of Griffith and Gance.
2. Both Griffith and Eisenstein could be said to have been interested in what Eisenstein called "intellectual" or "dialectical montage". Using <u>Intolerance</u> and <u>October</u>, examine the ways each of these filmmakers constructed wholes out of fragments and arguments out of cuts. Do not repeat information from Part II.
3. Both Griffith and Pudovkin could be said to have been interested in what Pudovkin called "linkage" or "constructive editing". Using <u>Mother</u> and any one of the Biograph films, examine the ways each of these filmmakers constructed wholes out of fragments. Do not repeat information from Part II.
4. Trace the relationship between Ufa and the American studio system.
5. Discuss the art of acting in a film. On the basis of films shown in class, which strike you as the most successful <u>silent</u> acting techniques, and how did the coming of sound affect those techniques?
6. Discuss the art of set design in film, using examples from films shown in class.
7. Discuss the art of cinematography, using examples from films shown in class.
8. Compare and contrast <u>McTeague</u> and <u>Greed</u>.
9. Discuss the use of dreams in <u>The Life of an American Fireman</u>, <u>Meshes of the Afternoon</u>, and any film (shown in class or not) of your choice.
10. Discuss the use of the climactic chase in any Griffith film, any other film shown in class, and any film released in the last ten years.
11. Discuss the use of physical comedy in any two films shown in class and in any film released in the last ten years.
12. Analyze in detail any single film shown in class this term.

<u>Note</u>: Turn in your bluebooks when you are done. You may keep this exam sheet for reference

FS/Hum 306: Film History 2
Fine Arts N-141
M W 3-6:30 (sometimes to 7 PM)

Prof. Bruce Kawin
Office: Dennison 146 A
Hours M Th 12-2
Phone 492-6471

Syllabus: FILM HISTORY 2

Texts:
1. The films. Attendance is mandatory. No repeat showings are possible.
2. Gerald Mast, A Short History of the Movies, 4th edition (Macmillan).
3. Bruce Kawin, How Movies Work [not available till early March] (Macmillan).

Exams:
Two quizzes will cover objective material, e.g., titles, dates, names related to films shown in class and material from assigned reading. A final exam will include both objective and subjective questions.

Showings, etc., by class meeting:

1-Wed, Jan 14 (=W J 14). Introduction. Duck Amuck. Olympia diving sequence.
   Singin' in the Rain.
2-W J 21. The Coming of Sound [compilation]. Enthusiasm. Mast, pp. 1-199, esp. ch. 9.
3-M J 26. Scarface. Vampyr. Mast, chs. 10 & 11. [class may run late].
4-W J 28. Queen Christina.
5-M Feb 2. Fury. Mad Love. Review Mast, ch. 7. [class may run late].
6-W F 04. Grand Illusion. ==QUIZ.==
7-M F 09. Bringing Up Baby. Mast, ch. 12.
8-W F 11. Citizen Kane.
9-M F 16. The Magnificent Ambersons.
10-W F 18. Sullivan's Travels.
11-M F 23. It's A Wonderful Life.
12-W F 25. Open City. The Miracle. Mast, ch. 13.
13-M March 2. The Bicycle Thief. ==QUIZ==
14-W M 04. Gun Crazy. Detour.
15-M M 09. Niagara. It Came From Outer Space (in 3-D). Kawin, Part I. [class till 7]
16-W M 11. The Searchers.
17-M M 16. Vertigo. Kawin, "Moving Camera" in Part II.
18-W M 18. Seven Samurai. [class will certainly run till 7]

   SPRING BREAK

19-M M 30. The 400 Blows. Review Mast, ch. 13.
20-W April 1. Night and Fog. Hiroshima, mon amour. Kawin, Part II.
21-M A 06. My Life to Live (Vivre sa vie).
22-W A 08. Last Year at Marienbad. Also, assigned screening, International Film Series, Muenzinger Auditorium, one show at 7 PM: Red Planet Mars, My Son John.
23-M A 13. La Jetee. Muriel.
24-M A 15. 2 or 3 Things I know About Her. Kawin, Part III.
25-M A 20. Dr. Strangelove, or How I Learned To Stop Worrying and Love the Bomb.
26-W A 22. That Obscure Object of Desire. Mast, chs. 14, 16.
27-M A 27. The Godfather. Mast, chs. 15, 17.
28-M A 29. The Godfather, Part II. [class will run late].
29-M May 4. Days of Heaven.

   Saturday, May 9: Final Exam

Film History II   Quiz #1   Kawin

This is a take home quiz that may prove useful as a study-sheet for the final. It will not be turned in or graded, but it is meant to be answered completely.

I. Define the following terms:
shot, scene, sequence, track shot, telephoto lens, depth of field, depth of focus, rack focus, Vitaphone, Movietone, Phonofilm, Tri-Ergon process, post-dubbing, wild sound, montage, mise en scene, pixillation, anamorphic lens, rear projection, dissolve, paradigm, syntagma, pan, tilt, zoom lens.

II. Arrange the following abbreviations in the proper order, starting with the shortest camera-to-subject distance, and then write out the terms in full and define them:
FS, MS, ECU, CU, ELS, LS.

III. Provide directors and release dates for the following films:
The Last Laugh
Vampyr
The Lights of New York
The Jazz Singer
The Blue Angel
Steamboat Willie
42nd Street

IV. Name the principal cinematographer on the following films:
The Last Laugh
Vampyr
Mad Love
Citizen Kane

V. Name the principal screenwriter on the following films:
The Blue Angel
Vampyr

VI. Discuss the use of sound in Land Without Bread. In what ways is it "commentative", in what ways "contrapuntal"?

VII. Discuss the use of silence in Study in Choreography for Camera.

VIII. Discuss the use of titles in The Last Laugh and Vampyr.

IX. Compare and contrast silent and sound acting technique; begin with Emil Jannings in Last Laugh and Blue Angel, then go on to discuss other actors and actresses before arriving at any generalizations.

X. The first sound/film apparatus was invented by _____ for Edison in the year _____ and was called the _____.

XI. Discuss the use of color in Samadhi, Composition in Blue, and any recent narrative film (e.g. The Godfather, Star Wars, Alien).

XII. To what extent is The Jazz Singer a reflexive film?

XIII. Briefly characterize (short history, basic qualities, etc.) the following studios:

Ufa
Warner Brothers
Paramount

XIV. Discuss any contemporary film in terms of its relation to the works of Lumiere and Melies.

FILM and HISTORY: the 1930s	Fall, 1987	Daniel J. Leab

> "...the very nature of film as a supremely popular art guarantees that it is the carrier of deep if enigmatic truths. Individuals create plays, novels, landscapes. But the creation of a movie is a mass undertaking, involving directors, writers, producers, cinematagrophers, players, and an army of technicians; the artifact is delivered by an intricate assembly line to a vast and anonymous audience. The production process, an unstable merger of commerce and art, is intimately interwoven with the mentality of the society. If as Ralph Waldo Emerson said and cultural historians have always assumed, "no man can quite emancipate himself from his age and country, or produce a model in which the education, the religion, the politics, messages, and arts of his time shall have no share," how much truer this must be for the art created by a crowd. What succeeds at the time in the movies, what is remembered later (often two separate things) obviously offer the social and intellectual historian significant clues to the tastes, apprehensions, myths, inner vibrations of the age."
>
> Arthur Schlesinger, Jr., American historian

> "I had a monumental idea this morning, but I did not like it...."
>
> Samuel Goldwyn, American film producer

This course is an inquiry into the relatonship between film and history. We will look not only at the development of the movie industry in the United States during the 1930s, but also at how movies shaped popular images in their representations of the present and the past.

Given the developments that took place in the movie industry in the 1930s, it is possible to divide the course into two parts, one dealing with images before the "Code" made itself felt in 1934, and the other dealing with the movies after censorship (morally, ethically, and politically) had become effective.

We will be paying special attention to the issue of film as historical evidence and the ways in which the film of the 1930s presented or ignored political, social, and economic issues of the day. The Leuchtenburg and Commager readings are designed to present the historical framework in which the other reading fit.

The REQUIREMENTS of the course are :
--a midterm exam (to be given Tuesday November 24th)
--a takehome final (must be typed)
--an annotated bibliography dealing with a particular genre, seminal film, or important development in the history of 1930s movies in the United States. The topic to be chosen with the approval of the instructor from the attached list.

The readings are drawn from the following:

Andrew Bergman, WE'RE IN THE MONEY
Henry Steele Commager, DOCUMENTS IN AMERICAN HISTORY
William Leuchtenburg, FDR AND THE NEW DEAL
Gerald Mast, THE MOVIES IN OUR MIDST
Robert Sklar, MOVIE-MADE AMERICA
John O'Connor/Martin Jackson, AMERIAN HISTORY/AMERICAN FILM
Gerald Weales, CANNED GOODS AS CAVIAR:AMERICAN FILM COMEDY OF THE 1930s

The Warshow reading will be available in copy form.

1. Introduction: Film and History-- the 1930s
    Film: <u>The 1930s</u> (newsreel compilation)
    O'Connor and Jackson, pp. ix-xxix

2. The Urbanization of America
    Film: <u>The Front Page</u>
    Bergman, pp. xi-xvii, xix-xxiii, 18-29
    Sklar, pp. 122-157
    Mast, pp. 228-236, 241-254, 282-302
    Leuchtenburg, Chapter I
    Commager, "Hoover's Rugged Individualism Speech:
        "Vanzetti's Last Statement in Court"

3. "Tough Guys Fight Back"
    Film: <u>Little Caesar</u>
    Bergman, pp. 3-17
    Leuchtenburg, Chaper 2
    Commager, "Democratic Party Platform of 1932"
        "Hoover's Veto of the Muscle Shoals Bill"
    Robert Warshow, "The Gangster as Tragic Hero"

4. Foreign Policy and Anarchistic-Nihilist Laff Riots
    Film: <u>Duck Soup</u>
    Bergman, pp. 30-48
    Leuchtenburg, Chapter 3
    Commager, "Kellog Peace Pact"
        "Stimson Doctrine"
        "The Johnson Act"

5. Sex and Personal Relations
    Film: <u>She Done Him Wrong</u>
    Bergman, pp. 49-61
    Mast, pp. 317-344
    Sklar, pp 161-174
    Leuchtenburg, Chapter 4
    Commager, "U.S. vs. One Book Called <u>Ulysses</u>"

6. Social Conciousness
    Film: <u>I Am A Fugitive From A Chain Gang</u>
    Bergman, pp. 92-100
    Leuchtenburg, Chapter 5
    Commager, "Mooney-Billings Case"
        "Herndon vs. Lowery"

7. Dancing your Way Through the Depression
    Film: <u>Forty Second Street</u>
    Bergman, pp. 62-65
    Leuchtenburg, Chapter 6
    Commager, "F.D. Roosevelt's First Innaugural Address"

8. Waving The Red Flag
    Film: <u>Modern Times</u>
    Bergman, pp. 69-82
    Leuchtenburg, Chapters 7-8
    Commager, "National Labor Relations Act"
              "National Recovery Act"
              "Cotton Textile Code"
              "Social Security Act"
              "Republican Platform of 1936"

9. "Many a Truth is Spoken in Jest": Screwball Comedy
    Film: <u>My Man Godfrey</u>
    Bergman, pp. 132-148
    Leuchtenburg, Chapters 9-10
    Weales, chapter on "My Man Godfrey"
    Commager "West Coast Hotel Co. v. Parrish"

10. Foreign Affairs
    Film: <u>Charge of the Light Brigade</u>
    Sklar, pp. 215-246
    Leuchtenburg, Chapter 12
    Commager, "Recognition of Soviet Russia"
              "Abrogation of the Platt Amendment"
              "Neutrality Act of 1937"

11. The Men in the White Hats
    Films: <u>The Bronze Buckaroo</u>; <u>Randy Ridews Alone</u>
    Leuchtenburg, Chapter 11
    Commager, "Economic Conditions in the South"
    Daniel J. Leab, <u>From Sambo to Superspade</u>, excerpts, xerox handout

12. <u>America, America</u>
    Film: <u>Drums Along The Mohawk</u>
    John O'Connor, "Drums Along The Mohawk," in O'Connor and Jackson
    Leuchtenburg, Chapters 13-14
    Bergman, pp. 149-173
    Commager, "Hands Off The Western Hemisphere"
              "Neutrality Act of 1939"
              "Alien Registration Act"

N.B.: Depending on availability specific films may change but it is not likely.

Topics for Annotated Bibliography

EPIC
The Dies Committee
Nykino
The Legion of Decency
The Hays Office
The U.S. Film Service
Pare Lorentz
"The French Turn"
A.J. Muste
The "Third Period"
J. Edgar Hoover
Kidnapping
Homer Cummmings
The Blue Eagle
Floyd Olsen
The Committee for Industrial Organization
The Unemployed Councils
David Lasser
Paramount Studios
Gabriel Over The White House
The Abraham Lincoln Brigade
The Smith Act
G-Men
Garbo
The Wagner Act
The Moscow Trials
F. Scott Fitzgerald in the 1930s
Earl Browder
The Nye Committee
Herbert Hoover
The Federal Theatre Project
It Can't Happen Here
Huey Long
The German-American Bund
Confessions of a Nazi Spy
Grand Hotel
Scarface
Al Capone
TVA
Blockade
Ernst Lubitsch
Aimee Semple McPherson
The "Memorial Day Massacre"
The Scottsboro Boys

Popular Culture 355

THE AMERICAN SILENT CINEMA   Spring 1986

Instructor: Jack Nachbar
Office: Popular Culture Building (Corner of Wooster and S. College)
Phone: 372-2982
Office Hours: 11:30-12:00 MWF; 204 TR and by appointment

Texts: THE RISE OF THE AMERICAN FILM by Lewis Jacobs
       THE SILENT CLOWNS by Walter Kerr
       Kinkos Notes (Buy these at Kinkos)

Course Requirements:

1. Tests. There will be FOUR tests in the course, three periodic in-class exams, and one take-home exam.

2. Journal. During the semester it is assumed that you will take class notes about class discussions and the movies you are watching. These should be important for studying for exams and for doing the take-home test. At the same time, you should be getting some ORIGINAL ideas of your own about what we are seeing and discussing. These ideas are interesting, maybe even valuable, but probably won't be covered on any of the tests. For instance, a particular shot from a film might be especially important to the meaning of the movie. Or maybe you notice a symbol in a film that we didn't discuss. Or maybe you have a good argument why a point made in class is wrong but you didn't get a chance to disagree. The journal is intended to give you some credit for these original thoughts. In your journal you are to consider ONE point about twelve different movies we see this semester. These must be a collection of ideas NOT DISCUSSED IN CLASS that you yourself discover in your personal watching or thinking. Each journal entry should be about 2/3 to one page. Completed four-entry journals will be turned in three times in the course.

3. Papers or projects. If you have a special interest you want to explore in detail that relates to the subject matter we are studying during any one period, you may substitute a paper or project for one of the tests. The paper or project must be approved by Nachbar AT LEAST ONE FULL WEEK before it is due and must be turned in the evening the rest of the class takes their period exam.

Grading will be as follows:

    Three In-class exams   60%
    Three Journals (4 items each) 20%
    One Take-home exam   20%

Other stuff: Class attendance is not required. BUT all assignments, all movies and all class discussions are fair game for the exams. Besides, with movies in almost every class, who would want to miss?????????

We will try to take a break every hour or so. Food and drink are NOT prohibited. Feel free to bring these sorts of goodies if they will help you enjoy the movies.

American Silent Cinema
Very Tentative Schedule Part A   1986

Part I The Movies Grow Up

Week One Jan. 14   General Introduction to the Course
                    Films: A TRIP TO THE MOON; Lumiere Shorts
                    Assign: Jacobs, pp. 3-77 (ouch!!! Sorry.)

         Jan. 16   The Era of the Nickelodeon, Part I
                    Films: THE GREAT TRAIN ROBBERY; THOSE AWFUL HATS
                    Assign: Jacobs, 81-94, Kinkos, 6-24, 47-50

Week Two Jan. 21   The Era of the Nickelodeon, Part II
                    Films: BRONCHO BILLY AND THE GREASER
                           RESCUED FROM AN EAGLE'S NEST
                    Assign: Jacobs, 202-206 (Ince stuff); Kinkos 25-46, 51-55

         Jan 23   Nickelodeon, final comments
                    The Movies Begin to Mature
                    Films: THE INVADERS; THE PERILS OF PAULINE, Chapter one,
                    Assign: Jacobs, pp. 136-156; Kinky's 56-58

Week Three Jan. 28 Maturity Continues
                    Film: THE BATTLE AT ELDERBUSH GULCH
                    Assign: Jacobs, 136-156

           Jan. 30 American Mindset, Pre World War One
                    Film: HELL'S HINGES; THE TOLL GATE
                    Assign: Nuthin! Get caught up.

Week Four Feb. 4   Some Complications in the American Mindset
                    Films: THE CHEAT; A FOOL THERE WAS
                    Assign: Jacobs, 95-119

Part II D. W. Griffith and Some Elements of the American Vision

          Feb. 6   An Introduction to D. W. Griffith
                    Film: THE LONELY VILLA
                    Assign: STUDY FOR TEST

Week Five Feb. 11   TEST NUMBER ONE
                    Assign: Jacobs, 171-201

          Feb. 13   Film: BIRTH OF A NATION (3 1/2 hours, get psyched!)
                    Assign: Kinkos, 73-74

PC 355 SCHEDULE

Week Six Feb. 18   Discussion of BIRTH, Part I
                    Film: BROKEN BLOSSOMS
                    Assign: Kinkos 61; 66-72

         Feb. 20   Discussion of BIRTH, Part II
                    Discussion of Broken Blossoms
                    Film: TOLABLE DAVID
                    Assign: Kinkos, 75-79, Jacobs 384-394; 248-263

Week Seven Feb. 25 A Note on WWI and the Movies
                    The Decline of D. W. Griffith
                    Assign: Jacobs, 343-354   (Von Stroheim stuff)

         Feb. 27   TAKE-HOME TEST ASSIGNED
                    An Introduction to the Roaring 20s
                    Film: GREED
                    Assign: Jacobs, 393-415; 335-343 (De Mille Stuff)

Part III The Manners and Morals of the 201 as Seen in the Movies

Week Eight Mar. 4   Film: SON OF THE SHEIK

Popular Culture 355
American Silent Movies   Take Home Test

General Directions: Do the following assignment in about 1000-1500 words
(4-6 typed pages)
The test is due in class on Tuesday, March 18

Imagine that you have fallen into a time warp. You suddenly find yourself in Hollywood, California in the year 1921, the beginning of "the jazz age."

Luckily for you, your trip back in time has not left you unemployed. You have a job working for the biggest and richest of the studios, Paramount, as an assistant production supervisor.

Well, kiddo, your first taste of Hollywood anxiety is about to commence. When you walked into your office this morning the first thing you spotted on your desk was the attached memo from the nasty old man himself, Adolph Zukor. Now it's up to you to produce or else!!!!!!

WRITE A MEMO TO ZUKOR EXPLAINING WHO YOU ARE GOING TO HIRE AND WHY.
(Be sure to also include detailed reasons why you are NOT going to hire the other two.)

Use details from the films we have seen, your readings about these folks, class handouts and what you have learned about the industry and the audiences of the era.

Note: Special bonus source of information:
Before you decide about the three applicants, you consult your friendly Beverly Hills soothsayer. She describes to you in general terms the directions the careers of these three directors are *probably* going to go during the next ten years. Naturally, you will use this information to help you reach a final decision.

Final hint:

The chief assistant head of production is this guy named Nachbar. You may, if you wish, want to let him take a peek at your memo before you send it off to the old man.

Popular Culture 355   American Movies of the 1930s   Spring, 1982

Instructor: Jack Nachbar
Office: Popular Culture Bldg.
Office Hours: 1-2:30 TR; 9:30-10:30 W and by Appointment

Texts: 1. HOLLYWOOD IN THE THIRTIES by John Baxter
        2. BROTHER CAN YOU SPARE A DIME by Milton Meltzer
        3. WE'RE IN THE MONEY by Andrew Bergman
        4. THE HOLLYWOOD PROBLEM FILM
        5. Selected handouts and assigned reserve readings.

Grading:

There will be five components to the Course Grade. Each component will be worth 20 percent.

1. Two papers. These will be assigned well ahead of time. Each paper should be about 5 typed (or equivalent) pages (1200-1600 wds).
   a. You will be asked to research an aspect of movie going during the 30s.
   b. You will be asked to research some movies of the 30s not seen in class.

2,3,4. In class examinations. These will be about 90 minutes and of the essay variety. They will cover everything since the previous test including lectures, readings and movies. Samples from another course will be passed out before the first test.

5. Take-Home Final Examination. This will be a test with a page limit of 6 pages. It will cover all the materials of the course and will be due on the day of the scheduled final examination.

Objectives:

1. To gain an overall perspective about the kinds of films during the 1930s. This includes style, stars, studios, etc., so that a viewer might later view 1930s films with a fuller understanding and appreciation of their context.

**2. To come to both an intellectual and emotional understanding of the Great Depression in America by a close examination of the films produced for mass audiences of the period. The assumption in this regard is that movies of any era offer a fantasized reflection of the hopes, fears and values of their audiences. (See introduction to Berman text for a discussion of this assumption.)

> We thought American business was the Rock of Gibralter. We were the prosperous nation, and nothing could stop us now. A brownstone house was forever. You gave it to your kids and they put marble fronts on it. There was a feeling of continuity. If you made it, it was there forever. Suddenly the big dream exploded. The impact was unbelievable.
>
> E.Y. (Yip) Harburg
> Lyricist for song, "Brother Can You Spare a Dime."

Tentative Schedule

American Movies of the 1930s

Week One
T. March 30   General Introduction to the Course
               Assign: Brother: 2-33; Bergman: Introduction; Baxter 7-15;
                       Problem Film: 1-11
               Film: The Movies Learn to Talk

R. Apr. 1   The Coming of Sound and the Movie Crisis of the Early 30s
               Assign: Brother: 23-76; Bergman:3-29; Problem Film: 15-30;
                       Baxter: 16-49.
               Film: The Virginian with Gary Cooper

Week Two
T. Apr. 6   The American Depression under Herbert Hoover
               Assign: Brother: 77-105; Problem Film: 31-45; Baxter 50-69
               Film: Scarface with Paul Muni and George Raft.

R. Apr. 8   Movies of the 30s and their times. The Gangster movie and
                       the early 30s.
               Assign: Brother: 106-145; Problem Film: 46-64;
                       Baxter: 70-86
               NO FILM TONITE

Week Three
T. Apr. 13   Early Horror and the Mood of Cynicism. How to Study for Test I.
               Assign: Bergman: 30-48; Problem Film: 65-77
               Film: Dracula with Bela Lugosi

R. Apr. 15   Films: (See at UAO 105 Hanna at 8:00) Duck Soup with the Marx
                       Bros. and It's a Gift with W.C. Fields.
               Assign: Bergman: 49-61; STUDY FOR THE TEST.

Week Four
T. Apr. 20   TEST NUMBER I
               A Note about Women in the Movies of the 30s
               Assign: Brother: 146-168; Problem Film: 65-77; Handout.
               Film: Three "Betty Boop" Cartoons

R. Apr. 22   The Production Code Administration
               Assign: Bergman: 69-82
               Film: Golddiggers of 1933 with Ruby Keeler and Dick Powell.

Week Five
T. Apr. 27   1933-A Transition year in the Movies
               Assign: Bergman: 132-148; Problem Film: 91-103
               Film: King Kong with Fay Wray and a big monkey.

R. Apr. 29   Film: You Can't Take It With You with Jimmy Stewart
                       and Jean Arthur (UAO 8:00 in 105 Hanna)
               Assign: Problem Film: 179-189; Baxter 87-104;

Week Six T. May 4		Capra, Screwball Comedies and Parables of Reconciliation FIRST PAPERS ARE DUE TONITE Film: <u>It Happened One Night</u> with Clark Gable and Claudette Colbert.
R. May 6		Parables of Reconcilliation, Continued. Assign: Study for second test. Film: <u>Top Hat</u> with Fred Astaire and Ginger Rogers.
Week Seven T. May 11		TEST II Assign: Reserve Readings; Baxter: 104-123. Film: <u>Flash Gordon</u>, Chapter 1.
R. May 13		A Word about Fred and Ginger A "Typical" Night at the Movies in the 30s Films: <u>Flash</u>, Chapter 6; <u>Judge Priest</u> with Will Rogers. Assign: Bergman: 92-131; 146-154. Finish Papers.
Week Eight T. May 18		Will Rogers and FDR Assign: Bergman: 83-91; Problem Film: 122 134 Film: <u>The Roaring 20s</u> with Jimmy Cagney.
R. May 20		The New Look of the Gangster Documentaries in the 30s SECOND PAPERS DUE Assign: Problem Film: 104-120; 155-162. Films: <u>Land of Cotton</u> (<u>March of Time</u>); The Plow that Broke the Plains.
Week Nine T. May 25		Labor in the 30s Assign: Bergman: 149-166; Problem Film: 135- 145. Film: <u>Modern Times</u> with Charlie Chaplin
R. May 27		Youth Assign: Bergman: 167-174; Problem Film: 165-178; 190-199. Study for Test. Films: <u>They Made Me a Criminal</u> with John Garfield, Dead End Kids. <u>Flash</u> #10
Week Ten T. June 1		TEST III; Discussion of Take-Home Final Exam. Film: <u>Flash</u> #11.
R. June 3		Final Thoughts; Class Evaluation. Films: Last Capter of <u>Flash</u>; <u>The Wizard of Oz</u> with Judy Garland.
Week Eleven		Take-Home Final Exam Due by 4:00 the day of the scheduled Test. Nachbar in his office beforehand to give you personal help on it.

Popular Culture 355 Spring, 1979
American Films of the 1940s

Instructor: Jack Nachbar
Office: Pop Culture Bldg. (Corner of Wooster and S. College)
Office Hrs: 9:30-10:20 M-F; 11:30-12 M-R and by Appt. 372-2981

Texts:
1. HOLLYWOOD IN THE FORTIES Higham and Greenberg
2. SCOUNDREL TIME by Lillian Hellman
3. DAYS OF SADNESS, YEARS OF TRIUMPH by Geoffrey Perrett
4. Selected reserve reading to be assigned.

Course Objectives:

Movies of the 40s are especially interesting because:
 a. They were at their all-time height of popularity in America.
 b. America itself was going through revolutionary changes during this period.
 c. The trials and troubles of these changes can be felt through an examination of the films people flocked to see during the period.

The aim of the course is therefore NOT to examine the greatest films of the period for their quality (though often we will do this) but rather to study the films of the 40s for hints and clues of what dreams and fears drove this country into the modern, atomic era.

Grading:

Three tests, in-class, short essay. (See attached schedule.)
Each test will cover only that material since the last test.

Note: No attendance will be kept. You are, however, responsible for everything, including films. The movies cannot be reshown so if for some reason you can't make it, either go to the library for some information or check with someone who took good notes.

The third test will also include one question that will cover the entire course. To be used if your grade is in doubt.
Each test will be 20% of the course grade.

Two papers.   20% each

The first paper will be based on an interview with a person who went to the movies during WW II.

The second paper will be a group project. The class will be divided into ten groups. Each group will be assigned one year of the 40's and will produce together a 10-15 page paper entitled, "America And Its Movies in 194?"

These papers will be dittoed and distributed to the class. Thus, as a class, we will write our own book.

Popular Culture 355
American Films of the 1940s
Tentative Schedule

Part I   Oh What a Lovely War

Week One   Introduction and the Pre-War Mindset
                Reading: Days of Sadness Chapters 1-8; Hollywood pp. 7-19

Mond. Mar 26   General Introduction.
                Dividing into small groups for second papers.
                Film: FOUR SONS with Don Ameche

Wed. Mar. 28   Hollywood's Attitudes towards the war in Europe
                Paper #1 Assigned.
                Film: TRAIL TO SANTE FE with E. Flynn and O. DeHavilland

Week Two   The War Movies
                Assign: D. of S.Chapters 9-15; Hollywood pp. 86-103

Mon. April 2   A General Introduction to WW II Movies
                Paper #2 (Group Papers) will be assigned.
                Film: WAKE ISLAND with Brian Donlevy, William Bendix.

Wed. April 4   American values as seen through the war films.
                Film: SAHARA with H. Bogart.

Week Three   Other Perspectives on the War
                Reading: D of S Chap. 16-20; Hollywood, pp. 36-50.

Mon. April 9   The War Documentary
                Small Group Meeting
                Films: PRELUDE TO WAR
                       THE BATTLE OF SAN PIETRO

Wed. Apr. 11   Real vs. Fictional Views of War
                Film: CASABLANCA with H. Bogart and I. Bergman

Week Four   Images of Life Back Home
                Reading: D of S Chapter 21-23; Hollywood, pp. 170-182

Mon. April 16   Film: SINCE YOU WENT AWAY with C. Colbert, J. Jones
                Each small group will meet with Nachbar sometime
                during the week in his office to report on their
                research progress.

Wed. Apri. 18   The longing for Normalcy
                        PAPER # 1 IS DUE
                Film: MEET ME IN ST. LOUIS with J. Garland, M. O'Brien.

        NOTE: THE FIRST TEST WILL COVER MATERIAL TO THIS POINT

Part II   Postwar Problems and Readjustments

Week Five   Where We Have Been and Where We Are Going
                Reading: Hollywood, pp. 139-154.

Mon. Apr. 23   Film: THE BEST YEARS OF OUR LIVES with F. March.
                    D. Andrew
                    Note: Study for Test

Wed. April 25   FIRST TEST
                    Discussion of LIVES and the problems the film reveals.

Week Six   More Signs of Postwar Restlessness and Renewal
                    Reading: D of S. Chap. 24-30

Mon. April 30   Small Group Meeting (Last One in Class)
                    The Western during the 40s.
                    Film: THE ANGEL AND THE BADMAN with John Wayne

Wed. May 2   The Lost Search for Old American Values
                    Film: IT'S A WONDERFUL LIFE with J. Stewart, D. Reed.

Week Seven   Great Directors Look at the 40s.
                    Reading: Finish D of S

Mon. May 7   John Ford and the Affirmation of America
                    Film: FORT APACHE

Wed. May 9   A Note of the 40s Sex Goddess
                    Hitchcock and European Scepticism
                    Film: NOTORIOUS with C. Grant and I. Bergman

Week Eight   The Silly and the Serious
                    Reading: Hollywood, pp. 68-86; 154-170-104-124.

Mon. May 14   Comedy Films in the 40s
                    Film: THE ROAD TO RIO with Crosby, Hope, Lamour.

Part III   Postwar Anxieties, Fears, and Betrayals

Wed. May 16   SECOND TEST
                    Film: HOME OF THE BRAVE

Week Nine   Hollywood in Crisis and the American Nightmare
                    Reading: SCOUNDREL TIME

Mon. May 21   Problem movies of the 40s and what they suggest.
                    Shocking upheavals in Hollywood.

Wed. May 23   An Introduction to Film Noir
                    Film: DETOUR   GROUP PAPERS DUE

Week Ten   More of the American Nightmare
                    Reading: Hollywood, pp. 19-36

Mon. May 28   NO CLASS

Wed. May 30   More of Film Noir
                    Film: DOA

Week Eleven That's All Folks
Mon. June 4   Final Thoughts   Film: THE RAW DEAL

Final Test Night THIRD TEST

Spring, 1984

Popular Culture 355
American Movies of the 1950s

Instructor: Jack Nachbar
Office: Popular Culture Bldg. (Corner of Wooster and S. College) 372 2981
Office Hours: TWR 10-12 and by appointment

Texts: THE CATCHER IN THE RYE by J.D. Salinger
NAMING NAMES by Victor Navasky
THE CRUCIAL DECADE and AFTER by Eric Goldman
ON THE VERGE OF REVOLT by Brandon French
THE FILMS OF THE 50S by Douglas Brode. There will also be several handouts.

Grading Requirements:

A. Three Tests.
1. Dates: Thursd. Feb. 23 (15%)
Thursd. Mar. 27 (15%)
Tuesd. May 8 (Final Exam Week [30%])

2. Type: Short answer essay covering material since the last test. The third test will also include a longer essay covering material over the entire course.

B. Two Papers. (20% each)

2. Due Dates:
Thursday, March 8
Thursday, April 19

Course Approach to the Films:

There are any number of ways to study a movie. We could concentrate on the film as representative of a director's skills and philosophy. Or we could look at how other movies are like or unlike the film being studied. These and other ways of studying movies are all worthwhile. However, we are going to take another approach. The most common name for this approach is socio-cultural. This approach assumes that popular movies are a product created mainly for commercial profit. In order to be profitable, movies must give their audiences what people want to see. And mainly people want to see films that reflect their moral, philosophical beliefs as well as stories that are entertaining. Therefore, movies provide us with invaluable clues to the world views of the crowds who go to them. By studying the movies we are also studying the culture out of which they come. Hints as to how to relate movies to the culture will be provided throughout the course.

Course objectives:

1. To come to a greater understanding of U.S. culture during the 1950s through a close examination of the movies made and shown during that period.

2. To come to a greater understanding of the movies of the 1950s by placing them in their appropriate cultural context.

Popular Culture 355
Schedule for Part I of Course

Week One
Tuesd. Jan 17   Basic Introduction to course.
                      Why movies tell us about their audience.
                      Assign: Brode, 69-74; Goldman, 3-45.

Thusd. Jan 19   Film: SINGIN IN THE RAIN
                      Assign: Goldman, 46-113.

Week Two
Tuesd. Jan 24   An Introduction to some major concerns of the 1950s
                      SINGIN as an idealized view.
                      Assign: Brode, 103-105; Navasky VII-XXIII

Thur. Jan 26   Film: SHANE
                      Assign: Brode, 99-101; Navasky, 3-69.

Week Three
Tues. Jan 31   Film: FROM HERE TO ETERNITY
                      Assign: 71-143 in Navasky

Thur. Feb 2   More thoughts about the basic fifties as revealed in
                      SHANE and ETERNITY
                      Film: THE CAINE MUTINY (8:00, UAO)
                      Assign: Navasky, 97-143.

                      PART II The Cold War and the HUAC Hearings

Week Four
Tuesd. Feb. 7   Background of the Cold War and the HUAC Hearings.
                      Film: RED NIGHTMARE
                      Assign: Navasky, 144-195, Brode, 65-68.

Thursd. Feb. 9   Initial Discussion of Navasky
                      Film: HIGH NOON (8:00, UAO)
                      Assign: Navasky 199-329.

Week Five
Tuesd. Feb 14   (Happy Valentine's Day)
                      Discussions of Navasky and HIGH NOON as related to the Cold War
                      Assign: Navasky 333-370; Brode, 43-44, 107-108

Thursd. Feb 16   Introd to Monster movies of 50s
                      Film: IT CAME FROM BENEATH THE SEA
                      Assign: Rest of Navasky; Brode 171-173.

Week Six
Tuesd. Feb 21   Film: INVASION OF THE BODY SNATCHERS
                      Assign: Study for the TEST

Thursd. Feb 23   7:00 Review session for the test
                      8:00 TEST NUMBER ONE
                      Assign: 113-133 in Goldman; French XIII-22.

112

Popular Culture 355   Films of 1950s

Schedule for Part II

DOMESTIC HARMONIES AND DISHARMONIES

Week Seven
Tues. Feb 28   An Introduction to American Domesticity in the 1950s.
                    Films: Two 50s TV situation comedies
                    Assign: Brode, 167-168; French, Chapter 3 and 8.

Thur. Mar 1   The influence of TV on the movies.
                    Film: MARTY
                    Assign: Brode, 135-139; Goldman, Chap. 6; MM Handout
                            FIRST PAPER WILL BE ASSIGNED

Week Eight
Tues. Mar. 6   Brief discussion of MARTY
                    Film: THE SEVEN YEAR ITCH
                    Assign: Brode, 86-87; Goldman, Chap. 7 and 8.

TROUBLE IN PARADISE: YOUTH ON THE LOOSE

Thursd. Mar.   Discussion of ITCH as a comment on Domesticity.
                    An Intro. to JDs in the 50s
                    Film: THE WILD ONE
                    Assign: James Dean Handout; Goldman, Chap. 9 and 10;
                            Brode, 163-166; 193-194.

Week Nine
Tues. Mar. 13   (Red Jacket and T-Shirt Nite -- Come Prepared!!!!!)
                    Film: REBEL WITHOUT A CAUSE
                    Assign: Brode, 252-253; finish papers.

Thur. Mar. 15   PAPER #1 IS DUE
                    What's wrong with those kids?
                    The rise of 50s exploitation movies.
                    Film: HIGH SCHOOL CONFIDENTIAL
                    Assign: Beat Poetry Handout; read CATCHER IN THE RYE

                    HAPPY SPRING VACATION!!!!!!

Week Eleven
Tues. Mar. 27   (Beatnik Nite -- Wear proper clothing, Daddio!)
                    The Beats and Rebellion and Youth
                    Assign: Study for Test.

Thur. Mar 29   TEST #2 (Note: This is a 2 day postponement from the date
                    on the original syllabus)

                    Like Cool. You dig?

Popular Culture 355
American Movies of the 1950s

Schedule for Part III

Week Twelve
Tuesd. April 3 Film: ON THE WATERFRONT
                Assign: Finish First Papers
                Finish reading Catcher in the Rye. Brode. 115-117.

Thursd. April 5 FIRST PAPERS DUE
                 Discuss Catcher in Rye and 50s rebellion.
                 Brief discussion of Method Acting
                 Discuss WATERFRONT as a movie that sums up what we have done
                 in class so far.
                 Assign: Verge of Revolt Chapt. 10; Brode 175-177.

STEREOTYPES IN THE FILMS OF THE 50S

Week Thirteen
Tuesd. April 10 Film: PICNIC
                 Assign: Crucial Decade, Chapt. 11

Thursd. April 12 Images of Women in 50s films
                  Discussion of Picnic
                  Assign: Brode, 266-267; Crucial Decade, Chapt. 12.

Week Fourteen
Tuesd. April 17 Film: PILLOW TALK
                 Assign: Crucial Decade, Chapt. 13; Verge of Revolt, Chapt. 2

Thursd. April 19 Images of Men in the 1950s
                  Discussion of PILLOW TALK
                  Assign: Crucial Decade, Chapt. 14; Brode, pp. 211-216,
                          258-259, 268-270.

ODDS AND ENDS

Week Fifteen
Tuesd. April 24 Film: PEYTON PLACE
                 Assign: Finish Papers #2, Brode, 200-202
Thursd. April 26 Some Notes on the Film Industry in the 50s
                  Discussion of PEYTON PLACE -- PAPER #2 DUE
                  Assign: Crucial Decade, Epilogue

Week Sixteen
Tuesd. May 1 Film: WRITTEN ON THE WIND
              Assign: VERGE OF REVOLT, Chapt. 9, 11

Thursd. May 3 Other Manias of the 50s
               Discuss WRITTEN ON THE WIND
               Assign: STUDY FOR 3rd TEST

THE THIRD EXAM WILL BE TUESDAY, MAY 8 -- 8:15-10:15
                We will have the regular length test to be followed by
                a parting gift: A Surprise Movie !!!!!!

WINTER 1988
COMMUNICATION 521
FILM HISTORY

Class Time: Tuesday/Thursday, 2-4 p.m.
Instructor: Jimmie L. Reeves
Office: 2008C Frieze Building
Office Hours: Monday 1-4 p.m. or by appointment
Telephone: 763-1144

THE COURSE

Emphasizing the history of the Hollywood studio system during the 1930s and 1940s, this course will challenge students to make sense of the complex aesthetic, technological, economic, and social influences that governed the development of the American sound film.

REQUIRED READING MATERIAL

   1. *Film History: Theory and Practice* by Robert C. Allen and Douglas Gomery (New York: Alfred A Knopf, 1985).
   2. *The Movies in Our Midst* edited by Gerald Mast (Chicago: The University of Chicago Press, 1982).
   3. Additional readings that will be made available at Kinkos.

ASSIGNED READINGS AND ATTENDANCE

   Plan on reading *every* assignment and attending *every* class. Daily reading assignments are listed on the class schedule. Since the readings will both inform and enhance material covered during class, I expect you to complete the reading assignments prior to the class meeting time. Also, because of the scope of this course, lecture material will be covered at a brisk pace--and absentees will not have the luxury of an encore presentation by the instructor.

TESTS

   1. Unscheduled (pop) tests. These tests are designed to encourage good reading habits and reward class attendance. Questions on these tests will be limited to: (a) lecture material presented at the most recent class meeting held prior to the testing day; (b) viewing material screened during the most recent class meeting held prior to the testing day; (c) reading material assigned for the testing day. Students who keep up with the reading and review their notes prior to class generally do very well on these tests.

As a matter of strict policy, students who are absent when I administer a "pop" test will be assigned a grade of zero (0), and students who are present but miss every question will be assigned a grade of fifty (50). To account for extraordinary circumstances that may cause you to miss one or two class meetings, at the end of the term I will drop your lowest grade on this type of test.

    2. The Mid-Term Exam. Currently scheduled for March 10, 1988, this test will be of the fill-in-the-blank and essay variety. To do well on this exam, you must master the readings, be familiar with the lectures, and attend all the viewing sessions.

    3. The Final Examination. A comprehensive test intended to make you re-think all of the material covered during this term, the final exam will also be made up of fill-in-the-blank and essay questions.

FINAL PROJECT

Discussion of Final Project: March 1
Topic Proposal and Preliminary Research Plan Due: March 8
Project Due: April 12
Graded Project Returned: April 19

    The final project for this course is an 8 to 10 page historical paper based on original research of primary source material. This paper should be typed (double-spaced) and it should include extensive footnotes. The paper should conform to the format for primary film historical research presented by Allen and Gomery (p. 47). According to Allen and Gomery, this format includes:

    1. Statement of the problem investigated;

    2. Review of pertinent literature dealing with that problem;

    3. Posing of the specific research question answered or hypothesis tested;

    4. Discussion of the method used;

    5. Presentation of the data generated by the study;

    6. Conclusions derived from the data;

    7. Suggestions for further research.

These papers should also be neat and readable. Since this is a 500-level course, I expect every student to be able to write clear, concise prose. Therefore, I will deduct points from the project for spelling, punctuation, grammar, and typographical errors.

DEADLINES

Paper topics, research plans, and final projects turned in after the beginning of class on the scheduled due dates are *late*. To encourage students to meet these deadlines, I will assign hefty grade penalties for late work.

GRADES

A ten point system will be used in determining final grades.
The following is a breakdown of how the final grades will be calculated:

```
            Unscheduled Tests  . . . . . . 20%
            The Mid-Term Exam  . . . . . . 20%
            The Final Project
                a. Topic Proposal and Research
                   Plan  . . . . . . . . .  5%
                b. Paper  . . . . . . . . 25%
            The Final Examination . . . . 30%
            Total                        100%
```

CLASS SCHEDULE

Jan. 7
    Syllabus Discussed.

Jan. 12
    Lecture: Film History as History
    Reading: Allen & Gomery, Chapter 1.
    Viewing: Film Firsts, I

Jan. 14
    Lecture: Researching Film History
    Reading: Allen & Gomery, Chapter 2.
    Viewing: Film Firsts, II

Jan. 19
    Lecture: Reading Film History
    Reading: Allen & Gomery, Chapter 3.
    Viewing: The History of Animation.

Jan. 21
    Viewing: Life Goes to the Movies, Parts I, II, & III.

Jan. 26
    Viewing: Life Goes to the Movies, Parts IV & V.

Jan. 28
    Lecture: Aesthetic Film History I--Continuity Editing.
    Reading: Allen & Gomery, Chapter 4.
    Viewing: 1. Illustration of Basic Film Editing Techniques.
              2. Film Editing Interpretations and Values.

Feb. 2
    Lecture: Aesthetic Film History II--Formalism and Realism.
    Viewing: 1. Art of Film Series--Camera.
              2. Art of Film Series--Edited Image.

Feb. 4
    Lecture: Aesthetic Film History III--The Auteur Policy.
    Viewing: Art of Film Series--Director.

Feb. 9
    Viewing: Sunrise.

Feb. 11
    Lecture/Discussion: Semiotics and Sunrise.

Feb. 16
Lecture: Technological Film History I--Technological Determinism.
Reading: Allen & Gomery, Chapter 5
Viewing: Connections Series--No. 9--Countdown.

Feb. 18
Lecture: Technological Film History II--The Coming of Sound.

Feb. 23
Mid-Winter Recess

Feb. 25
Mid-Winter Recess

Mar. 1
Discussion of Final Project
Reading: Allen & Gomery, Chapter 8.

Mar. 3
Guest Lecturer: Economic Film History.
Reading: 1. Allen & Gomery, Chapter 6
2. Zukor, "Origin and Growth of the Movies," (Mast, pp. 112-121).
3. Hays, "The Motion Picture Industry" (Mast, pp. 205-212).
4. Huettig, "The Motion Picture Industry Today" (Mast, pp. 383-391).
5. "Loew's Inc." (Mast, pp. 392-402).

Mar. 8
Paper Topic and Preliminary Research Plan Due.
Test Review

Mar. 10
Mid-Term Examination.

Mar. 15
Viewing: A Star is Born.

Mar. 17
Lecture: Social Film History I--An Introduction.

Reading: 1. Allen & Gomery, Chapter 7.
2. Powdermaker, "Hollywood and the USA" (Mast, pp. 620-633).

Mar. 22/24
Lecture/Viewing: David King on Writing as an Occupation--Getting an Agent/The Screenwriter's Guild/The Collaborative Production Process.
Viewing/Lecture: Sunset Boulevard.
Reading: Reeves, "Rewriting Newhart: A Dialogic Analysis" (available at Kinkos).

Mar. 29
  Lecture: Social Film History II--Controlling Motion Picture Content.
    Reading: 1. United States Supreme Court, "Mutual Film Corp. v. Industrial Commission of Ohio" (Mast, pp. 136-143).
    2. "The Sins of Hollywood" (Mast, pp. 176-182).
    3. "The Don'ts and Be Carefuls" (Mast, pp. 213-214).
    4. Moley, "The Birth of the Production Code" (Mast, pp. 317-320).
    5. "The Motion Picture Production Code" (Mast, pp. 321-332).
    6. Martin, "The Legion of Decency Campaign" (Mast, pp. 333-339).
    7. Quigley, "Decency in Motion Pictures" (Mast, pp. 340-343).
    8. Production Code Administration, "Code Seal and Letter" (Mast, p. 344).
    9. Westin, "The Miracle Case: The Supreme Court and the Movies" (Mast, pp. 604-609).

Mar. 31
    Viewing: A Face in the Crowd

Apr. 5
    Lecture: Image Studies--The Role of Stardom in Film History.
    Viewing: Art of Film Series--The Role of Women in the Movies.

Apr. 7
    Guest Lecturer: The Popcorn Venus--Women in the Movies.

Apr. 12
    Final Project Due.
    Viewing: Star 80.

Apr. 14
    Lecture: Final Words on The Studio System, Stardom, and Film History.

Apr. 19
    Review for Final Exam.
    Return Final Project.
    Conduct Course Evaluation.

To Be Announced: Final Exam.

EARLY FOREIGN CINEMA
A film/lecture course on
the history of cinema in
foreign countries during
the silent era: 1895-1930.

Instructor: Adam Reilly
University of Colorado at Boulder
Fall, 1984
Tuesdays, 5:30-9:30 p.m.
Course # 234/334
At the Denver Center Cinema

OBJECTIVES OF THE COURSE

1. To provide an introduction and overview of the first three and one half decades of the movies, concentrating on the development of the art and the technology of the medium and the people who made it happen in key foreign countries.
2. To give the student an opportunity to view as much material from the silent era as possible, with lectures and discussion to help situate the films in the context of the work of the filmmakers, the conventions of the genres, the social milieu in which each was produced, the characteristics of various national cinemas, and the contributions, if any, each film made toward advancing the art form.
3. To develop in the student a critical sense and appreciation for the films of this particular era.

TEXTS:

I have not assigned a particular text book for this course since there is no single book that covers the material the way we will be approaching it. There are, however, several basic film history books which will give you a good overview and a sense of chronology. Each of them will include a large dose of early American film as well, which is unavoidable, but is not the specific subject of this class. It won't hurt for you to know what was going on in the United States at the same time! (That will be the subject of my class next semester.) See the bibliographies for each class and the general bibliography in these pages.

STUDENT REQUIREMENTS FOR THE COMPLETION OF THE COURSE:

1. Preparation for class by reading the noted assignments.
2. Regular, punctual and active attendance of classes. Film can only be studied and appreciated by actually seeing the films themselves. Most of the films to be shown in this class are rarely screened elsewhere. So each class must be considered a unique, one-chance-only opportunity to view these movies. Attendance will be taken and will count for 10% of your final grade.
3. Completion of assignments:
   a) A book report, due in our sixth class, which will count for 25% of final grade.
   b) A brief, objective quiz, given in our ninth class, consisting of 15 short questions, based on the time-line and list of significant names and films included in these pages. This will count for 15% of your final grade.
   c) A critique of a silent feature film, due at our twelfth class, which will make up 25% of your final grade.
   d) A final take-home paper, to be turned in at the fifteenth class, or by the end of exam week, which will count for 25% of the final grade.
4. While not required, the students will be encouraged to see other silent films outside of class at various film societies, the Ogden, and the Denver Center Cinema.

INSTRUCTOR:

Adam Reilly obtained his M.A. in Cinema Studies at New York University in 1969. He has taught film at Marymount Manhattan College, The New School for Social Research, was book review editor for *Filmmakers Newsletter* for five years, authored *Harold Lloyd: The King of Daredevil Comedy* (Macmillan, 1977), was director of the American Film Institute Theater at the Kennedy Center in Washington, D.C. for two and one half years, and is currently director of the Denver Center Cinema. Phone: 893-4000 (work), 863-9218 (home)

COURSE OUTLINE

Aug 28	1.	INTRODUCTION	Nine short films from France, Germany, Great Britain, Italy, and Russia, and one feature from Italy, <u>Antony and Cleopatra</u>.
Sep 4	2.	GERMANY I	The Spiders and <u>The Cabinet of Dr. Caligari</u>.
Sep 11	3.	GERMANY II	<u>Nosferatu</u> and <u>The Last Laugh</u>.
Sep 18	4.	GERMANY III	<u>The Student of Prague</u> and <u>Metropolis</u>.
Sep 25	5.	GERMANY IV	<u>Variety</u> and <u>The White Hell of Pitz Palu</u>.
Oct 2	6.	FRANCE I	<u>Queen Elizabeth</u>, <u>Mater Dolorosa</u> and <u>Catherine</u>. **BOOK REPORT DUE THIS CLASS**
Oct. 9	7	FRANCE II	<u>Entr'acte</u>, <u>The Crazy Ray</u>, <u>The Imaginary Voyage</u> and <u>The Italian Straw Hat</u>.
Oct 16	8.	FRANCE III	<u>La P'tite Lilie</u>, <u>Charleston</u>, <u>The Little Match Girl</u> and <u>Nana</u>.
Oct 23	9.	FRANCE IV	<u>The Smiling Madame Beudet</u>, <u>Menilmontant</u>, <u>Rien que les Heures</u>, <u>Ballet Mechanique</u>, <u>Marche des Machines</u>, <u>L'Etoile de Mer</u>, <u>Un Chien Andalou</u>. **QUIZ GIVEN IN THIS CLASS**
Oct 30	10.	U.S.S.R. I	<u>Battleship Potemkin</u> and <u>October</u>.
Nov 6	11.	U.S.S.R. II	<u>Mother</u> and <u>Storm Over Asia</u>.
Nov 13	12.	U.S.S.R. III	<u>The Man With the Movie Camera</u> and <u>Bed and Sofa</u>. **FILM CRITIQUE DUE THIS CLASS**
Nov 20	13.	NORWAY/ SWEDEN	<u>Growth of the Soil</u>, <u>Thomas Graal's Best Child</u>, <u>Phantom Chariot</u>

Nov 27	14.	DENMARK	Master of the House and The Passion of Joan of Arc.
Dec 4	15.	BRITAIN	The Lodger and The Manxman. **ESSAY DUE THIS CLASS**
Dec 11	16.	SOUND	Blackmail and Ecstasy

ADDITIONAL SCREENINGS (OPTIONAL) AT THE DENVER CENTER CINEMA:
You may have four (4) free passes to each of these programs.

Sep 15	Show People	Nov 29	Homecoming
Sep 19	Battleship Potemkin	Dec 4	Tramp, Tramp, Tramp
Oct 6	The Gold Rush	Dec 8	Backstairs/Destiny
Oct 18	The Great Love	Dec 11	The Strongman
Nov 15	Erotikon	Dec 18	Long Pants
Nov 18	Easy Virtue/Warning Shadows	Dec 20	The Greatest Thing in Life

ADDITIONAL OPTIONAL SCREENINGS AT MY HOUSE:

dates to be arranged (usually on a Saturday or Sunday)

    Napoleon
    Siegfried/Krimhild's Revenge

        Adam Reilly
        1276 Emerson St
        on Capital Hill
        863-9218

CLASS #1   INTRODUCTION   AUGUST 28, 1984

FILMS TO BE SCREENED IN CLASS:

   Lumiere's First Programs (France, Lumiere Brothers, 1895-1900, b&w, 7 min.)
   Max Skladanowsky Pioneer Films (Germany, 1895-1896, b&w, 5 min.)
   A Trip to the Moon (France, George Melies, 1902, b&w, 12 min.)
   Rescued by Rover (Great Britain, Cecil Hepworth, 1905, b&w, 8 min.)
   The Red Spectre (France, Pathe, c.1907, hand-colored, 10 min.)
   The Nobleman's Dog (France, Pathe, c.1908, hand-colored, 10 min.)
   Don Juan's Wedding (Germany, H. Bolten-Baeckers, 1909, b&w, 8 min.)
   The Revenge of the Cameraman (Russia, L. Starevitch, 1912, b&w, 10 min.)
   The Fall of Troy (Italy, Giovanni Pastrone, 1910 b&w, 18 min.)
   Antony and Cleopatra (Italy, Enrico Guazzioni, 1913, b&w, 55 min.)

RECOMMENDED READING:

   Barsacq, Leon, Caligari's Cabinet and Other Grand Illusions; ch. 1: "Painted Sets, The
      French Primitives," and ch 2: "Constructed Sets, Italy, 1910-1915."
   Katz, Ephraim, The Film Encyclopedia, "Italy," "Germany," "France," "Soviet Union,"
      "United Kingdom," "Melies," "Lumiere."
   Mast, Gerald, A Short History of the Movies, ch 1, 2, 3.
   Robinson, David, The History of World Cinema, ch 1: "Heritage," ch 2: "Discovery."
   plus the following notes for class #1

SUGGESTED READING:

   Brownlow, Kevin, The Parade's Gone By, ch 45: "The Silent Film in Europe."
   Casty, Alan, Development of the Film, ch 1, pt 1: "Beginnings."
   Ceram, C.W., Archeology of the Cinema.
   Film Society Programmes: "A Trip to the Moon."
   Frazer, John, Artificially Arranged Scenes: The Films of George Melies.
   Hammond, Paul, Marvellous Melies.
   Jacobs, Lewis, The Emergence of Film Art, Pt One, I: "George Melies."
   Quigley, Martin Jr, Magic Shadows: The Story of the Origin of the Motion Picture.
   Rotha, Paul, The Film Till Now, Pt One I: "The Development of the Film," and Pt
      One, VIII: "The French Film."
   Roud, Richard (ed), Cinema: A Critical Dictionary, "French Cinema--Origins,"
      "German Cinema--Its Origins," "Italian Silent Cinema," "Georges Melies."
   Sadoul, Georges, Dictionary of Film Makers, "Cohl," "Lumiere," "Pathe," "Melies,"
      "Zecca," "Pastrone," "Hepworth," "Skladanowsky," "Starevitch,"
   Sadoul, Georges, Dictionary of Films, "Lumiere Films," "Voyage dans la Lune,"
      "Rescued by Rover."
   Thurman, J&D, The Magic Lantern: How Movies Got to Move.
   Low, Rachel, The History of the British Film: 1896-1906.

CLASS #2   GERMANY I   SEPTEMBER 4, 1984

FILMS TO BE SCREENED IN CLASS:

The Spiders, Episode 1 (Fritz Lang, 1919, color-tinted, music track, 56 min.)
The Cabinet of Dr. Caligari (Robert Wiene, 1919, b&w, music track, 62 min.)

RECOMMENDED READING:

Beaver, Frank, On Film: A History of the Motion Picture, ch 6: "Germany."
Eisner, Lotte, The Haunted Screen, ch 2: "The Cabinet of Dr. Caligari," ch 14: "The Spiders."
Mast, Gerald, A Short History of the Movies, ch 6: "The German Golden Age."
Robinson, David, The History of World Cinema, ch 4: "Apogee: 1918-1927."

SUGGESTED READING:

Andrew, Dudley, The Major Film Theories, II-5: "Siegfried Kracauer."
Casty, Alan, Development of the Film, ch 4: "The Germans and Expressionism."
Film Society Programmes, "The Cabinet of Dr. Caligari."
Katz, Ephraim, The Film Encyclopedia, "Wiene," "Lang," "Germany."
Jensen, Paul M., The Cinema of Fritz Lang, ch 2: "The Silent Era."
Kracauer, Siegfried, From Caligari to Hitler, Pts I, II, III.
Lennig, Arthur, The Silent Voice, "The Cabinet of Dr. Caligari."
Manvell, Roger, The German Cinema, Ch I: "Pioneers in a New Art, 1895-1918," ch 2: "The Nineteen Twenties."
New York Times Film Reviews, "The Cabinet of Dr. Caligari," Mar 20, 1921.
Ott, Frederick, The Films of Fritz Lang, "The Spiders."
Rotha, Paul, The Film Till Now, Pt One, VII: "The German Film."
Roud, Richard, Cinema: A Critical Dictionary, "German Cinema," "The Cabinet of Dr. Caligari," "Fritz Lang."
Sadoul, Georges, Dictionary of Film Makers, "Wiene," "Lang."
Sadoul, Georges, Dictionary of Films, "Cabinet des Dr. Caligari."
Solomon, Stanley, The Classic Cinema, "The Cabinet of Dr. Caligari."
Variety Film Reviews, "The Cabinet of Dr. Caligari," Apr 8, 1921.
Cowie, Peter, A Concise History of the Cinema, ch 5: "Germany and Austria."

CLASS #3   GERMANY II   SEPTEMBER 11, 1984

FILMS TO BE SCREENED IN CLASS:

    Nosferatu (F.W. Muranu, 1922, b&w, silent, 55 min.)
    The Last Laugh (F.W. Murnau, 1924, b&w, silent, 80 min.)

RECOMMENDED READING:

    Eisner, Lotte, The Haunted Screen, ch 6: "Nosferatu," ch 12: "The Last Laugh."
    Eisner, Lotte, Murnau
    Roud, Richard (ed), Cinema: A Critical Dictionary, "F.W. Muranu."

SUGGESTED READING:

    Barsacq, Leon, Caligari's Cabinet and Other Grand Illusions, ch 3: "Toward a Film Aesthetic."
    Film Society Programmes, "Dracula."
    Katz, Ephraim, The Film Encyclopedia, "Murnau."
    Lennig, Arthur, Film Notes, "Nosferatu."
    New York Times Film Reviews, "Nosferatu," Jun 4, 1929; "The Last Laugh," Jan 28, 1925.
    Sadoul, Georges, Dictionary of Film Makers," "Murnau."
    Sadoul, Georges, Dictionary of Films, "Nosferatu," "Letzte Mann."
    Variety Film Reviews, "Nosferatu: Phantom der Nacht," Jan 24, 1929.

CLASS #4　　　　　　　GERMANY III　　　　　　SEPTEMBER 18, 1984

FILMS TO BE SCREENED IN CLASS:

The Student of Prague (Henrik Galeen, 1926, b&w, silent, 80 min.)
Metropolis (Fritz Lang, 1927, b&w, silent, 80 min.)

RECOMMENDED READING:

Eisner, Lotte, The Haunted Screen, ch 6: "The Demoniac Bourgeois," "The Sway of the Doppelganger;" ch 13: "Metropolis."
Eisner, Lotte, Fritz Lang.
Roud, Richard, Cinema: A Critical Dictionary, "Fritz Lang: German Period."

SUGGESTED READING:

Hammen, Scott, Film Notes, "Metropolis."
Katz, Ephraim, The Film Encyclopedia, "Lang," "Galeen," "Veidt."
New York Times Film Reviews, "Metropolis," Mar 7, 1927
Ott, Frederick, The Films of Fritz Lang, "Metropolis."
Sadoul, Georges, Dictionary of Film Makers, "Lang," "Galeen."
Sadoul, Georges, Dictionary of Films, "Metropolis."
Variety Film Reviews, "Student of Prague," Nov 24, 1926; "Metropolis," Feb 23, 1927, Mar 16, 1927.

CLASS #5   GERMANY IV   SEPTEMBER 25, 1984

FILMS TO BE SCREENED IN CLASS:

   Variety (E.A. Dupont, 1925, b&w, silent, 60 min.)
   The White Hell of Pitz Palu (Fanck/Pabst, 1929, b&w, music score, 75 min.)

RECOMMENDED READING:

   Atwell, Lee, G.W. Pabst.
   Roud, Richard (ed), Cinema: A Critical Dictionary, "Pabst."

SUGGESTED READING:

   Hinton, David, The Films of Leni Riefenstahl, ch 1: "The Blue Light and the Mountain Films."
   Katz, Ephraim, The Film Encyclopedia, "G.W. Pabst," "Leni Riefenstahl," "Dr. Arnold Fanck," "E.A. Dupont."
   New York Times Film Reviews, "White Hell of Pitz Palu," Sept 27, 1930; "Variety," June 28, 1926.
   Sadoul, Georges, Dictionary of Film Makers, "Pabst," "Fanck," "Dupont."
   Sadoul, Georges, Dictionary of Films, "Variete."

CLASS #6   FRANCE I   OCTOBER 2, 1984

FILMS TO BE SCREENED IN CLASS:

   Queen Elizabeth (Louis Mercanton; w/Sarah Bernhardt, 1912, bw, silent, 40 min.)
   Mater Dolorosa (Abel Gance, 1917, bw, silent, 44 min.)
   Catherine (Albert Dieudonne/Jean Renoir, 1924, bw, silent, 55 min.)

RECOMMENDED READING:

   Beaver, Frank, On Film, ch 7: "France--Eclecticism."
   Mast, Gerald, A Short History of the Movies, ch 10: "France Between the Wars."
   Roud, Richard, Cinema: A Critical Dictionary, "Renoir," "Gance."

SUGGESTED READING:

   Bazin, Andre, Jean Renoir.
   Kramer and Welsh, Abel Gance.
   Renoir, Jean, My Life in Films.
   Rotha, Paul, The Film Till Now, "France."
   Sadoul, Georges, Dictionary of Film Makers, "Renoir," "Gance."
   Sadoul, Georges, Dictionary of Films, "Les Amours de la Reine Elisabeth," "Mater Dolorosa."

CLASS #7   FRANCE II   OCTOBER 9, 1984

FILMS TO BE SCREEN IN CLASS:

Entr'acte (Rene Clair, 1924, b&w, silent, 15 min.)
The Crazy Ray (Rene Clair, 1924, b&w, silent, 40 min.)
The Imaginary Voyage (Rene Clair, 1926, b&w, silent, 53 min.)
The Italian Straw Hat (Rene Clair, 1927, b&w, silent, 75 min.)

RECOMMENDED READING:

McGerr, Celia, Rene Clair, Boston, Twayne, 1980.
Clair, Rene, Cinema Yesterday and Today.
Roud, Richard (ed), Cinema: A Critical Dictionary, "Clair."

SUGGESTD READING:

Bardeche and Brasillach, The History of the Motion Pictures, pt 5, I: French Film.
Sadoul, Georges, Dictionary of Film Makers, "Clair."
Sadoul, Georges, Dictionary of Films, "Entr'acte," "Paris qui Dort," "Un Chapeau de Paille d'Italie."

CLASS #8   FRANCE III   OCTOBER 16, 1984

FILMS TO BE SCREENED IN CLASS:

Nana (Jean Renoir, 1925, b&w, silent, French titles, 111 min.)
Charleston (Jean Renoir, 1927, b&w, silent, no titles, 15 min.)
La P'tite Lilie (Alberto Cavalcanti; Renoir as actor; 1927; b&w, silent, French titles, 18 min.)
The Little Match Girl (Jean Renoir, 1928, b&w, silent, French titles, 28 min.)

RECOMMENDED READING:

Bazin, Andre, Jean Renoir.
Leprohon, Pierre, Jean Renoir.
Roud, Richard (ed), Cinema: A Critical Dictionary, "Renoir."

SUGGESTED READING:

Braudy, Leo, Jean Renoir: The World of His Films.
Durgnat, Raymond, Jean Renoir.
Faulkner, Christopher, Jean Renoir: A Guide to References and Resources.
Renoir, Jean, My Life in Films.
Sadoul, Georges, Dictionary of Film Makers, "Renoir."
Sadoul, Georges, Dictionary of Films, "Nana," "Petite Marchande d'Allumettes."

CLASS #9   FRANCE IV   OCTOBER 23, 1984

FILMS TO BE SCREENED IN CLASS:

    The Smiling Madame Beudet (Germain eDulac, 1922, b&w, silent, French titles, 28 min.)
    Menilmontant (Dimitri Kirsanov, 1926, b&w, silent, 25 min.)
    Rien Que Les Heures (Alberto Cavalcanti, 1926, b&w, silent, French titles, 18 min.)
    Ballet Mecanique (Fernand Leger, 1924, b&w, silent, French titles, 10 min.)
    Marche des Machines (Eugene Deslaw, 1928, b&w, silent, no titles, 5 min.)
    L'Etoile de Mer (Man Ray, 1928, b&w, silent, French titles, 10 min.)
    Un Chien Andalou (Louis Bunuel/Salvador Dali, 1928, b&w, music track, French titles, 15 min.)

RECOMMENDED READING:

    Curtis, David, Experimental Cinema.
    Lawder, Standish, The Cubist Cinema.
    Renan, Sheldon, An Introduction to the American Underground Film.

SUGGESTED READING:

    Morrison, George, "The French Avant-Garde" in Lewis Jacobs' The Emergence of Film Art.
    Sadoul, Georges, Dictionary of Film Makers, "Dulac," "Kirsanov," "Leger," "Deslaw," "Ray," "Bunuel."

CLASS #10   U.S.S.R. I   OCTOBER 30, 1984

FILMS TO BE SCREENED IN CLASS:

Battleship Potemkin (Sergei Eisenstein, 1925, b&w, silent, 55 min.)
October (Sergei Eisenstein, 1927, b&w, music track, 100 min.)

RECOMMENDED READING:

Eisenstein, Sergei, Film Form and Film Sense.
Leyda, Jay, Kino.
Roud, Richard (ed), Cinema: A Critical Dictionary, "Eisenstein."

SUGGESTED READING:

Andrew, J. Dudley, The Major Film Theories, I,3: "Sergei Eisenstein."
Barna, Yon, Eisenstein.
Barsacq, Leon, Caligari's Cabinet and Other Grand Illusions, ch 4: "Natural Scenery--Russia, 1914-1930."
Casty, Alan, Development of the Film, ch 3: "The Russians and Epic Montage."
Film Society Programmes: "October."
Hammen, Scott, Film Notes, "October."
Katz, Ephraim, The Film Encyclopedia, "Eisenstein," "The Soviet Union."
Lennig, Arthur, The Silent Voice, "Eisenstein," "October."
Leyda, Jay, and Z. Voynow, Eisenstein at Work.
Macdonald, Dwight, "Eisenstein, Pudovkin and Others," in Lewis Jacobs' The Emergence of Film Art.
Mast, Gerald, A Short History of the Movies, ch 8: "Soviet Montage."
Moussinac, Leon, Sergei Eisenstein.
New York Times Film Reviews, "October," Nov 3, 1928.
Rotha, Paul, The Film Till Now, Pt One, VI: "The Soviet Film."
Schnitzer, L & J, Cinema in Revolution.
Swallow, Norma, Eisenstein: A Documentary Portrait.

CLASS #11   U.S.S.R. II   NOVEMBER 6, 1984

FILMS TO BE SCREENED IN CLASS:

   Mother (V.I. Pudovkin, 1926, b&w, silent, 100 min.)
   Storm Over Asia (V.I. Pudovkin, 1928, b&w, silent, 80 min.)

RECOMMENDED READING:

   Pudovkin, V.I., Film Technique and Film Acting.

SUGGESTED READING:

   Film Society Programmes, "Mother"
   Katz, Ephraim, The Film Encyclopedia, "Pudovkin"
   Lennig, Arthur, The Silent Voice, "Pudovkin," "Mother"
   New York Times Film Reviews, "Mother" Jan 8, 1928; "Storm Over Asia" Sep 8, 1930.
   Roud, Richard (ed), Cinema: A Critical Dictionary, "Pudovkin"
   Sadoul, Georges, Dictionary of Film Makers, "Pudovkin"
   Sadoul, Georges, Dictionary of Films, "Mat," "Potomok Chingis-Khan"

CLASS #12   U.S.S.R. III   NOVEMBER 13, 1984

FILMS TO BE SCREENED IN CLASS:

   The Man With The Movie Camera (Dziga Vertov, 1929, b&w, silent, 65 min.)
   Bed and Sofa (Abram Room, 1927, b&w, silent, 65 min.)

RECOMMENDED READING:

   Roud, Richard, Cinema: A Critical Dictionary, "Vertov," "Room."

SUGGESTED READING:

   Film Society Programmes, "Man with the Movie Camera," "Bed and Sofa."
   Hammen, Scott, Film Notes, "Man with the Movie Camera."
   Katz, Ephraim, The Film Encyclopedia, "Vertov," "Room"
   Lennig, Arthur, The Silent Voice, "Bed and Sofa"
   Sadoul, Georges, Dictionary of Film Makers, "Vertov," "Room"
   Sadoul, Georges, Dictionary of Films, "Chelovek s Kinoapparotom."
   Sitney, P. Adams, The Essential Cinema, ch 5: "From Magician to Epistomologist: Vertov's The Man With the Movie Camera."

CLASS #13   NORWAY/SWEDEN   NOVEMBER 20, 1984

FILMS TO BE SCREENED IN CLASS:

The Growth of the Soil (Norway, Gunnar Sommerfled, 1921, b&w, silent, 55 min.)
Thomas Graal's Best Child (Sweden, Mauritz Stiller, 1918, b&w, silent, 53 min.)
The Phantom Chariot (Sweden, Victor Sjostrom, 1920, b&w, silent, 63 min.)

RECOMMENDED READING:

Hardy, Forsyth, ScandinavianCinema.
Roud, Richard (ed), Cinema: A Critical Dictionary, "Stiller," "Sjostrom"

SUGGESTED READING:

Barsacq, Leon, Caligari's Cabinet and Other Grand Illusions, ch 3: "Towards a Film Aesthetic: Sweden and Germany, 1917-1922"
Cowie, Peter, A Concise History of the Cinema, ch 6: "Scandinavia"
Katz, Ephraim, The Film Encyclopedia, "Stiller," "Sjostrom"
Pensel, Hans, Sjostrom and Stiller in Hollywood.
Robinson, David, Hollywood in the Twenties, ch 4: "Invaders: Sjostrom & Stiller"
Sadoul, Georges, Dictionary of Film Makers, "Stiller," "Sjostrom"
Sadoul, Geroges, Dictionary of Films, "Korkarlen"
Walker Arts Center, The Rivals of D.W. Griffith, "Thomas Graal's Best Child"

CLASS #14   DENMARK   NOVEMBER 27, 1984

FILMS TO BE SCREENED IN CLASS:

 The Master of the House (Denmark, Carl-Theodor Dreyer, 1925, b&w, silent, 80 min.)
 The Passion of Joan of Arc (France, Carl-Theodor Dreyer, 1928, b&w, silent, 85 min.)

RECOMMENDED READING:

 Bordwell, David, The Films of Carl-Theodor Dreyer
 Milne, Tom, The Cinema of Carl Dreyer
 Roud, Richard (ed), Cinema: A Critical Dictionary, "Dreyer--Early Works"

SUGGESTED READING:

 Danish Institute, The Story of Danish Film.
 Film Society Programmes, "The Passion of Joan of Arc"
 Katz, Ephraim, The Film Encyclopedia, "Dreyer," "Denmark"
 New York Times Film Reviews, "The Passion of Joan of Arc" five entries
 Potamkin, Harry Alan, "The Passion of Joan of Arc" in Lewis Jacobs' The Emergence of Film Art.
 Sadoul, Georges, Dictionary of Film Makers, "Dreyer"
 Sadoul, Georges, Dictionary of Films, "Le Passion de Jeanne d'Arc," "Du Skal Aere Din Hustru"
 Skoller, Donald, Dreyer in Double Reflection
 Solomon, Stanley, The Classic Cinema, "The Passion of Joan of Arc"

CLASS #15   GREAT BRITAIN   DECEMBER 4, 1984

FILMS TO BE SCREENED IN CLASS:

    The Lodger (Alfred Hitchcock, 1926, b&w, silent, 65 min.)
    The Manxman (Alfred Hitchcock, 1929, b&w, silent, 80 min.)

RECOMMENDED READING:

    Low, Rachel, The History of the British Film, 1896-1929, 4 vols.
    Roud, Richard (ed), Cinema: A Critical Dictionary, "Hitchcock," (2 articles)
    Truffaut, Francois, Hitchcock.

SUGGESTED READING:

    Cowie, Peter, A Concise History of the Cinema, ch 2: "Britain."
    Harris, Robert, The Films of Alfred Hitchcock.
    Katz, Epharim, The Film Encyclopedia, "Hitchcock," "United Kingdom."
    New York Times Film Reviews, "The Manxman," Dec 17, 1929.
    Perry, George, The Great British Picture Show.
    Rotha, Paul, The Film Till Now, Pt One, XI: "The British Film."
    Sadoul, Georges, Dictionary of Film Makers, "Hitchcock."

CLASS #16   THE COMING OF SOUND   DECEMBER 11, 1984

FILMS TO BE SCREENED IN CLASS:

    Blackmail (Great Britain, Alfred Hitchcock, 1929, b&w, sound, 93 min.)
    Ecstasy (Czechoslovakia, Gustav Machaty, 1933, b&w, sound, 80 min.)

RECOMMENDED READING:

    Cavalcanti, Alberto, "The Sound Film," in Lewis Jacobs' The Emergence of Film Art.
    Mast, Gerald, A Short History of the Movies, ch 9: "Sound."
    Robinson, David, The History of World Cinema, ch 5: "Revolution: 1927-1930"

SUGGESTED READING:

    Brownlow, Kevin, The Parade's Gone By, ch 47: "The Talking Picture."
    Everson, William K., American Silent Film, ch 19: "Transition to Sound."
    Geduld, Harry, The Birth of the Talkies.
    Jacobs, Lewis, The Rise of the American Film, ch 22: "Refinements in Technique."
    Walker, Alexander, The Shattered Silents: How the Talkies Came to Stay.

A film/lecture course on the
history of American cinema in
the silent era: 1895-1929.

Instructor: Adam Reilly
University of Colorado at Boulder
Fall, 1981
Tuesdays, 5:15 to 9:00 pm

BEFORE TALKIES: EARLY AMERICAN FILM

Texts:

The assigned text book for the course is Kevin Brownlow's The Parade's Gone By... published by the University of California Press in paperback. This book is not designed as a text book as such, but is rather a unique compendium of interviews with the pioneers of the film industry giving first-hand accounts of life and work in those days. The book also reproduces many rare photographs from the era. Additional factual material and supplementary readings will be handed out in class to augment the above book.

Objectives of the Course:

1. To provide an introduction and overview of the first three and one half decades of the movies, concentrating on the development of the art and the technology of the medium and the people who made it happen.
2. To give the student an opportunity to view as much material from the silent era as possible, with lectures and discussion to help situate the films in the context of the work of the filmmakers, the conventions of the genres, the social milieu in which each was produced, and the contributions, if any, each film made toward advancing the art form.
3. To develop in the student a critical sense and appreciation for the films of this particular era.

Student Requirements for the Completion of the Course:

1. Preparation for class by reading the noted assignments.
2. Regular, punctual and active attendance of classes. Film can only be studied and appreciated by actually seeing the films themselves. Most of the films to be shown in this class are rarely screened elsewhere. So each class must be considered a unique, one-chance-only to view these films.
3. Completion of assignments:
   a. a brief objective quiz, given in class, based on the time-line and list of significant names and films (pages 0:5, 0:6, and 0:7 of these notes); this will be in our 6th class, Oct. 6th.
   b. a book report due at our 9th class, Oct 27th.
   c. critique of a silent film, dut at our 12th class, Nov 17th.
   d. a final take-home paper due at the close of the semester.
4. While not required, the students will be encouraged to see other films outside of class at various film societies, the Ogden, and the Denver Center Cinema.

Instructor:

Adam Reilly obtained his M.A. in Cinema Studies at New York University in 1969. He has taught film at Marymount Manhattan College, The New School for Social Research, was book review editor of Filmmakers Newsletter for five years, is the author of Harold Lloyd: The King of Daredevil Comedy (Macmillan, 1977), was director of the American Film Institute Theater at the Kennedy Center in Washington, D.C. for 2½ years, and is currently director of the Denver Center Cinema. Daytime phone: 893-4432 (Denver Center Cinema).

COURSE OUTLINE

1) Sep 01   **INVENTION**: The invention of the movies, the inventors, the machines, the primitive films; Thomas Edison, Edwin Porter, D.W. Griffith, the Biograph studios, etc.

2) Sep 08   **NARRATIVE I**: The first attempts at real storytelling; "Traffic in Souls," "The Whip," "Judith of Bethulia."

3) Sep 15   **NARRATIVE II**: D.W. Griffith refines and defines the art; "The Birth of a Nation."

4) Sep 22   **NARRATIVE III**: A more mature Griffith, "Broken Blossoms;" Henry King--Master Storyteller, "Tol'able David."

5) Sep 29   **THE DIRECTORS**: Cecil B. DeMille, "Male and Female."

6) Oct 06   **THE DIRECTORS**: Erich von Stroheim, "Greed," "The Wedding March."

7) Oct 13   **THE DIRECTORS**: Clarence Brown, "Smouldering Fires," "The Goose Woman."

8) Oct 20   **THE DIRECTORS**: Ernst Lubitsch, "The Marriage Circle," and Mal St. Clair (under Lubitsch), "Are Parents People?"

9) Oct 27   **THE STARS**: Rudolph Valentino, "The Eagle," "Son of the Shiek."

10) Nov 03   **THE STARS**: Lon Chaney, "The Penalty," "Phantom of the Opera."

11) Nov 10   **THE GENRES--COMEDY**: Charlie Chaplin, "The Pilgrim," Harold Lloyd, "Why Worry?" Buster Keaton, "Seven Chances," Harry Langdon, "Saturday Afternoon."

12) Nov 17   **THE GENRES--HORROR/SCI FI**: Shelton Lewis' "Dr Jekyll and Mr Hyde," Harold Lloyd's "Haunted Spooks," Paul Leni's "The Cat and the Canary," Willis O'Brien's "The Lost World."

13) Nov 24   **THE GENRES--THE WESTERN**: "The Great Train Robbery," "The $5000 Elopement," "The Iron Horse."

14) Dec 01   **THE GENRES--ANIMATION/SPECIAL EFFECTS**: selection of early cartoons: Bowers' "AWOL," Earl Hurd's "Bobby Bumps and the Speckled Death," Raoul Barre's "Cartoons on the Beach," Paul Terry's "Farmer Al Falfa," Winsor McCay's "Gertie the Dinosaur," J. Stewart Blackton's "Princess Nicotine," Walt Disney's "Puss in Boots," Pat Sullivan's "Felix Gets the Can," and Bud Fisher's "Mutt and Jeff." Plus a selection of American avant-garde films: Steiner's "H2O," Robert Florey's "The Life and Death of a Hollywood Extra," Herman Weinberg's "Autumn Fire," Weber and Watson's "The Fall of the House of Usher," plus their "Lot in Sodom."

15) Dec 08   **THE COMING OF SOUND**: "The Jazz Singer" [excerpt], "The Lights of New York" [excerpt], Robert Benchley's "The Sex Life of a Polyp," "George Bernard Shaw Talks for Movietone News," Mickey Mouse in "Steamboat Willie," plus Harold Lloyd's first talking feature, "Welcome Danger."

(Note: several titles may change due to availability of prints.)

University of Southern California
Fall Semester of 1987
Cinema 502a

Instructor: David Shepard
Phone: (818) 769-9247 (home)

COURSE OUTLINE: INTERNATIONAL SILENT CINEMA

"In the glorious period between 1912 and 1928, the new medium threw up fantastic showmen who projected exciting new images onto the silent screen:

> D.W. Griffith and Abel Gance
> Rex Ingram and Rene Clair
> Erich von Stroheim and Josef von Sternberg
> Fritz Lang and Victor Sjostrom
> Carl Dreyer and Jean Renoir
> Alfred Hitchcock and Anthony Asquith
> Ernst Lubitsch and Charlie Chaplin
> Douglas Fairbanks and Mary Pickford
> Walt Disney and Mickey Mouse
> Buster Keaton and Max Linder
> Laurel and Hardy
> Eisenstein and Pudovkin
> John Ford and Fred Niblo
> Allan Dwan and William Wellman
> Cecil B. DeMille

... to pick a handful of memorable names out of hundreds that are forgotten. What a blazing glory of talent and impudence! These men created the motion picture, the silent motion picture, long before a black-face comedian started to cry for his "Mammy". These pioneer directors came from everywhere and nowhere. From vaudeville, from the circus, from the gutter. They took silent movies for their own. The sky was the limit. When I was sixteen these men were gods to me.

I am writing this sixty-five years later and the names come up as fresh and green and inspiring as ever. I need no reference books. They are the creators and designers of my medium, they are my Leonoardo, my Chardin, my Daumier. They saw instinctively the limitations and advantages of a two-dimensional picture. Where there is no depth, movement must be lateral, particularly in comedy. The pioneers soon discovered that the camera can photograph thought as well as action. They discovered the power of mime. They discovered that in this wonderful medium, emotion could be shared between the actor and actress, the director and the audience ...

That was the silent film, that was! The greatest medium of communication, the greatest storytelling medium that has ever been invented ...

Silent films flowered in a decade of astonishing and unforgettable achievement, then withered at the trumpet of sound. But not and never to those of us who worked on them. Let my works bear witness for me."

-- Michael Powell

A Life in Movies (1987)

FORMAT

The purpose of this course is to excite and inform your interest in silent narrative film. We will view, read about and discuss complete works and excerpts from films produced prior to 1934 in light of some aesthetic, social, technological and economic considerations surrounding them. Every week includes +/- four hours of screening and discussion. As there is no way to "make up" missed films and insights with notes, your commitment to this class must include faithful attendance and participation.

You are expected to be familiar with the broad outline of film history and for that reason, no survey text is assigned. If the names of most filmmakers on this outline are unfamiliar to you, you should assume the extra responsibility of learning about them from such general books as A History of Narrative Film by David Cook.

In lieu of a single text, topical readings are due each week as noted. All are available as a xerox packet for purchase, and are on reserve in complete form. Dates are cited for all works prior to 1960. Country of origin is cited for films of other than U.S. production.

A term project will develop your special interest in silent film under the instructor's guidance. You are expected to complete your work by December 1st. It may be unusual in format but must be responsive both to your own interest and to the course content. Once you have chosen your subject, you must obtain the instructor's advance approval.

Your grade will reflect attendance, participation and attitude (30%), two short reading quizzes (15%), the term project (30%), and your final examination (25%).

Supplementary Screenings are offered on two Saturdays: October 10th and November 14th. Attendance is optional. If you attend, you will almost certainly find the films very interesting and well worth the time in the dark!

SCHEDULE

September 1 SILENT FILM: IMAGE AND METAPHOR

View:
"Fantasmagorie" (1907, France, Emil Cohl)
"The Automatic Moving Company" (1912, Italy, Romeo Bossetti)
"Dream of a Rarebit Fiend" (1906, E.S. Porter)
"The Acrobatic Fly" (1908, England, F. Percy Smith)
"Amor Pedestre" (1913, Italy, attributed to M. Fabre)
"The High Sign" (1920, Buster Keaton)
"Old Heidelberg" (1927, Ernst Lubitsch)

September 8 DISCONTINUOUS TO CONTINUOUS NARRATIVE 1886-1906

Read: Tino Balio, "A Novelty Spawns Small Businesses" in The American Film Industry (revised ed.), 3-25; W.K.L. Dickson, "A Brief History of the Kinetograph, the Kinestoscope and the Kineto-phonograph" (1933) and Louis Lumiere, "The Lumiere Cinematograph" (1936) in Fielding (ed.), A Technological History of Motion Pictures and Television, 9-16 and 49-51; Tom Gunning, "The Non-Continuous Style of Early Film (1900-1906);" N.Y. Daily Tribune, "From What Strange Source" (1903) in Deutelbaum (ed.), "Image" on the Art and Evolution of the Film, 32-37; Iris Barry, "George Melies: Magician and Film Pioneer" (1939), in Bandy (ed.), Rediscovering French Film, 42-43; John Fell, "Dissolves by Gaslight" in Film and the Narrative Tradition, 12-36; Frank Norris, McTeague (1899), excerpt from Chapter 6.

View: "Lumiere's First Picture Show" (compilation of 1895-1896 French films)
"Peep Show Films" (compilation, 1895-1902)
"Jack and the Beanstalk," "How They Do Things on the Bow'ry," "Life of an American
   Fireman," "The Great Train Robbery," "The Train Wreckers" (1902-1905, E.S.
   Porter)
"Rescued by Rover" (2 versions), "A Day With the Gipsies" (C. Hepworth, England,
   1905-06)
"The Palace of the Arabian Nights" (1905, G. Melies)
"Humorous Phases of Funny Faces" (1906, Vitagraph Co.)

September 15 THE NICKELODEON ERA

Read: Russell Merritt, "Nickelodeon Theaters 1905-1914: Building an Audience for the Movies" in Balio, 83-102; Linda Arvidson, When the Movies Were Young (1925), 29-36 and 45-61; Rick Altman, "'The Lonely Villa' and Griffith's Paradigmatic Style," in Quarterly Review of Film Studies 6, No. 2, 123-131; Merritt, "Mr. Griffith, 'The Painted Lady,' and the Distractive Frame" in Deutelbaum, 147-152; Robert Anderson, "The Motion Picture Patents Company: A Reevaluation" in Balio, 133-152; George Pratt, "See Mr. Ince," in Deutelbaum, 85-93; Camille, original review in Pratt (ed.), Spellbound in Darkness, 115-116; Richard Roud, "Louis Feuillade and the Serial" in Bandy, 44-51.

View: "Seeing Boston by Streetcar" (1906, Biograph)
"Those Awful Hats" (1909, D.W. Griffith)
"Troubles of a Grasswidower" (1908, Max Linder, France)
"Flying at Rhiems" (1908, Pathe Freres, France)
"The Lonely Villa" (1909), "Corner in Wheat" (1909), "The Painted Lady" (1912), "The
   Girl and Her Trust" (1912), D.W. Griffith
"Camille" (1912, Andre Calmettes, France, excerpt)
"Juve vs. Fantomas" (1913, Louis Feuillade, France, excerpt)
"Blazing the Trail" (1912, Thos. H. Ince)
"Suspense" (1913, Lois Weber)

"Mabel's Married Life" (1914, Mabel Normand)

September 22 THE FIRST FEATURES

Read: Victor O. Freeburg, The Art of Photoplay Making, (1918), 7-25; David Bordwell, Kristin Thompson, Janet Staiger, The Classical Hollywood Cinema, 128-153; Richard Koszarski, "Maurice Tourneur: the First of the Visual Stylists" in Film Comment 9, No. 2, 24-31; Raoul Walsh, Each Man in His Time, 114-121.

View: "Cabiria" (1914, Giovanni Pastrone, Italy, excerpt)
"The Cheat" (1915, Cecil B. DeMille)
"The Wishing Ring" (1914, Maurice Tourneur)
"Regeneration" (1915, Raoul Walsh, excerpt)

September 29 AMERICAN FILM AND THE FIRST WORLD WAR

Read: Raoul Sobel and David Francis, Chaplin, Genesis of a Clown, 87-120; Lewis Jacobs, The Rise of the American Film (1939), 248-263; Kristin Thompson, Exporting Entertainment, 61-99; Balio, "Stars in Business" in Balio, 152-172.

READING QUIZ

View: "Unknown Chaplin: My Happiest Years" (1982, Kevin Brownlow and David Gill, England)
"The Moving Picture Boys in the Great War" (1974, David Shepard and Larry Ward)
"Shoulder Arms" (1918, Charles Chaplin)

October 6 DEFINING SCREEN CHARACTER

Read: Freeburg, 192-203; Peter Milne, Motion Picture Directing (1922), 38-46; Dudley Andrew, Film in the Aura of Art 16-27; Arthur Lennig, The Silent Voice, 189-193, 198-202.

View: "The Parson's Widow" (1920, Carl Th. Dreyer, Sweden)
"The Phantom Chariot" (1920, Victor Sjostrom, Sweden, excerpt only)
"Miss Lulu Bett" (1921, William C. deMille)
"Broken Blossoms" (1919, D.W. Griffith, excerpt)

October 10 OPTIONAL SUPPLEMENTARY SCREENING
"PROGRAM PICTURES" FROM THE U.S.A.

9:30 "Hell's Hinges" (1916) Ince-produced Western starring William S. Hart
10:30 "A Movie Romance" (1917) An abridgement of a feature directed by Maurice Tourneur which depicts movie making of the period
11:00 "The Mark of Zorro" (1920) Douglas Fairbanks' first costume swashbuckler, exhilarating, directed by Fred Niblo.
1:30 "Smouldering Fires" (1924) A "woman's film," starring Pauline Frederick

2:40	and brilliantly directed by Clarence Brown. "For Heaven's Sake" (1926) Harold Lloyd "gag" comedy -- really funny, and with great L.A. locations.
3:45	"The Kiss" (1929) Greta Garbo and Lew Ayres, directed by Jacques Feyder. The last silent film from a major studio (MGM), of interest also for stunning art deco sets by C. Gibbons.
October 13	DEPICTING THE SUBJECTIVE STATE
Read:	Richard Abel, French Cinema, the First Wave, 279-294, 340-344, 367-373, 395-402; Lotte H. Eisner, The Haunted Screen, 9-27, 207-221; Lennig, 211-222.
View:	"La souriante Madame Beudet" (1923, Germaine Dulac, France) "The Cabinet of Dr. Caligari" (1919, Robert Wiene, Germany, excerpt only) "Le brasier ardent" (1923, Ivan Mosjoukine, France, excerpt only) "The Last Laugh" (1924, F.W. Murnau, Germany, excerpt) "Menilmontant" (1925, Dimitri Kirsanov, France)
October 20	REALISM, STYLIZATION AND ACTUALITY I.
Read:	Richard Koszarski, The Man You Loved to Hate, 114-149; Norris, McTeague, chapters 1 and 2 (1899)l; Jean Renoir, "Memories" (1938) in Bandy, 97-101.
View:	"Greed" (1924, Erich von Stroheim) "Nana" (1926, Jean Renoir, France, excerpt only) "Ueberfall" (1929, Erno Metzner, Germany)
October 27	LEGEND
Read:	Abel, 241-275, 428-455; Eisner 44-59, 64-74, 151-170, 223-236, 385-293.
View:	"Der Golem" (1920, Paul Wegener and Karl Boese, Germany, excerpt) "Siegfried: (1923, Fritz Lang, Germany, excerpt) "Faust" (1926, F.W. Murnau, Germany, excerpt) "Metropolis" (1926, Fritz Lang, Germany, excerpt) "The Miracle of the Wolves" (1924, Raymond Bernard, France, excerpt) "Napoleon" (1927, Abel Gance, France, excerpts)
November 3	CONCEPTS OF MONTAGE IN SOVIET FILM I.
Read:	David Bordwell, "The Idea of Montage in Soviet Art and Film" in Cinema Journal 11, No. 2, 11-17; V.I. Pudovkin, Film Technique (1929), 26-33, 38-50, 93-136; Vance Kepley, "Pudovkin and the Classical Hollywood Tradition"; Herbert Marshall, Masters of the Soviet Cinema; 10-14, 16-24; Anatoli Golovnia, "Broken Cudgels" in Schnitzler (3d.), Cinema in

Revolution, 133-149.

View: short excerpts from "Intolerance" and "Way Down East" (1916, 1920, D.W. Griffith) and "Mother" (1926, V.I. Pudovkin, U.S.S.R.)

"Storm Over Asia" (1928, V.I. Pudovkin, U.S.S.R.)
"Strike" (1924, S.M. Eisenstein, U.S.S.R., excerpt)

November 10 CONCEPTS OF MONTAGE IN SOVIET FILM II.

Read: Jay Leyda, Kino, 245-276; Lennig 341-343, 347-356.
READING QUIZ

View: "Bed and Sofa" (Abram Room, 1926, U.S.S.R.)
"A Fragment of an Empire" (Friedrich Ermler, 1929, U.S.S.R.)

November 14 OPTIONAL SUPPLEMENTARY SCREENING:
FILM CLASSICS YOU SHOULD SEE IF YOU HAVEN'T

9:30 GRASS (1925, Schoedsack and Cooper)
10:30 MOR VRAN (1930, Jean Epstein, France)
11:00 THE PASSION OF JOAN OF ARC (1928, Carl Dreyer, France)
1:35 SPIONE (1928, Fritz Lang, Germany)
3:15 PANDORA'S BOX (1928, G.W. Pabst, Germany)

November 17 REALISM, STYLIZATION AND ACTUALITY II

Read: Frances H. Flaherty, "The Odyssey of a Film-Maker"; Paul Rotha, Robert J. Flaherty (1959) 106-139, 337-340

View: "How the Myth Was Made" (1978, George C. Stoney)
"Man of Aran" (1934, Robert Flaherty, England)

November 24 REALISM, STYLIZATION AND ACTUALITY III

Read: Standish D. Lawder, The Cubist Cinema, 35-64; Joris Ivens, The Camera and I (1940) 34-41; William C. Uricchio, "Ruttman's 'Berlin' and the City Film to 1930" (excerpt, unpublished); Vance Kepley, In the Service of the State, 75-84.

View: German experimental films: "Symphonie Diagonale" (1921, Eggling); Rhythmus 21," "Filmstudie" (1925-26, Richter), Lichtspiel, Opus 1 (1921, Ruttmann)
"Berlin, the Symphony of a Great City" (1927, Walther Ruttmann, Germany)
"Rain" (1929, Joris Ivens, Netherlands)
"Earth" (1930, Alexander Dovzhenko, Ukraine)

December 1   THE AMERICAN FILM INDUSTRY AND ITS AUDIENCE

TERM PROJECTS DUE!

Read: Jacobs, 395-415; Bordwell et al, 281-293; Halsey, Stuart & Co., "The Motion Picture Industry as a Basis for Bond Financing" (1927) and Douglas Gomery, "U.S. Film Exhibition: The Formation of a Big Business" in Balio, 193-228; Lennig 123-126; Deutelbaum, "King Vidor's 'The Crowd' in Deutelbaum, 166-170

December 8   THE END OF THE SILENT ERA

Read: Benjamin Hampton, A History of the Movies (1931), 326-347; Robert C. Allen, "William Fox Presents 'Sunrise', Steven Lipkin, "'Sunrise': A Film Meets Its Public", and Dudley Andrew, "The Gravity of 'Sunrise'", in Quarterly Review of Film Studies, 2, No. 3, 327-387; William C. deMille, Hollywood Saga, 266-293.

View: "Sunrise" (1927, F.W. Murnau)

FINAL EXAMINATION

Department of Cinema Studies
Tisch School of the Arts
New York University

Fall Term, 1987
Mon., 6-9:30 p.m.

H72.2106   AMERICAN FILM, 1945-1960

Professor Robert Sklar

Schedule of Lectures, Screenings, and Reading Assignments

Sept. 21   Screening: THEY LIVE BY NIGHT (Nicholas Ray, RKO, 95 min., 1948)

No Reading Assignment

Sept. 28   Screening: IN A LONELY PLACE (Ray, Columbia, 94 min., 1950)

1. Peter Biskind, "THEY LIVE BY NIGHT by Daylight," S&S 45 (Autumn 1976), 218-22
2. Michael Wilmington, "Nicholas Ray: The Years at RKO (Part One)," VLT 10 (Fall 1973), 46-5:
3. Victor Navasky, Naming Names (1980), 78-195, 436-441

Oct. 5   Screening: ACE IN THE HOLE (Billy Wilder, Paramount, 112 min., 1951)

1. J.P. Telotte, "Film Noir and the Dangers of Discourse," QRFS 9 (Sp. 1984), 101-12
2. Manny Farber, "The Gimp," [1952] in Negative Space, 71-83
3. Robert K. Merton, "Social Structure and Anomie," Social Theory and Social Structure, 185-21

Oct. 12   Screening: THE NAKED SPUR (Anthony Mann, MGM, 91 min., 1953)

1. Jim Kitses, Horizons West (1969), 29-80
2. Robert Warshow, "Movie Chronicle: The Westerner," The Immediate Experience, 135-54
3. Edward Buscombe, "The Idea of Genre in the American Cinema," in Grant, ed., Film Genre Reader, 11-25

Oct. 19   Screening: PICKUP ON SOUTH STREET (Samuel Fuller, 20th-Fox, 80 min., 1953)

1. Frank McConnell, "PICKUP ON SOUTH STREET and the Metamorphosis of the Thriller," Film Heritage 8 (1973), 9-18
2. Jack Shadoian, Dreams and Dead Ends: The American Gangster/Crime Film (1977), 221-233
3. David Riesman, The Lonely Crowd (1950), 66-82

Oct. 26   Screening: JOHNNY GUITAR (Ray, Republic, 110 min., 1954)

1. Michael Wilmington, "Nicholas Ray's JOHNNY GUITAR," VLT 12 (1974), 19-25
2. Jacqueline Levitin, "The Western: Any Good Roles for Feminists?" FR 5 (1982), 95-108
3. Rebecca Bell-Metereau, Hollywood Androgyny, 80-95, 242-243

Nov. 2   Screening: ON THE WATERFRONT (Elia Kazan, Columbia, 108 min., 1954)

1. Kenneth R. Hey, "Ambivalence as a Theme in ON THE WATERFRONT (1954): An Interdisciplinary Approach to Film Study," in Rollins, ed., Hollywood as Historian, 159-189
2. P. Biskind, "The Politics of Power in ON THE WATERFRONT," FQ 29 (Fall 1975), 25-38
3. Navasky, Naming Names, 199-222, 441-42

AMERICAN FILM, 1945-1960, page 2

Nov. 9 Screening: KISS ME DEADLY (Robert Aldrich, United Artists, 105 min., 1955)

1. Carol Flinn, "Sound, Woman and the Bomb: Dismembering the 'Great Whatsit' in KISS ME DEADLY," Wide Angle 8:3/4 (1986), 115-127
2. J.P. Telotte, "Talk and Trouble: KISS ME DEADLY's Apocalyptic Discourse,' Journal of Popular Film and Television 13:2 (1985), 69-79
3. Erik H. Erikson, Identity: Youth and Crisis (1968 [1956]), 208-231

Nov. 16 Screening: REBEL WITHOUT A CAUSE (Ray, Warner Bros., 111 min., 1955)

1. P. Biskind, "REBEL WITHOUT A CAUSE: Nicholas Ray in the Fifties," FQ 28 (Fall 1974), 32-38
2. John Francis Kreidl, Nicholas Ray (1977), pp. 73-146.
3. Robert Lindner, "The Mutiny of the Young," Must You Conform? (1956), 3-28

Nov. 23 Screening: THERE'S ALWAYS TOMORROW (Douglas Sirk, Universal, 84 min., 1956)

1. Laura Mulvey, "Notes on Sirk and Melodrama," Movie No. 25 (Winter 1977/78), 53-56
2. Rainer Werner Fassbinder, "Fassbinder on Sirk," Film Comment 11 (Nov. 1975)
3. Thomas Elsaesser, "Tales of Sound and Fury: Observations on the Family Melodrama," in Nichols, ed., Movies and Methods, Vol. II, 165-189

Nov. 30 Screening: BIGGER THAN LIFE (Ray, 20th-Fox, 95 min., 1956)

1. Roger D. McNiven, "The Middle-Class American Home of the Fifties: The Use of Architecture in Nicholas Ray's BIGGER THAN LIFE and Douglas Sirk's ALL THAT HEAVEN ALLOWS," CJ 22:4 (Summer 1983), 38-57
2. D.N. Rodowick, "Madness, Authority, and Ideology in the Domestic Melodrama of the 1950s," VLT 19 (1982), 40-45
3. C. Wright Mills, White Collar: The American Middle Classes (1951), 239-286

Dec. 7 Screening: WRITTEN ON THE WIND (Sirk, Universal, 92 min., 1956)

1. Christine Saxton, "The Collective Voice as Cultural Voice," CJ 26:1 (Fall 1986), 19-30
2. Christopher Orr, "Closure and Containment: Marylee Hadley in WRITTEN ON THE WIND," WA 4:2 (1980), 28-35
3. Barbara Klinger, "'Cinema/Ideology/Criticism' Revisited: The Progressive Genre," in Grant, Film Genre Reader, 74-90

Dec. 14 Screening: SOME CAME RUNNING (Vincente Minnelli, MGM, 137 min., 1958)

1. T. Elsaesser, "Vincente Minnelli," in Altman, ed., Genre: The Musical: A Reader, 8-27
2. Geoffrey Nowell-Smith, "Minnelli and Melodrama," in Movies and Methods, Vol. II, 190-194
3. Arnold W. Green, "Why Americans Feel Insecure," in Brossard, The Scene Before You: A New Approach to American Culture (1955), 161-179

Jan. 11 Screening: IMITATION OF LIFE (Sirk, Universal, 125 min., 1959)

1. Marina Heung, "'What's the Matter with Sara Jane?': Daughters and Mothers in Douglas Sirk's IMITATION OF LIFE," CJ 26:3 (Spring 1987), 21-43
2. Thomas Schatz, Hollywood Genres, 221-260
3. Erving Goffman, "Performances," The Presentation of Self in Everyday Life (1959), 17-76

Department of Cinema Studies
Tisch School of the Arts
New York University

Spring Term, 1987
Weds., 6-9 p.m.

H72.1100   FILM HISTORIOGRAPHY

Professor Robert Sklar

Schedule of Lectures, Screenings, and Reading Assignments

February 4   Introductory Lecture, No Reading Assignment

Case Study #1: Kracauer and Weimar Cinema

February 11   Screening: DAS CABINET DES DR. CALIGARI [THE CABINET OF DR. CALIGARI]
(Robert Wiene, Germany, 1919)

1. Walter Benjamin, "Theses on the Philosophy of History," Illuminations, 253-264
2. Paul Ricoeur, The Contribution of French Historiography to the Theory of Histo:
3. Dominick LaCapra, "Rhetoric and History," History & Criticism, 15-44

February 18   1. Siegfried Kracauer, From Caligari to Hitler: A Psychological Study of the Germa Film, 3-11, 61-76, 96-106
2. Patrice Petro, "From Lukacs to Kracauer and Beyond: Social Films Histories and the German Cinema," Cinema Journal, 22:3 (Spring 1983), 47-70
3. Hayden White, "Interpretation and History" and "Historicism, History and the Figurative Imagination," Tropics of Discourse, 51-80, 101-120

February 25   Screening: HINTERTREPPEN [BACKSTAIRS]
(Leopold Jessner, Germany, 1921)

1. Noel Carroll, "THE CABINET OF DR. CALIGARI," Millennium Film Journal, 1:2 (1978), 77-85
2. Lotte Eisner, The Haunted Screen, 9-37
3. Thomas Elsaesser, "Social Mobility and the Fantastic: German Silent Cinema," Wide Angle, 5:2 (1982), 14-25

March 4   Screening: SCHERBEN [SHATTERED]
(Lupu Pick, Germany, 1921)

1. Martin Jay, "The Extraterritorial Life of Siegfried Kracauer," Salmagundi, Nos. 31-32 (1975-76), 49-106
2. Michel Foucault, "What Is an Author?", Language, Counter Memory, Practice, 113-138
3. Robert C. Allen & Douglas Gomery, Film History: Theory and Practice, 153-172

March 11   1. Thomas Elsaesser, "Film History and Visual Pleasure: Weimar Cinema," Cinema Histories, Cinema Practices, 47-84
2. Allen & Gomery, Film History: Theory and Practice, 3-23
3. Christine Faure, "Absent from History," Signs, 7:1 (1981), 71-80

March 18   Mid-Term Essays and Class Presentations due

FILM HISTORIOGRAPHY, Spring Term, 1987, page 2

Case Study #2: A Japanese World War II Film

April 1   Screening: TATAKAU HEITAI [THE SOLDIERS AT THE FRONT]
             (Fumio Kamai, Japan, 1940)

             1. Joseph L. Anderson and Donald Richie, The Japanese Film, 126-158
             2. Tadao Sato, Currents in Japanese Cinema, 100-115
             3. Noel Burch, To the Distant Observer: Form and Meaning in the Japanese Cinema,
                25-54, 262-269

April 8   1. Michel Foucault, "Nietzsche, Genealogy, History," Language, Counter-Memory,
                Practice, 139-164
             2. Hayden White, "Foucault Decoded: Notes from Underground," Tropics of Discourse
                230-260
             3. Giuliana Bruno, "Toward a Theorization of Film History," Iris, 2:2 (1984), 41-

Case Study #3: Film Noir

April 15   Screening: THE DARK CORNER (Henry Hathaway, 20th-Fox, 1946)

             1. David Bordwell, "Lowering the Stakes: Prospects for a Historical Poetics of
                Cinema," Iris, 1:1 (1983), 5-18
             2. Kristin Thompson, "Cinematic Specificity in Film Criticism and History,"
                Iris 1:1 (1983), 39-49
             3. David Bordwell, "The Bounds of Difference," The Classical Hollywood Cinema, 70

April 22   Screening: CRISS CROSS (Robert Siodmak, Universal, 1949)

             1. Siegfried Kracauer, "Hollywood's Terror Films," Commentary, 2 (1946), 132-136
             2. Martha Wolfenstein and Nathan Leites, Movies: A Psychological Study, 175-242
             3. Paul Jensen, "The Return of Dr. Caligari: Paranoia in Hollywood,"
                Film Comment, 7:4 (1971-72), 36-45

April 29   Screening: DOUBLE INDEMNITY (Billy Wilder, Paramount, 1944)

             1. James Damico, "Film Noir: A Modest Proposal," Film Reader 3, (1978), 48-57
             2. Paul Schrader, "Notes on Film Noir," Film Comment, 8 (Spring 1972), 8-13
             3. Robert G. Porfirio, "No Way Out: Existential Motifs in the Film Noir,"
                Sight & Sound, 45:4 (1976), 212-217

May 6   Screening: OUT OF THE PAST (Jacques Tourneur, RKO, 1947)

             1-3. E. Ann Kaplan, ed., Women in Film Noir, the following essays: Sylvia Harvey
             "Women's Place: The Absent Family of Film Noir," 22-34; Janey Place, "Women in
             Film Noir," 35-67; Claire Johnston, "DOUBLE INDEMNITY," 100-111

May 13   1. Richard Maltby, "Film Noir: The Politics of the Maladjusted Text,"
                Journal of American Studies, 18:1 (1984), 49-71
             2. Philip Kemp, "From the Nightmare Factory: HUAC and the Politics of Noir,"
                Sight & Sound, 55:4 (1986), 266-270
             3. Thomas Elsaesser, "The New Film History," Sight & Sound, 55:4 (1986), 246-251

Department of Cinema Studies
Tisch School of the Arts
New York University

Spring Term, 1988
Weds., 6-9 p.m.

H72.1100   FILM HISTORIOGRAPHY

Professor Robert Sklar

Schedule of Lectures, Screenings, and Reading Assignments

February 3   Introductory Lecture, No Reading Assignment

                  Screening: LADRI DI BICICLETTE (Vittorio de Sica, Italy, 1948, 87 min.)
                  [U.S. title, THE BICYCLE THIEF]

Historiography and Historical Theory

February 10   1. Walter Benjamin, "Theses on the Philosophy of History," Illuminations, 253-264
                2. Paul Ricoeur, The Contribution of French Historiography to the Theory of Histor
                3. Dominick LaCapra, "Rhetoric and History," History & Criticism, 15-44

                Screening: M (Fritz Lang, Germany, 1931, 90 min.)

February 17   1. Louis Althusser, "Ideology and Ideological State Apparatuses," in
                  Lenin and Philosophy, 127-186
                2. Raymond Williams, "Base and Superstructure in Marxist Cultural Theory," in
                  Problems in Materialism and Culture, 31-49
                3. Richard Johnson, "Three Problematics: Elements of a Theory of Working-Class
                  Culture," in Working Class Culture: Studies in History and Theory
                  eds. J. Clarke, C. Critcher, and R. Johnson, 201-237, 282-288

                Screening: Films of Edwin S. Porter, U.S., 1904-1908

February 24   1. Michel Foucault, "Nietzsche, Genealogy, History," Language, Counter-Memory,
                  Practice, 139-164
                2. Mark Poster, "A New Kind of History," Foucault, Marxism & History, 70-94
                3. Hayden White, "Interpretation and History" and "Historicism, History and the
                  Figurative Imagination," in Tropics of Discourse, 51-80, 101-120

          Case Study #1: Early American Silent Cinema

March 2   1. Robert Sklar, "Oh! Althusser!: Historiography and the Rise of Cinema Studies,"
                  forthcoming in Radical History Review 41 (Spring 1988)
                2. Robert C. Allen, "Contra the Chaser Theory," Wide Angle 3:1 (1979), 4-11
                3. Charles Musser, "Another Look at the 'Chaser Theory'," response by Allen,
                  reply by Musser, Studies in Visual Communication 10:4 (Fall 1984), 24-52

March 9   1. Noel Burch, "Porter, or Ambivalence," Screen 19:4 ((Winter 1978/9), 91-105
                2. Kristin Thompson and David Bordwell, "Linearity, Materialism, and the Study
                  of Early American Cinema," Wide Angle 5:3 (1983), 4-15
                3. Charles Musser, "The Nickelodeon Era Begins: Establishing a Framework for
                  Hollywood's Mode of Representation," Framework 22/23 (Autumn 1983), 4-11

FILM HISTORIOGRAPHY, Spring Term, 1988, page 2

March 16
1. Michel Foucault, "What Is an Author?", Language, Counter-Memory, Practice, 113-138
2. Tom Gunning, "Non-Continuity, Continuity, Discontinuity: A Theory of Genres in Early Film," Iris 2:1 (1984), 101-112
3. Miriam Hansen, "Early Silent Cinema: Whose Public Sphere?" New German Critique 29 (Winter 1983), 147-184

March 23
Mid-term Essays due; No Class meeting

Case Study #2: M and Weimar Cinema

April 6
1. Siegfried Kracauer, From Caligari to Hitler: A Psychological Study of the German Film, 3-11, 215-222
2. Patrice Petro, "From Lukacs to Kracauer and Beyond: Social Film Histories and the German Cinema," Cinema Journal, 22:3 (Spring 1983), 47-70
3. Thomas Elsaesser, "Film History and Visual Pleasure: Weimar Cinema," Cinema Histories, Cinema Practices, 47-84

April 13
1. Noel Burch, "Fritz Lang: German Period," in Cinema, A Critical Dictionary: The Major Film-Makers, Vol. 2, ed. Richard Roud, 583-599
2. Eric Rhode, "Fritz Lang (The German Period: 1919-1933), Tower of Babel: Speculations on the Cinema, 85-105
3. Noel Carroll, "Lang, Pabst, and Sound," Cine-Tracts 2:1 (Fall 1978), 15-23

April 20
1. Patrice Petro, "Modernity and Mass Culture in Weimar: Contours of a Discourse on Sexuality in Early Theories of Perception and Representation," New German Critique 40 (Winter 1987), 115-146
2. Christine Faure, "Absent from History," Signs, 7:1 (1981), 71-80
3. Thomas Elsaesser, "Social Mobility and the Fantastic: German Silent Cinema," Wide Angle, 5:2 (1982), 14-25

Case Study #3: LADRI DI BICICLETTE and Italian Neorealism

April 27
1. Andre Bazin, "An Aesthetic of Reality: Neorealism" and "Bicycle Thief," in What Is Cinema?, Vol. II, 16-40, 47-60
2. Roy Armes, Patterns of Realism, 17-28, 141-156
3. Millicent Marcus, Italian Film in the Light of Neorealism, 3-29

May 4
1. Peter Bondanella, Italian Cinema: From Neorealism to the Present, 31-73
2. Mira Liehm, Passion and Defiance: Film in Italy from 1942 to the Present, 60-89
3. Millicent Marcus, Italian Film in the Light of Neorealism, 54-75

May 11
1. Mario Cannella, "Ideology and Aesthetic Hypotheses in the Criticism of Neo-Realism," Screen 14:4 (Winter 1973/4), 5-60
2. Eric Rhode, "Why Neo-Realism Failed," Sight & Sound 30:1 (Winter 1960/1), 26-32
3. Geoffrey Nowell-Smith. "Cinema Nuovo and Neo-Realism," Screen 17:4 (Winter 1976/7), 111-117

Film/English 215   Introduction to American Film   Winter 87   T. Sobchack

Course Objectives: To examine the growth and development of the forms of American film. Hollywood is both a place and an idea. It is a part of the entertainment industry, and it has set the standard for the theatrical fiction film all over the world. But it has also fostered world class filmmakers who are revered by critics and scholars everywhere. This course will investigate the Hollywood form, the idea of genre, the notion of cultural production, and some of the individual directors who have created individual films and bodies of work of great distinction.

Text: An Introduction to Film, 2nd ed., Sobchack & Sobchack

Class Schedule:

Week of	Title	Topic	Reading
1/5	ROBIN HOOD (Silent)	Film History	Intro. pp. 44-53, 104-11, 163-9, Ch. 1.
1/12	SINGIN' IN THE RAIN	The Coming of Sound	Intro. Ch. 4.
1/19	GOLDDIGGERS OF 1933	Genre Comedy	Intro. Ch. 2, Ch. 5, Schatz (on reserve)
1/26	STAGECOACH	Auteurs	Intro. Ch. 3, Ch. 6.
1/28	FIRST PAPER DUE	(Read Intro. Ch. 9 before writing paper.)	
2/2	THREE MUSKETEERS (Kelly)	Genre Melodrama	Intro. Ch. 5.
2/9	THREE MUSKETEERS (Lester)	Genre Parody	Intro. Ch. 5.
2/16	DOUBLE INDEMNITY	Film Noir	Intro. Ch. 5.
2/23	S.O.B.	Hollywood Business	Intro. Ch. 1, Ch. 6.
3/1	BADLANDS	Artists	Intro. Ch. 6.
3/3	SECOND PAPER DUE		
3/8	BIRTH OF A NATION	Artists	Historical Overviews Ch. 2,3,4,5

Student Responsibility: Readings must be completed before the Thursday class meeting so that everyone can participate in the class discussion. There will be a mid-term and a final exam (dates to be announced) which will contain both short answer and essay questions. Two short papers on topics relative to the quarter's work will also be prepared. Directions to follow.

Theater Arts 181B: Silent Film History
German Expressionist & Soviet Cinemas
T/TH **3:15-5:15** p.m. + (Lecture & Screenings)
Evening Screenings: 7:30 p.m. (Thimann 3)
All screening & lectures in Thimann 3

Winter 1986
Vivian Sobchack
Office: D124 Porter
x4462;
x2951 message

REQUIRED TEXTS (Available at Bay Tree Bookstore and Bookshop Santa Cruz and on reserve in McHenry):

Eisner, Lotte H.	THE HAUNTED SCREEN
Leyda, Jay	KINO: A HISTORY OF THE RUSSIAN AND SOVIET FILM
Schnitzer & Marin, eds.	CINEMA IN REVOLUTION (photocopy) only at Campus Copy Center)
Willett, John	ART & POLITICS IN THE WEIMAR PERIOD

RECOMMENDED TEXT (Available at bookstores and on reserve in McHenry):

Kracauer, Siegfried   FROM CALIGARI TO HITLER

REFERENCE MATERIALS (On 2-hour reserve in McHenry. Other books of interest on regular loan.)

Barna, Yon.	EISENSTEIN: THE GROWTH OF A CINEMATIC GENIUS
Dovzhenko, Alexander (Ed. & trans. Marco Carynnyk)	ALEXANDER DOVZHENKO: THE POET AS FILMMAKER
Eisenstein, Sergei	FILM FORM & FILM SENSE NOTES OF A FILM DIRECTOR IMMORAL MEMORIES FILM ESSAYS AND A LECTURE BY SERGEI EISENSTEIN
Eisner, Lotte H.	MURNAU
Jensen, Paul M.	THE CINEMA OF FRITZ LANG
Kulesov, Lev. (Trans. Ron Levaco)	KULESHOV ON FILM
Michelson, Annette, ed.	THE WRITINGS OF DZIGA VERTOV
Nizhny, Vladimir	LESSONS WITH EISENSTEIN
Pudovkin, V.I.	FILM TECHNIQUE & FILM ACTING

FEES: There will be a $20.00 screening fee to help cover the film costs for the course. Unless the fee is paid, you will not receive credit for the course or be able to register for next quarter. You will be billed by mail; pay promptly to avoid a late charge. No money will be collected in class; I will give you a CLASS PASS upon receipt of your name, SS#, student ID#, and a current mailing address. You must have a class pass--whether or not you use it for admittance to evening screenings. BE ADVISED: If your pass has been used, even if you drop the course, you must pay the full $20.00 fee; no prorating allowed.

SCREENINGS: You are expected to see all films at least once and are encouraged to see them twice (if they are screened twice). Plan in

Theater Arts 181B   Winter 1986

advance for the few films screened only in the evening. Your CLASS PASS
will admit you to evening screenings. Please be advised that screenings
may go past scheduled class times on some occasions. (Prompt attendance
to class will help avoid this.) A very few films of interest will be
available on videotape at the Recordings Desk in McHenry, and it is
possible that additional screenings of related films may be arranged;
these will be announced as they are planned and are optional.

DISCUSSION SECTIONS: In addition to class time noted above, you will
also be required to sign up for and attend a discussion section ONE HOUR
PER WEEK. In section, you will discuss films, readings, and develop
class projects as assigned. You must attend the same section all the
time; no floating allowed. Section times will be arranged dependent
upon total enrollment but will be sometime on Wednesdays and Thursdays.

ASSIGNMENTS: Written work for the class will consist of two take-home
essay examinations--one at midterm (at the end of the unit on German
Expressionist cinema) and the other at the end of the course (on Soviet
cinema). Note information under class dates below. As well, students
will be required to complete and present a project of their choice: a
term paper, a film, a photographic/slide presentation, design materials,
etc. These projects may be done individually or in small groups and
must be approved by the instructor or TAs. At the end of the quarter,
the entire class will meet to hear and look at presentations.

SCREENINGS & READINGS BY CLASS MEETING: Readings are DUE on the date
specified. Film titles are indicated in upper case; filmmakers and
release dates are indicated in parentheses. Please note single
screenings, midterm, and quarter-end exam dates, etc.

T   1/7/86   Introduction
                 MAGIC MEMORIES 1901-1925 (Sampling of early films)
                 OVER THERE 1914-1918 (Jean Aurel, 1963)

T   7:30 p.m.   THE CABINET OF DR. CALIGARI (Robert Wiene, 1919)
                 NOSFERATU (F. W. Murnau, 1922)

TH   1/9   THE GREAT PRIMITIVES (A sampling of early silents)
                 THE CABINET OF DR. CALIGARI
                 Reading: Eisner: Forward; Chaps. 1 & 2

T   1/14   NOSFERATU
                 Reading: Eisner: Chaps. 3 & 6; Willett, pp. 7-66

T   7:30 p.m.   NOSFERATU THE VAMPYR (Werner Herzog, 1979)
                 ONLY SCREENING!

TH   1/16   DESTINY (Fritz Lang, 1921)
                 Reading: Eisner: Chaps. 5 & 8

T   1/21   FAUST (F. W. Murnau, 1926)
                 Reading: Willett, pp. 67-94; Eisner: Chaps. 16 & 18

Theater Arts 181B   Winter 1986

T   7:30 p.m.   METROPOLIS (Fritz Lang, 1926) This is the Giorgio Moroder
                  reconstruction in color and with rock music.
                  ONLY SCREENING!

TH   1/23   METROPOLIS (This is a longer version than above.)
                  Reading: Eisner: Chaps. 9 & 13

T   1/28   THE LAST LAUGH (F. W. Murnau, 1924)
                  Reading: Willett, pp. 95-149; Eisner:
                     Chaps. 11, 12 & 15

T   7:30 p.m.   THE LAST LAUGH
                  VARIETY (E. A. Dupont, 1925)

TH   1/30   VARIETY
                  Reading: Eisner: Chap. 17

T   2/4   PANDORA'S BOX (G. W. Pabst, 1928)
                  Reading: Willett, pp. 149-176; Eisner:
                     Chaps. 19 & 20

T   7:30 p.m.   PANDORA'S BOX

TH   2/6   THE BLUE ANGEL (Joseph von Sternberg, 1930)
                  Reading: Willett, pp. 177-229
                  TAKE-HOME MIDTERM DISTRIBUTED. DUE BACK TUES. 2/11!

T   2/11   M (Fritz Lang, 1931)
                  Reading: Eisner: Chap. 14
                  MIDTERMS DUE BACK TODAY! No Late Exams accepted.

T   7:30 p.m.   A SLAVE OF LOVE (Nikita Mikhalkov, 1978)

TH   2/13   A SLAVE OF LOVE
                  Reading: Leyda, pp. 11-16; Chap. I

T   2/18   POTEMKIN (Sergei Eisenstein, 1925)
                  Reading: Leyda: Chap. II & III
                  Cinema in Revolution (CIR): Intro. &
                  Sections 1, 2, 4 & 6

T   7:30 p.m.   MOTHER (V.I. Pudovkin, 1926)

TH   2/20   MOTHER
                  Reading: CIR: Sect. 8 & 9; Leyda: Chap. IV

T   2/25   BED AND SOFA (Abram Room, 1927)
                  Reading: Leyda: Chaps. V & VI; CIR: Sec. 7 & 11

T   7:30 p.m.   BED AND SOFA

TH   2/27   STORM OVER ASIA (V.I. Pudovkin, 1928)
                  Reading: Leyda: Chaps. VII & VIII

Theater Arts 181B   Winter 1986

T   3/4   THE END OF ST. PETERSBURG (V.I. Pudovkin, 1927)
                  Reading: Leyda: Chaps. IX, X & XI

T   7:30 p.m.   OCTOBER/TEN DAYS THAT SHOOK THE WORLD
                     (Sergei Eisenstein, 1928)

TH   3/6   OCTOBER
                  Reading: CIR, Sect. 3

T   3/11   EARTH (Alexander Dovzhenko, 1930)
                  Reading: Leyda: Chap. XII; CIR, Sect. 10

T   7:30 p.m.   MAN WITH A MOVIE CAMERA (Dziga Vertov, 1929)

TH   3/13   MAN WITH A MOVIE CAMERA
                  Reading: CIR, Sect. 5 & 12
                  TAKE-HOME FINAL DISTRIBUTED.   DUE BACK IN MY OFFICE
                  (D124 Porter) no later than 5 p.m. on TUES. 3/18

                  CLASS PROJECT MEETING TO BE ARRANGED

Films on reserve in Recordings on video (Theater Arts tapes)

GRIFFITH BIOGRAPH PROGRAM (5 short silents directed by Griffith c. 1909)

THE BLUE ANGEL (DER BLAUE ENGEL)   Be advised that subtitles are virtually
                                   unreadable on the tape--basically good
                                   for reviewing visuals if you've already
                                   seen the film.

"M" (Same problem as above tape)

EISENSTEIN (This is a documentary--with clips from E's films--made in
           the Soviet Union. It runs about an hour.)

THE MAN WITH A MOVIE CAMERA

Videos of interest held in McHenry

BEFORE MICKEY: AN ANIMATED ANTHOLOGY (a compilation of animated silents
                covering period 1898-1928)

Theater Arts 181A; Silent Film History
American and French Silent Cinemas
T/TH 3:15 plus pm Screenings & Lecture
W 7:30 pm Screenings
All screening & lectures in Thimann 3

Winter 1985
V. Sobchack
Office: D124
Porter College

Required Texts

Brownlow, Kevin. The Parade's Gone By . . . Berkeley: University of California Press, 1968.
Brownlow, Kevin. Napoleon: Abel Gance's Classic Film. New York: Alfred A. Knopf, 1983.
Mast, Gerald. A Short History of the Movies. Third Edition Indianapolis: Bobbs-Merrill, 1981.

Reserve Readings (Required readings are starred)

*Abel, Richard. "The Contribution of the French Literary Avante-Garde to Film Theory and Criticism (1907-1924)." Cinema Journal 14 (Spring 1975), 18-40.
Abel, Richard. French Cinema: The First Wave, 1915-1929. Princeton: Princeton University Press, 1984.
*Aiken, Edward A. "Reflections on Dada and the Cinema." Post Script 3 (Winter 1984), 5-20.
*Bunuel, Luis. "Notes on the making of Un Chien Andalou." From Art in Cinema, ed. Frank Stauffacher. San Francisco: Art in Cinema Society, San Francisco Museum of Modern Art, 1947, pp. 29-30.
Hammond, Paul. The Shadow and its Shadow: Surrealist Writings on Cinema. London: British Film Institute, 1978.
King, Norman. "The Sound of Silents." Screen 25 (May-June 1984), 2-15.
*Liebman, Stuart, "French Film Theory, 1910-1921." Quarterly Review of Film Studies 8 (Winter 1983), 1-23.
Mast, Gerald, ed. The Movies in Our Midst: Documents in the Cultural History of Film in America. Chicago: University of Chicago Press, 1982.
Matthews, J. H. Surrealism and Film. Ann Arbor: University of Michigan Press, 1971.
*Michelson, Annette. "Dr. Crase and Mr. Clair." October 11 (Winter 1979), 31-53.
Rosen, Philip. "Securing the Historical: Historiography and the Classical Cinema." In Cinema Histories, Cinema Practices, eds. Patricia Mellencamp and Philip Rosen. Frederick, MD: American Film Institute, 1984, pp. 17-31.
Sobchack, Thomas and Vivian. An Introduction to Film. Boston: Little, Brown, 1980.

Fees

There will be a $15.00 screening fee to help cover the costs of film rentals as films are your primary texts. Unless the fee is paid, you will not get credit for this class nor be able to register for spring quarter. Upon receipt of your name, student ID number, and a current mailing address, you will receive a class pass which will allow you to see repeated films twice if you wish and also get you into the two films which are going to be screening in the evening only. You will be billed by mail for the pass! Your pass is nontransferable and, once used, non-returnable even if you drop the class.

Screenings

Please be advised that class screenings may extend beyond the 5:15 hour. This may occur because of the length of an individual film combined with lecture and/or quiz. Please also note that only some of the films screened in the afternoon will be repeated in the evening and three major films for the course will be shown in the EVENING ONLY! Intolerance will be shown January 16, and The Wind on February 20 at 7:30 p.m. only, and the other is the four hour epic, Napoleon, which will screen only on Wednesday, March 13 and will begin at 7:00 p.m. because of its length! Please note these dates and times. In addition to scheduled class films, other films may be screened for your benefit and pleasure. These will be announced as their occasion arises and are optional.

Discussion Sections

In addition to the above specified class times, you will also be required to sign up for and regularly attend a discussion section which meets one hour per week. In this more intimate group, you will discuss films and readings and research strategies. The sections will meet on Wednesday and Thursday and times will be determined during the first week of class. All sections will meet in the Film Lab in Porter D140.

Papers and Quizzes

There will be three short answer quizzes administered in the large class on dates specified. In addition, there will be a take-home final examination requiring essay-length responses; this will be given out on the last day of class and will be due back by 5:00 p.m. on the Monday of exam week (March 18). Students must also plan and complete a research project related to course concerns; this can be a written research paper of 15 pages, or some approved alternative. Be advised: There will be no make-up quizzes, and late work will be considered unacceptable without consent of instructor and a very good reason.

Screenings and Readings (by class meeting)

Readings are due on the date indictated. Quiz dates are also indicated. Films are underlined. Approximate running times are also provided although these can be way off at times due to problems with catalog listings, etc. Please also note those films which play only in the evening: The Wind and Napoleon (and the latter's special time). Oops . . . Intolerance is also only going to be shown in the evening.

T	1/8/85	The Great Primitives (selections from the work of Thomas Edison, Auguste and Louis Lumiere, George Melies, Edwin S. Porter, and Cecil Hepworth). 1894-1905. (54 min.) The Age of Ballyhoo (a documentary on American culture during the silent period.) (55 min.)
W	1/9	NO EVENING SCREENING. SERIES STARTS NEXT WEEK!
TH	1/10	Griffith Biograph Program: The Lonely Villa (1909); A Corner in Wheat (1909); The Lonedale Operator (1911, with Blanche Sweet); The Musketeers of Pig Alley (1912, with Lillian Gish); The New York Hat (1912, with Mary Pickford and scenario by Anita Loos). Program 75 min. READING: Parade: Sections 1, 2, 3, 4, 5, (pp. 1-40); History: Chaps, 1, 2, 3 (pp. 1-44)
T	1/15	The Birth of a Nation (D. W. Griffith, 1915). With Lillian Gish, Mae Marsh, H. B. Walthall. 130 min. with added music track. READING: Parade: Section 6 (41-63) and 8 (77-93); History: Chap. 4 (45-75). Also highly recommended is the reserve article on historiography by Rosen (which deals with Birth of a Nation as well as interrogating the writing of history).
W	1/16pm	Intolerance (D. W. Griffith, 1916). 164 min. ONLY SCREENING!
TH	1/17	Tol'able David (Henry King, 1921). With Richard Barthelmess. 95 min. READING: Parade: Sections 10 (105-117), 21 (259-267), and 31 (343-353).
T	1/22	Foolish Wives (Erich von Stroheim, 1922). 128 min. READING: History: Chap. 6 (104-118); Parade: Sections 30 (337-341), 37 (415-420), and 38 (421-427).
W	1/23pm	Foolish Wives
TH	1/24	The Blot (Lois Weber, 1929). 104 min. READING: Parade: Sections 22 (268-278), 23 (279-287), 25 (301-305).

T	1/29	QUIZ #1 Tillie's Punctured Romance (Mack Sennett and Charlie Chaplin, 1914). With Chaplin, Mabel Normand, and Marie Dressler. Added music track. 50 min. The Tramp (1915) 20 min. with music track. The Adventurer (1916) 20 min. with music track. READING: History: Chap. 5 (76-92); Parade: Sections 17 (211-221) and 24 (289-299)
W	1/30pm	Tillie's Punctured Romance; The Tramp; The Adventurer
TH	1/31	The Gold Rush (Chaplin, 1925). 85 min. With music track. READING: Parade: Section 44 (495-507)
T	2/5	The General (Buster Keaton, 1926). 108 min. with music track (?) READING: Parade: Sections 40 (435-445) and 43 (473-494); History: Chap. 6 (118-128)
W	2/6pm	The General and Cops
TH	2/7	Cops (Buster Keaton, 1922) 20 min. High and Dizzy (Harold Lloyd and Hal Roach, 1920) 36 min. Harold Lloyd's World of Comedy (documentary compilation) 30 min. Big Business (Laurel and Hardy, 1929) 20 min. READING: Parade: Sections 27 (313-324) and 42 (458-472)
T	2/12	Sunrise: A Song of Two Humans (F. W. Murnau, 1927). 95 min. with music track. READING: History: Chap. 7 (129-149); Parade: Sections 18 (224-235) and 19 (237-245)
W	2/13pm	Sunrise
TH	2/14	Reel of Silent Trailers (1924). 14 min. Dancing Mothers (Herbert Brenon, 1926), with Clara Bow. 70 min. READING: Parade: Sections 7 (65-75) and 28 (325-327)
T	2/19	Holiday--but keep up with the reading! READING: Parade: Sections 29 (330-335) and 45 (509-516); History: Chap. 8 (150-180)
W	2/20pm	The Wind (Victor Seastrom, 1928) with Lillian Gish. 120 min. ONLY SCREENING OF THIS FILM

TH	2/21	QUIZ #2 Paris from 1900 (documentary on period to 1914) 76 min. Gaumont Newsreel (1917) 10 min. Georges Melies: Cinema Magician (documentary compilation). 25 min. READING: History: Chap. 10 (193-217)
T	2/26	The Smiling Madame Beudet (Germaine Dulac, 1922) 40 min. Retour a la Raison (Man Ray, 1923) 4 min. Ballet Mecanique (Fernand Leger, 1924) 14 min. La Fille de l'eau (Jean Renoir, 1924) 5 min. Entr'acte (Rene Clair, 1924) 14 min. Un Chien Andalou (Luis Bunuel and Salvador Dali 1928) 16 min. READING: All on reserve: the articles by Abel, Aiken, Bunuel, and Liebman. Highly recommended are the 1st chapter of Matthews book and browsing through Hammond.
W	2/27pm	The Smiling Madame Beudet and The Crazy Ray (Paris Qui Dort)
TH	2/28	The Hasher's Delirium (Emile Cohl, 1906) 3 min. Fantasmagorie and The Automatic Moving Company (Cohl, 1906) 14 min. The Crazy Ray/Paris Qui Dort (Rene 'Clair, 1923) 66 min. READING: On reserve: Michelson article. Napoleon: 9-65.
T	3/5	Crainquebelle (Jacques Feyder, 1923). 55 min. The Little Match Girl (Jean Renoir, 1928). 27 min. with music track. READING: Napoleon: 67-176
W	3/6pm	Crainquebelle and The Little Match Girl
TH	3/7	Menilmontant (Dmitri Kirsanov, 1925) 40 min. Charleston (Jean Renoir, 1927) 24 min. Le Petit Lilie (Alberto Cavalcanti, 1928) 10 min. with music track READING: Napoleon: 178-228
T	3/12	QUIZ #3 Abel Gance: The Charm of Dynamite (Kevin Brownlow, 1968) 52 min. READING: Napoleon: 229-289. Recommended: reserve article by King.

W	3/13pm	Napoleon (Abel Gance, 1927) 240 min. with music. THIS SCREENING BEGINS AT 7:00 pm! Be early; no seats will be saved and it is likely to sell out!
TH	3/14	The Passion of Joan of Arc (Carl Dreyer, 1928) 82 min. READING: History: Chap. 9 (181-192); Parade: Section 47 (565-577) and recommended is Section 46 (517-564) Take Home Final will be given out. Due back (typed) on Monday, March 18 by 5:00 pm.

Theater Arts 162B: Sound Film History   T/TH 3:15-5:15+ Thiman 3
Film & Historiography: "The Sound of Canons"   W 7:30pm Screenings Classroom
Vivian Sobchack (D1124 Porter)   Unit 11

Required Texts

Mast, Gerald, A Short History of the Movies, Third Edition
Mast, Gerald, ed. The Movies in our Midst.

Recommended Texts (on sale & or reserve in McHenry)

Carr, Edward H., What is History?
Sobchack & Sobchack, An Introduction to Film. (This latter book is helpful for those of you who have not previously studied film aesthetics and need a basic understanding and vocabulary. As well, there is a chapter on writing papers about film from various aesthetic and cultural perspectives.)

Fees: There is a $15.00 screening fee to assist covering costs of film rentals. Unless the fee is paid, you will not be considered registered for this class and cannot get credit; as well, a hold will be put on further registration. You will be billed by mail upon receipt of your name, student ID# and a current mailing address. You will receive a "CLASS PASS" enabling you to attend evening screenings where the pass must be shown to differentiate you from the general university public. (Also be advised that you need the pass whether you go to evening screenings or not.)

Assignments: You will be required to attend class meetings and one hour of discussion section each week. Attendance at evening screenings is not mandatory-- except in the instances when that is the only time a particular film will be shown (as indicated below). The screenings, however, are highly recommended. Make sure you see each film at least once! In addition to the readings and screenings, you will be required to write three short (5-8 pp.) typed pages each) papers relating to course concepts. There will be no final examination. There may be short spot quizzes on aspects of reading.

Sections: All sections will be held in the Porter Film Study Center (D 140). You are not allowed to section-hop, but must sign up for a section and stick with it. You are required to attend, and if you cannot do so, don't take the course. Hours will be arranged dependent upon enrollment and general desire, but they will be held between Tuesday evening and Thursday afternoon.

Screenings and Readings: Readings are to be done by the date indicated, and they are generally relevant to the films being screened that date. Be aware that, on occasion, screenings may go over 5:15 mark. Also watch for those very few films that will be screened on Wednesday evenings only!

T	4/3	Introduction: What is Film History? Why "The Sound of Canons"? Technological History. THE MOVIES LEARN TO TALK (26 min.) LA CUCARACHA (1934, 19 min.) First film made in 3-color Technicolor.
W pm	4/4	SINGIN' IN THE RAIN (1952, Gene Kelly & Stanley Donen, USA. 101 min.)
TH	4/5	Genre History meets Technological History: SINGIN' IN THE RAIN Reading: History: Chap. 9; Anthology: "Pictures that Talk" (241-43); "The Vitaphone" (254-57); "Color and Sound on Film" (302-8); and "The Don'ts and Be Carefuls" (213-14).
T	4/10	Black History: BLACK SHADOWS ON THE SILVER SCREEN (55 min.) SECTION SIGN-UP!!! Reading: Anthology: Pieces on BIRTH OF A NATION controversy (122-35); "The Voice of Vitaphone" (243-54); "Warner Bros. Innovates Sound: A Business History" (267-82); Aldous Huxley & Robert Sherwood debate on sound film (282-9).
W pm	4/11	HALLELUJAH! (1929, King Vidor, USA. 100 min.) with BLACK SHADOWS ON THE SILVER SCREEN
TH	4/12	Black History meets Genre History Out of Technological History HALLELUJAH! Reading: Anthology: "The Cultural Influence of the 'Talkies'" (291-4); "The Birth of the Production Code" (317-21); "The Motion Picture Production Code of 1930" (321-33).
T	4/17	Aesthetic History/Auteur History CITIZEN KANE (1941, Orson Welles, USA. 119 min.) Reading: History: Chapters 10 & 11; Anthology: "Moving-Picture and Radio Propaganda" (476-88).
W pm	4/18	GRAND ILLUSION (1937, Jean Renoir, France. 111 min.) ONLY SCREENING!!!
TH	4/19	History of Film Movements: Italian Neo-Realism ROMA: OPEN CITY (1945, Roberto Rossellini, Italy. 103 min.) Reading: History, pp. 280-87 only + Chapter 12.
T	4/24	Political History: Writings & Re-writings HOLLYWOOD ON TRIAL (1976, David Helpern, USA. 100 min.) Reading: Anthology pp. 441-4 + HUAC Hearing Transcripts (496-535); "Hollywood on Trial" (536-45).
W pm	4/25	HOLLYWOOD ON TRIAL
TH	4/26	THE FRONT (1976, Martin Ritt, USA. 94 min.) Reading: Anthology: "Report on Blacklisting" (570-88).
T	5/1	SALT OF THE EARTH (1954, Herbert Biberman, USA. 94 min.) Reading: Anthology: "Documentation of the Red Stars in Hollywood (545-9); "Communist Infiltration of Hollywood Motion Picture Industry" (550-70); "Hollywood and the U.S.A." (620-34).
W pm	5/2	NEWSFRONT (1978, Phillip Noyce, Australia. 110 min.)
TH	5/3	NEWSFRONT Reading: Anthology: "Freedom of the Movies" (488-96); "The Paramount Case and its Legal Background" (594-99).

T	5/8	Political History meets Genre History through Technological History IT CAME FROM OUTER SPACE (1953, Jack Arnold, USA. 80 min.) in 3-D!!! Reading: Anthology "Hollywood in the Television Age" (634-39+ 643-51); "3-D High, Wide, and Handsome" (646-55); "Hollywood Faces the World" (667-73).
W pm	5/9	IT CAME FROM OUTER SPACE
TH	5/10	STRANGER THAN SCIENCE FICTION (27 min. made in 1969) THE SHAPE OF FILMS TO COME (26 min. made in 1968) Reading: Anthology: "The New Hollywood: Myth and Anti-Myth." (683-93); "On the Future of Movies" (734-44).
T	5/15	Auteur History ECLIPSE (1962, Michelangelo Antonioni, Italy, 123 min.) Reading: History: pp. 287-332. Anthology: "When the Movies Really Counted" (419-27).
W pm	5/16	A MARRIED WOMAN (1965, Jean-Luc Godard, France. 94 min.) Reading: Anthology: "Fantasies of the Art House Audience" (674-83)
T	5/22	Feminist History: Women's Pictures A VERY CURIOUS GIRL (1969, Nelly Kaplan, France. 105 min.) Reading: Anthology: "Sex Pictures" (194-200); "See No Evil" (693-704); "Linda Lovelace: The Blue-ing of America" (720-28); "Synaesthetic Cinema and Polymorphic Eroticism" (728-33).
W pm	5/23	A VERY CURIOUS GIRL
TH	5/24	UNION MAIDS (1975, 50 min.) THE LIFE & TIMES OF ROSIE THE RIVETER (1981, Lorraine Kahn, USA. 60 min.)
T	5/29	Third World History CEDDO (1977, Cusmene Sembane, Senegal. 120 min.) Reading: History: Chapter 14
W pm	5/30	LUCIA (1969, Humbetto Solas, Cuba. 160 min!!!) ONLY SCREENING!!!!!
TH	5/31	CHIQUIAGO (1977, Antonio Esquino, Bolivia. 87 min.) Reading: Anthology: "The Raise of the Year from a 'Board of Robots'" (744-49)
T	6/5	History as Production & Historical Consciousness BUFFALO BILL AND THE INDIANS, OR SITTING BULL'S HISTORY LESSON (1975, Robert Altman, USA. 123 min.) Reading: History: Chapters 15 & 16.
W pm	6/6	BUFFALO BILL AND THE INDIANS

Theater Arts 182A: Sound Film History   T/TH 3:15-5:15+ Thimann 3
Film & Ideology: "The Politics of Power"   W 7:30 pm Screenings
Vivian Sobchack (D124 Porter)   Thimann 3

Required Texts

Harvey, Sylvia, May '68 and Film Culture.
Mast, Gerald, A Short History of the Movies, Third Edition.
Mast, Gerald, ed. The Movies in our Midst.

Recommended Texts (on sale and on reserve in McHenry Library)

Sobchack & Sobchack, An Introduction to Film. (This latter book is helpful
    for those of you who have not previously studied film
    aesthetics and need a basic understanding and vocabulary.
    As well, there is a chapter on writing papers about
    film from various aesthetic and cultural perspectives).

Fees: There is a $15.00 screening fee to assist covering cost of film rentals. Unless the fee is paid, you will not be considered registered for this class and cannot get credit; as well, a hold will be put on further registration. You will be billed by mail upon receipt of your name, student ID#, social security # and a current mailing address. You will receive a "CLASS PASS" enabling you to attend evening screenings where the pass must be shown to differentiate you from the general university public. (Also be advised that you need the pass whether you go to evening screenings or not).

Assignments: You will be required to attend class meetings and one hour of discussion section each week. Attendance at evening screenings is not mandatory -- except in the instance when that is the only time a particular film will be shown (as indicated below). The screenings, however, are highly recommended. Make sure you see each film at least once! In addition to the readings and screenings, you will be required to write three short (5-8 pp. typed pages each) papers relating to course concerns. There will be no final examination. There may be short spot quizzes on aspects of reading and lectures.

Sections: All sections will be held in the Porter Film Study Center (D140). You are not allowed to section-hop, but must sign up for a section and stick with it. You are required to attend, and if you cannot do so, don't take the course. Hours will be arranged dependent upon enrollment and general desire, but they will be held between Tuesday evening and Thursday evening.

Screenings and Readings: Readings are to be done by the date indicated, and they are generally relevant to the films being screened that date. Be aware that, on occasion, screenings may go over 5:15 mark. Also watch for the single film that will be screened on Wednesday evenings only: (Grand Illusion 4/10).

Theater Arts   Spring 1985

T	4/2	Introduction: What is Film History? Why "The Politics of Power"? THE MOVIES LEARN TO TALK (26 min.) LA CUCARACH (1934, 19 min.) First live-action film in 3-strip Technicolor.
Wpm	4/3	GABRIEL OVER THE WHITE HOUSE (1933, Gregory LaCava, USA, 87 min.) With Walter Huston.
TH	4/4	GABRIEL OVER THE WHITE HOUSE Reading: History: Chap. 9 (Sound): Anthology: "Pictures that Talk" (241-43), "The Vitaphone" (254-57), "Color and Sound on Film" (302-8), and "The Don'ts and Be Carefuls" (213-14).
T	4/9	TRIUMPH OF THE WILL (1935, Leni Riefenstahl, Germany, 110 min.) Reading: History: Chap. 7 (The German Golden Age), and Chap. 10 (France between the Wars).
Wpm	4/10	GRAND ILLUSION (1937, Jean Renoir, France, 111 min.) THIS IS THE ONLY SCREENING OF THIS FILM! It is required.
TH	4/11	OPEN CITY: ROMA (1945, Roberto Rossellini, Italy, 103 min.) Reading: History: Chap. 13 (pp. 280-87); Anthology: "The War Abroad, a War at Home" (441-44), "War in the World of Make Believe " (445-53), and "The Movies" (453-467).
T	4/16	MR. SMITH GOES TO WASHINGTON (1939, Frank Capra, USA, 130 min.) With Jimmy Stewart and Jean Arthur. Reading: History: Chap. 11 (The American Studio Years 1930-1945); Anthology: "When the Movies Really Counted" (419-26).
Wpm	4/17	MEET JOHN DOE (1941, Frank Capra, USA, 135 min.) With Gary Cooper and Barbara Stanwyck.
TH	4/18	MEET JOHN DOE Reading: Anthology: "So Proudly We Fail" (467-70), "Is Hollywood Growing Up?" (470-75), "Moving-Picture and Radio Propaganda" (476-88), and "Freedom of the Movies: (488-96).
T	4/23	CITIZEN KANE (1941, Orson Welles, USA, 119 min.) Reading: History: Chap. 12 (Hollywood in Transition 1946-1965).

Theater Arts   Spring 1985

Wpm   4/24   ALL THE KING'S MEN (1949, Robert Rossen, USA, 109 min.)
               With Broderick Crawford and Mercedes McCambridge.

TH   4/25   ALL THE KING'S MEN
               Reading: "Hollywood in the Television Age" (634-45),
               "3-D: High, Wide, and Handsome" (647-655), "Hollywood
               Faces the World" (667-73).

T   4/30   SALT OF THE EARTH (1954, Herbert Biberman, USA, 94 min.)
               Reading: Anthology: "Hollywood on Trial" (536-45),
               "Hearings Regarding the Communist Infiltration of the
               Motion-Picture-Industry Activities in the United States"
               (496-535).

Wpm   5/1   A KING IN NEW YORK (1957, Charles Chaplin, USA, 105 min.)

TH   5/2   A KING IN NEW YORK
               Reading: Anthology: "Report on Blacklisting" (570-88),
               "Communist Infiltration of Hollywood Motion-Picture
               Industry" (550-70), "Hollywood and the U.S.A." (620-34).

T   5/7   LA CHINOISE (1967, Jean-Luc Godard, France, 96 min.)
               Reading: History: Chap. 13 (pp. 302-332); May '68,
               pp. 1-43, 121-5, 149-65.

Wpm   5/8   LA CHINOISE

TH   5/9   BATTLE OF ALGIERS (1966, Gillo Pontecorvo, France,
               123 min.)
               Reading: May '68, pp. 45-86.

T   5/14   THE CONFORMIST (1970, Bernardo Bertolucci, Italy, 116 min.)
               Reading: History: Chap. 13 (pp. 287-302); Chap. 14
               (pp. 333-61, 377-400).

Wpm   5/15   THE CONFORMIST

TH   5/16   THE CANDIDATE (1972, Michael Ritchie, USA, 111 min.)
               Reading: History: Chaps. 15 and 16 (The New Hollywood
               1966-1978, and A Sixth American Era?); Anthology:
               "The New Hollywood: Myth and Anti-Myth" (683-93).

T   5/21   MEMORIES OF UNDERDEVELOPMENT (1973, Tomas Guttierez
               Alea, Cuba, 97 min.)
               Reading: History: Chap. 14 (400-412); May '68:
               pp. 87-119.

Theater Arts   Spring 1985

Wpm	5/22	ONE WAY OR ANOTHER (1975-79), Sara Gomez, Cuba, 78 min.)
TH	5/23	ONE WAY OR ANOTHER Reading: May '68: pp. 139-48
T	5/28	THE LOST HONOR OF KATHERINA BLUM (1975, Volker Schlondorff and Margarethe von Trotta, West Germany, 102 min.) Reading: History: Chap. 14 (361-77)
Wpm	5/29	THE LOST HONOR OF KATHERINA BLUM
TH	5/30	LUCIA (1st story, 1972, Humberto Solas, Cuba) Reading: May '68: pp. 127-37.
T	6/4	COUP DE TORCHON (1982, Bertrand Tavernier, France, 128 min.) Reading: Anthology: "On the Future of Movies" (734-49)
Wpm	6/5	COUP DE TORCHON
TH	6/6	THE WILLMAR 8 (1980, Lee Grant, USA, 55 min.) Wrap-Up.

KEEP OUT OF THE HEAT? . . . GO TO A MOVIE!!

Theater Arts 171: Film Genres; Documentary
T/TH 10:45-12:45 pm Screenings, Discussion, & Lecture: Porter Film Lab #140
T   7:30 pm Screenings: Thimann Lecture Hall 3
Instructor: Vivian Sobchack (Office: D124 Porter; Phone: x 4462; Message: x2951)

Required Texts:
Barnouw, Erik. Documentary: A History of the Non-Fiction Film. New York: Oxford University Press, 1974.
Jacobs, Lewis. The Documentary Tradition, Second Edition. New York: W.W. Norton, 1979.

Recommended Texts:
Barsam, Richard M. Non-Fiction Film: Theory and Criticism.
Mamber, Stephen. Cinema Verite in America: Studies in Uncontrolled Documentary.
Sobchack, Thomas & Vivian C. An Introduction to Film. (This is recommended for those students who have no previous training in film analysis and aesthetics.)

Fees: There will be a $15.00 screening fee to help cover the costs of film rentals which are the primary texts for the class. You will be billed by mail. Unless fee is paid, you will not get credit for TA 171 nor be able to register for Spring quarter. Upon receipt of your name, mailing address, and student ID#, you will receive a class ticket which will alow you to see films in both afternoon and evening screenings. Your ticket is non-transferable and, once used, non-returnable even if you drop the class.

Screenings: Please be advised of the two locations for class and screenings (see above). Also note that the films screened during the day and night are not always the same. Some films will only be shown during the day, others only at night. PLEASE NOTE THE SINGLE 7:00 pm starting time for A MEMORY OF JUSTICE which runs 4½ hrs. It is also possible that additional screenings of available films may be arranged for your benefit and pleasure. These will be announced as they arise and are optional.

Written Work: Each student must keep on on-going Documentary Film Journal and make an entry for each film screened in class. The entry can engage the film with relevant readings and discussion, with other films, or raise theoretical and critical issues provoked by the film. Each entry must be legible and written to communicate to the instructor the depth and clarity of your thought (i.e., no cinematic grocery lists or poems allowed). The journal must be kept up to date and brought to class each meeting along with your texts. (I may ask for a presentation of an entry or for you to turn in the journal to date so I may share in your thoughts). In addition, a 15 page critical and/or theoretical paper on non-fiction film will be due at the quarter's end. (Topics should be checked with instructor well before beginning). Other small written assignments may be given during the quarter.

Screenings and Readings: (by class meeting). Readings are due on date indicated. Films are underlined and approximate running time given.

T   1/4/83   PIONEERS & EXPLORERS
               Cinematographie in 1895 (Lumiere films) 5 min.
               Moscow Clad in Snow (Pathe, 1909) 3 min.
               Nanook of the North (Robert Flaherty, 1921) 60 min.
T   7:30pm   Nanook of the North & Man of Aran
TH   1/6   Man of Aran (Robert Flaherty, 1934) 77 min.
               READING: Barnouw: "Prophet", pp. 1-30; "Explorer", pp. 33-51;
               Recommended, "Reporter", pp. 51-71; Jacobs: pp. 2-21, 25-28, 97-99

TA 171: Film Genres: Documentary

T	1/11	ADVOCATES & PAINTERS Night Mail (Basil Wright & Harry Watt, 1936) 24 min. The River (Pare Lorentz, 1937) 30 min. READING: Barnouw: "Advocates", pp. 85-139; Jacobs: pp. 72-76, 112-115, 123-125
T	7:30pm	Olympia, Part I (Leni Riefenstahl, 1938) 115 min. NIGHT ONLY
TH	1/13	Olympia (Diving Sequence only) 5 min. The City (Willard VanDyke & Ralph Steiner, 1939) 44 min. READING: Barnouw: "Painters", pp. 71-81; Jacobs: pp. 126-128, 131-135, 136-137, 138-140
T	1/18	BUGLER Divide and Conquer ("Why We Fight" Series, Frank Capra, 1943) 60 min. Battle of San Pietro (John Huston, 1944) 39 min. READING: Barnouw: "Buglers", pp. 139-172
T	7:30pm	Divide and Conquer & The Battle of San Pietro
TH	1/20	Prelude to War ("Why We Fight" Series, Frank Capra, 1942) 54 min. READING: Jacobs: pp. 167-174, 182-188, 213-223, 224-225, 205-210
T	1/25	CHRONICLER March of Time: Marriage and Divorce (Louis deRochemont, 1948) 20 min. Night and Fog (Alain Resnais, 1955) 31 min. READING: Barnouw: "Chronicler", pp. 172-182; Jacobs: pp. 104-111, 301-306, 276-282
T	7:30pm	City of Gold (Colin Low & Wolf Koenig, 1958) 23 min. NIGHT ONLY Dead Birds (Robert Gardiner, 1963) 83 min.
TH	1/27	Dead Birds 83 min. READING: Barnouw: pp. 198-212; Jacobs: pp. 430-436
T	2/1	PROMOTER Harvest of Shame (CBS, David Lowe, 1960) Edward R. Murrow narrator, 54 min. READING: Barnouw: "Promoter", pp. 213-228; Jacobs: pp. 327-333, 494-499
T	7:30pm	Grey Gardens (Maysles Brothers, 1976) 94 min.
TH	2/3	OBSERVER Grey Gardens 94 min. READING: Barnouw: "Observer", pp. 231-252; Jacobs: pp. 368-380, 400-406, 466-468. Recommended: Mamber, Cinema Verite in America
T	2/8	Lonely Boy (Wolf Koenig & Ralph Kroitor, 1961) 27 min. Happy Mother's Day (Richard Leacock & Joyce Chopra, 1964) 26 min. READING: Jacobs: pp. 406-419, 420-424. Also Mamber recommended.
T	7:30pm	High School (Frederick Wiseman, 1968) 75 min.
TH	2/10	High School 75 min. READING: Jacobs: pp. 459-461, 477-482, 536-550. Mamber recommended.
T	2/15	CATALYST No Lies (Mitchell Block 1973) 15 min. READING: Barnouw: "Catalyst", pp. 253-262
T	7:00pm	The Memory of Justice (Marcel Ophuls, 1976) 278 min. 4½ hrs. Begin Early! THIS IS THE ONLY SCREENING OF THIS FILM. PLAN FOR DINNER.
TH	2/17	READING: Jacobs: pp. 514-517, 521-522. Possibly one reel of above film may be screened.

TA 171: Film Genres: Documentary

T	2/22	GUERILLA The Selling of the Pentagon (CBS, Peter Davis, 1971) 52 min. READING: Barnouw: "Guerillas", pp. 262-287; Jacobs: pp. 518-520, 551-556
T	7:30pm	The Selling of the Pentagon and Interviews with MyLai Veterans
TH	2/24	Interviews with MyLai Veterans (Joseph Strick, 1970) 22 min.
T	3/1	PARTICIPANT Poto and Cabengo (Jean-Pierre Gorin, 1979) 77 min. READING: Barnouw: pp. 287-288
T	7:30pm	Poto and Cabengo & La Soufriere
TH	3/3	La Soufriere (Werner Herzog, 1977) 39 min. Land Without Bread (Luis Bunuel, 1932) 28 min. READING: Barnouw: "Poet", pp. 185-198; Jacobs: p. 146
T	3/8	RECLAIMERS & REVISIONISTS Right Out of History: The Making of Judy Chicago's Dinner Party (Johanna Demetrakas, 1980) 75 min. READING: Jacobs: pp. 523-535
T	7:30pm	Right Out of History & The Life and Times of Rosie the Riveter
TH	3/10	The Life and Times of Rosie the Riveter (1981) 60 min. READING: Jacobs: pp. 563-568

III. FILM GENRES

Spring 1988 Dr. Braudy
Tues, 12:30-3 CTC 205/7
English/Cinema-TV 579
SEMINAR IN GENRE THEORY

I. From Literature to Film: Some Basic Myths Reseen
Jan 12 Genre and Ritual: Horror as religion
James Whale, Frankenstein (1931)
Mary Shelley, Frankenstein (1819)

Jan 19 Todd Browning, Dracula (1931)
Bram Stoker, Dracula (1897)
Suggested: William Friedkin, The Exorcist (1973)
M. G. Lewis, The Monk (1796)

Jan 26 Genre and Gender: Horror and the Divided Self
Robert Louis Stevenson, The Strange Case of Dr. Jekyll and Mr. Hyde (1886)
Rouben Mamoulian, Dr. Jekyll and Mr. Hyde (1932)
Suggested: Victor Fleming: Dr. Jekyll and Mr. Hyde (1941)

Feb 2 Alfred Hitchcock, Shadow of a Doubt (1943)
Edgar Allan Poe (d. 1849): William Wilson; Murders in the Rue Morgue; The Purloined Letter

Feb 9 Genre and Pattern: The Detective Story
Howard Hawks, The Big Sleep (1946)
Dashiell Hammett, The Maltese Falcon (1930)
Arthur Conan Doyle, The Adventures of Sherlock Holmes
Suggested: John Huston, The Maltese Falcon (1941)

Feb 16 Robert Aldrich, Kiss Me, Deadly (1955)
Mickey Spillane, I, the Jury (1947)
Suggested: Ross Macdonald, Black Money (1966)

II. Genre and Film Form: The Possibilities of Self-Criticism
Feb. 23 Genre and History: The Western
Howard Hawks, Red River (1948)

March 1 John Sturges, Bad Day at Black Rock (1954)
Suggested: John Ford, Stagecoach (1939); The Searchers (1956);
The Man who Shot Liberty Valance (1962)
Robert Aldrich, Ulzana's Raid (1972)

March 8 Genre and Society: The Musical
Mark Sandrich, Shall We Dance? (1937)

March 15 Vincent Minnelli, The Pirate (1948)
Suggested: Robert Wise/Jerome Robbins, West Side Story (1961)
Perry Henzell, The Harder they Come (1973)

March 22 Genre and Gender: Crime and Comedy
Howard Hawks, Scarface (1932)

VACATION

Apr. 5 Fritz Lang, The Big Heat (1953)

Apr. 12 Billy Wilder, Some Like It Hot (1959)

Apr. 19 Genre and The Future: Technology and Politics
         Fritz Lang, Metropolis (1926)

Apr. 26 Christian Nyby/Howard Hawks, The Thing (1951)
Suggested: Robert Wise, The Day the Earth Stood Still (1951)
            Ridley Scott, Alien (1979)
            James Cameron, Terminator (1986)
            James Cameron, Aliens (1987)

Texts:

　　　　　Barry Keith Grant, ed., Film Genre Reader
　　　　　Gerald Mast, Marshall Cohen, Film Theory and Criticism
　　　　　Leo Braudy, The World in a Frame
　　　　　Jacques Derrida, "The Law of Genre"
　　　　　Robert Warshow, "The Westerner" and "The Gangster as
　　　　　　　Tragic Hero"
　　　　　Stanley Cavell, The World Viewed

BIBLIOGRAPHY

(Some useful works not included in Film Genre Reader bibliography)

Bateson, F.W. Toward an Ecology of Mind.

Bakhtin, M. M. The Dialogic Imagination.

---. See also Medvedev.

Cohen, Ralph. "On the Interrelation of Eighteenth-century Literary Forms," in New Approaches to Eighteenth-century Literature, ed. Phillip Harth.

Colie, Rosalie. The Resources of Kind: Genre Theory in the Renaissance.

De Lauretis, Teresa. Alice Doesn't: Feminism, Semiotics, Cinema.

Fowler, Alastair, Kinds of Literature: An Introduction to the Theory of Genre and Modes.

Frye, Northrop. A Natural Perspective.

Geertz, Clifford. The Interpretation of Cultures.

Gledhill, Christine, "Recent Developments in Feminist Criticism," in Film Theory and Criticism, eds. Gerald Mast and Marshall Cohen.

Guillen, Claudio. Literature as System: Essays toward the Theory of Literary History.

Hall, Edward. Beyond Culture.

---. The Silent Language.

Hernadi, Paul. Beyond Genre: New Directions in Literary Classification.

Jameson, Fredric. The Political Unconscious: Narrative as a Socially Symbolic Act.

Jauss, Hans Robert. Aesthetic Experience and Literary Hermeneutics.

Macherey, Pierre. A Theory of Literary Production.

Medvedev, P.N., and Bakhtin, M.M. The Formal Method in Literary Scholarship: A Critical Introduction to Sociological Poetics.

Metz, Christian. The Imaginary Signifier.

Mulvey, Laura. "Visual Pleasure and Narrative Cinema," in Film Theory and Criticism, eds. Gerald Mast and Marshall Cohen.

Scholes, Robert. Structuralism in Literature: An Introduction.

Silverman, Kaja. The Subject of Semiotics.

Todorov, Tzvetan. The Poetics of Prose.

Weimann, Robert. Shakespeare and The Popular Tradition in the Theater: Studies in The Social Dimension of Dramatic Form and Function.

Williams, Raymond. Culture.

---, Marxism and Literature.

Wolff, Janet. The Social Production of Art.

The Southern

A Regional Approach to Film

Edward D. C. Campbell, Jr.

Just as war movies, musicals, or detective stories, films of the South embrace certain conventions of plot, characterization, and often even cinematic style. And just as in westerns, movies about the South--southerns they might be called--are steeped in a mythology. Like the western, the southern presents a distinctive geographical area and, perhaps more important, a particular personality or temperament recognizable whether the production be a celebration of the region, as in Steamboat 'Round the Bend (1935), a gentle but respectful spoof, as in the musical comedy Mississippi (1935), or an indictment like Mandingo (1975).

Unlike the western, however, southerns have not necessarily produced an archetypal American hero; the region for all its seductive, mythological charm has its seamier side as well. For every graceful, paternal southern gentleman in So Red the Rose (1935), there is a grasping one in Bright Leaf (1950). The southern has, though, recorded in popular culture an evolving perception of a region's charms and faults and in so doing has also revealed the audiences' changing tastes and perceptions of a region and its history. Perhaps most important, southern films in many ways serve as benchmarks of race relations both in the region portrayed and in the nation as a whole.

The first screen images of the South date from the earliest days of film when a production's brief running time required themes that were already popular subjects that needed no explanation, subjects that were, in fact, instantly recognizable. For example, film pioneers like Thomas A. Edison shot scenes of Southern blacks dancing while his director, Edwin S. Porter, as early as 1903 presented the first film version of Uncle Tom's Cabin, complete with a grand riverside cotton plantation as the primary backdrop. With D. W. Griffith's Birth of Nation (1915) the southern mystique was complete, its primary settings and black and white characters already stereotyped.

Southern romanticism reached its height during Hollywood's golden era of the 1930s, with productions like Dixiana (1930), Steamboat 'Round the Bend (1935), and Gone With the Wind (1939). At even their simplest level, such productions with their large estates, loyal servants, and idealized belles—whether the stories were set in the pre- or post-Civil War South—served as a welcome escape from the harsh realities of the Depression.

A more honest view of the region developed during and after World War II. The war itself, the film industry's increasing business problems, the new competition later brought by television, and a by-then growing realization that the romanticism disguised some rather crucial problems together influenced film makers' perspectives. New films—Cat on a Hot Tin Roof (1958), To Kill a Mockingbird (1962), and Slaves (1969), for instance--addressed regional xenophobia, racism, and greed. Neither course--romanticism or reaction--has completely supplanted the other, thus making the genre one of the most instructive insights into film as popular culture.

Suggested Background Readings:

Each of the films listed below for course consideration was of necessity subjectively chosen; many other titles would also ably serve. The productions will, however, serve as a broad introduction to the southern's evolution and themes. For historical perspective or for additional film titles, the following studies are useful. Citations to works from which films were adapted are paperback editions suitable for classroom use.

Amberg, George, comp. The New York Times Film Reviews: A One-Volume Selection, 1913-1970. New York: Arno Press, 1971.

Ball, John. In the Heat of the Night. New York: Harper and Row, 1985.

Bogle, Donald. Toms, Coons, Mulattoes, Mammies and Bucks: An Interpretive History of Blacks in American Films. New York: Viking, 1973.

Campbell, Edward D. C., Jr. The Celluloid South: Hollywood and the

Southern Myth. Knoxville: University of Tennessee Press, 1981.

Cripps, Thomas J. Slow Fade to Black: The Negro in American Film, 1900-1942. New York: Oxford University Press, 1977.

Degenfelder, E. Pauline. "Rites of Passage, Novel into Film" [Intruder in the Dust]. In The Modern American Novel and the Movies, ed. by Gerald Peary and Roger Shatzkin. New York: Frederick Ungar, 1978.

Dixon, Thomas, Jr. The Clansman: An Historical Romance of the Ku Klux Klan. Lexington: University Press of Kentucky, 1970.

Fadiman, Regina K. Faulkner's Intruder in the Dust: Novel into Film. Knoxville: University of Tennessee Press, 1978.

Faulkner, William. Intruder in the Dust. New York: Random House, 1972.

_____. The Reivers. New York: Random House, 1962.

French, Warren, ed. The South and Film. Jackson: University Press of Mississippi, 1981.

Harwell, Richard B., ed. Gone With the Wind as Book and Film. Columbia: University of South Carolina Press, 1983.

Kawin, Bruce F. Faulkner and Film. New York: Frederick Ungar, 1977.

Kirby, Jack T. Media-Made Dixie: The South in the American Imagination. Athens: University of Georgia Press, rev. ed. 1987.

Lee, Harper. To Kill a Mockingbird. New York: Warner Books, 1982.

Mitchell, Margaret. Gone With the Wind. New York: Avon, 1973.

Onstott, Kyle. Mandingo. New York: Fawcett, 1986 [abridged].

Pyron, Darden Asbury, ed. Recasting: Gone With the Wind in American Culture. Miami: University Presses of Florida, 1983.

Silva, Fred, ed. Focus on The Birth of a Nation. Englewood Cliffs: Prentice-Hall, 1971.

Soderbergh, Peter A. "Hollywood and the South, 1930-1960." Mississippi Quarterly 19 (Winter 1965-1966): 1-19.

Stowe, Harriet Beecher. Uncle Tom's Cabin. New York: Harper and Row, 1981.

Thompson, Richard. "What's Your 10-20?" Film Comment 16 (July-August 1980): 34-42.

Warren, Robert Penn. All the King's Men. New York: Harcourt, Brace Jovanovich, 1982.

Walling, William. "In Which Humpty Dumpty Become King" [All the King's Men]. In The Modern American Novel and the Movies, ed. by Gerald Peary and Roger Shatzkin. New York: Frederick Ungar, 1978.

Williams, Tennessee. Cat on a Hot Tin Roof. New York: NAL, 1986.

Yacowar, Maurice. Tennessee Williams and Film. New York: Frederick Ungar, 1977.

Recommended Films:

Eight of the productions are set in the antebellum or Civil War periods; eleven are devoted to the postwar South. Separated, the two periods could serve as a distinct course or as a two-semester offering. Each title entry includes reviews from generally available periodicals recommended for assessing contemporary critical responses. For plot synopses, see Jay Robert Nash and Ralph Stanley, The Motion Picture Guide. 12 volumes (Chicago: Cinebooks, 1985-1987). For rental information, see J. L. Limbacher, Feature Films: A Directory of Feature Films on 16mm and Videotape Available for Rental, Sale, and Lease (New York: R. R. Bowker Co., 1985).

Adventures of Hucklebery Finn (MGM, 1939) 90 min.
Produced by Joseph L. Mankiewicz, directed by Richard Thorpe, written by Hugo Butler from the novel by Mark Twain. With Mickey Rooney, Walter Connolly, William Frawley, and Rex Ingram.

All the King's Men (1949) 109 min.
Produced and directed by Robert Rossen, written by Rossen from the novel by Robert Penn Warren. With Broderick Crawford, Joanne Dru, John Ireland, John Derek, Mercedes McCambridge, Sheppard Sturdwick, Ralph Dumke, Anne Seymour, Katherine Warren, and Raymond Greenleaf.

Birth of a Nation (Epoch, 1915) 180 min.
Directed by D.W. Griffith, written by Griffith and Frank E. Woods from the novel, The Clansman, by Thomas Dixon, Jr. With Henry B. Walthall, Mae Marsh, Miriam Cooper, Lillian Gish, Robert Harron, Wallace Reid, Donald Crisp, Joseph Henaberry, Raoul Walsh, Eugene Pallette, and Walter Long.

Can on a Hot Tin Roof (MGM, 1958) 108 min.
Produced by Lawrence Weingarten, directed by Richard Brooks, written by Brooks and James Poe from the play by Tennessee Williams. With Elizabeth Taylor, Paul Newman, Burl Ives, Jack Carson, Judith Anderson, Madeleine Sherwood, Larry Gates, and Vaughan Taylor.

Gone With the Wind (MGM, 1939) 222 min.
Produced by David O. Selznick, directed by Victor Fleming (and others), written by Sidney Howard (and others) from the novel by Margaret Mitchell. With Clark Gable, Vivien Leigh, Olivia DeHavilland, Leslie Howard, Thomas Mitchell, Barbara O'Neil, Hattie McDaniel, Butterfly McQueen, Victor Jory, and Ona Munson.

In the Heat of the Night (United Artists/Mirisch, 1967) 109 min.
Produced by Walter Mirisch, directed by Norman Jewison, written by Stirling Silliphant from the novel by John Ball. With Sidney Poitier, Rod Steiger, Warren Oates, Quentin Dean, James Patterson, and William Schallert.

Intruder in the Dust (MGM, 1949) 87 min.
Produced and directed by Clarence Brown, written by Ben Maddow from the novel by William Faulkner. With David Brian, Claude Jarman, Jr., Juano Hernandez, Porter Hall, Elizabeth Patterson, Charles Kemper, Will Geer, and David Clarke.

Jezebel (Warner Brothers, 1938) 104 min.
Produced by Hall B. Wallis and Henry Blanke, directed by William Wyler, written by Clements Ripley, Abem Finkel, John Huston, and Robert Bruckner from the play by Owen Davis. With Bette Davis, Henry Fonda, George Brent, Margaret Lindsay, Fay Bainter, Richard Cromwell, Donald Crisp, Eddie Anderson, and Theresa Harris.

The Little Foxes (RKO, 1941) 116 min.
Produced by Samuel Goldwyn, directed by William Wyler, written by Lillian Hellman, Arthur Kober, Dorothy Parker, and Alan Campbell from Hellman's play. With Bette Davis, Herbert Marshall, Teresa Wright, Richard Carlson, Charles Dingle, Dan Duryea, Carl Benton Reid, Patricia Collinge, Jessica Grayson, and Russell Hicks.

The Littlest Rebel (Fox, 1935) 73 min.
Produced by Darryl F. Zanuck and B.G. DeSylva, directed by David Butler, written by Edwin Burke and Harry Tugend from the play by Edward Peple. With Shirley Temple, John Boles, Jack Holt, Karen Morley, Bill Robinson, Willie Best, Frank McGlynn, and Bessie Lyle.

Mandingo (Paramount, 1975) 143 min.
Produced by Dino DeLaurtentis, directed by Richard Fleischer, written by Norman Wexler from the novel by Kyle Onstott and the play by Jack Kirkland. With James Mason, Susan George, Perry King, Richard Ward, Brenda Sykes, Ken Norton, Ben Masters, and Paul Benedict.

Norma Rae (Fox, 1979) 110 min.
Produced by Tamara Asseyev and Alex Rose, directed by Martin Ritt, written by Irving Ravetch and Harriett Frank, Jr. With Sally Field, Beau Bridges, Ron Leibman, Pat Hingle, Barbara Baxley, Gail Strickland, Morgan Paull, and Robert Broyles.

Nothing But a Man (DuArt/Cinema V, 1964) 95 min.
Produced by Robert Young, Michael Roemer, and Robert Rubin, directed by Roemer, written by Roemer and Young. With Ivan Dixon, Abby Lincoln, Gloria Foster, Julius Harris, Martin Priest, Leonard Parker, and Yaphet Kotto.

The Reivers (Duo-Solar, 1969) 111 min.
Produced by Irving Ravetch and Robert E. Relyea, directed by Mark Rydell, written by Ravetch and Harriett Frank, Jr. from the novel by William Faulkner. With Steve McQueen, Sharon Farrell, Will Geer, Michael Constantine, Rupert Crosse, Mitch Vogel, Lonny Chapman, Juano Hernandez, Clifton James, and Ruth White.

Slaves (Theatre Guild/Walter Read/Contionental, 1969) 103 min.
Produced by Philip Langer, directed by Herbert J. Biberman, written by Biberman, John O. Killens, and Alida Sherman. With Stephen Boyd, Dionne Warwick, Ossie Davis, Robert Kya-Hill, Barbara Ann Teer, and Marilyn Clark.

So Red the Rose (Paramount, 1935) 83 min.
Produced by Douglas McLean, directed by King Vidor, written by Laurence Stallings, Edwin Justus Mayer, and Maxwell Anderson from the novel by Stark Young. With Margaret Sullavan, Walter Connolly, Janet Beecher, Harry Ellerbe, Robert Cummings, Charles Starrett, Daniel Haynes, Randolph Scott, Elizabeth Patterson, Dickie Moore, and Clarence Muse.

Song of the South (Walt Disney, 1946) 94 min.
Produced by Walt Disney, directed by Harve Foster and Wilfred Jackson, written by Dalton Raymond, Morton Grant, and Maurice Rapf, from the Tales of Uncle Remus, by Joel Chandler Harris. With Ruth Warrick, James Baskett, Bobby Driscoll, Luana Patten, Lucile Watson, Hattie McDaniel, and Glen Leedy.

The Southerner (United Artists, 1945) 91 min.
Produced by David L. Loew and Robert Hakim, directed by Jean Renoir, written by Renoir, Hugo Bulter, William Faulkner (uncredited), and Nunnally Johnson, from the novel Hold Autumn in Your Hand by George Sessions Perry. With Zachary Scott, Betty Field, Beulah Bondi, Jean Vanderwilt, Jay Gilpin, Percy Kilbride, Blanche Yurka, J. Carrol Naish, and Norman Lloyd.

To Kill a Mockingbird (Universal, 1962) 129 min.
Produced by Alan J. Pakula, directed by Robert Mulligan, written by Horton Foote, based on the novel by Harper Lee. With Gregory Peck, Mary Badham, Phillip Alford, John Megna, Frank Overton, Rosemary Murphy, Ruth White, Brock Peters, Estelle Evans, Paul Fix, Collin Wilcox, James Anderson, Alice Ghostley, and Robert Duvall.

Teaching "Film Images of World War II"
Geoffrey Cocks and Paul Loukides

Film Images of World War II is among the most popular elective courses taught at Albion College. Offered in alternate years, the class typically fills (55 students) with juniors and seniors despite the fact that it fulfills neither major nor core requirements, requires a lab fee, extensive reading and the writing of 2 major papers, and is rigorously graded (median grade below all-campus average). While popularity per se should not be used to justify offering a course, it does help us justify the relatively high cost of a team-taught course for which both instructors receive a full unit of teaching credit. The administration has had no difficulty seeing 25 to 30 students per instructor unit as reasonably cost effective but concurs that team-taught courses can offer students an enriched educational experience by providing a depth of interdisciplinary expertise that no one instructor can provide.

Initially, part of the popularity of the course seemed to reflect a not entirely healthy interest in violence, Nazis, weapons and battles on the part of at least some of the students. Of the 55 students who first enrolled in the course, none were pacifists and only three were women; World War II seemed to be for many Albion students a John Wayne movie with incredibly good special effects. Within this group anti-war films were severely criticized in discussion. However, as the nature of the course became clear within the student community, the composition of students enrolled began to change. At present more than 30% of the students are women. Many students who are less than enthusiastic about war and the military take the course even though they find many of its images and arguments distressing; militarists and neo-fascists take the course although they must confront the war as something other than a simple morality play or opportunity for sadistic self-indulgence. A large middle group helps insure that the mixture is a dynamic one.

As the course outline makes clear, "Film Images of World War II" has been designed to be truly interdisciplinary in its perspective. While literature, film study and history constitute the core of the course and reflect our primary areas of expertise, more than a little attention is paid to sociology, economics, psychology and popular culture. The design of the course, which has evolved over eight years, reveals a set of problems and solutions to the task of creating a critical perspective on World War II and its representations in history, film, and literature.

Perhaps the most difficult questions we have faced in designing and redesigning the course have been questions of focus. The material on World War II — both film and text — is immense. In our initial conversations we very quickly generated a list of more than 100 available feature and documentary films dealing with World War II; since then our list of film options had more than doubled. Texts - including histories, novels, poems and articles — number in the thousands. Our individual interests range over dozens of topics including psychohistory, weaponry, clandestine warfare, comparative propaganda, the literature of the Holocaust, individual campaigns, naval and air warfare, the artifacts of popular culture and many more. We could, with little difficulty, design an entire course around any one of those areas and still have prodigious amounts of material worth studying.

As our planning discussions proceeded, it became clear that what we wished to do was show World War II as a complex human social enterprise with consequences which ranged far beyond the grim statistics of warfare and the reshaping of geopolitical structures in the postwar world. By using film and a variety of texts and short readings we hoped to show students something of the immense complexity of World War II and its consequences by focusing on a limited number of thematic concerns.

Our course outline called for dividing materials into two separate but intertwined strands. The first strand, around which the second revolved, was the war itself in fundamental outline. Dates, battles, leaders, weapons, casualties, and the broad outlines of social change occasioned by the war formed the body of this strand. Lectures and texts provided the basic outlines for this motif.

The second, and more complex, strand focused on the experience, interpretation and reinterpretation of aspects of the conflict before, during, and after the war. Central to this component of the course was a focus on several motifs: the experience of combat, the effect of total war on non-combatants, strategy and tactics, the economics of total war, and the role of women in war. Using films, novels, poems, songs, essays, and interviews, we worked at showing the evolution of representations of World War II from the most blatant propaganda to the most subtle analyses and disputes.

The class format has had a great deal to do with the success of the class. The group meets twice weekly for two hours per session; except on days when feature films are shown, there is one three-to-five minute break between hours. The class sessions -- with the with the exception of discussion periods -- are crowed with materials presented by the instructors. In the ten minutes before class begins, there is likely to be music of World War II playing in the foreground, a series of slides of World War II photographs, propaganda posters or cartoons projected on the wall, two or three new contemporary newsclippings about World War II - related subjects posted on the board and one or more handouts for students to collect. Lectures are typically an hour long and profusely illustrated by film clips, slides, and quoted texts.

On the other hand, discussions, while often intense, are never rushed; the goal of the course, after all, is to engage the student intellectually in an examination of images of World War II. The texts, lectures, handouts, and films are only the beginning points of what we hope to achieve; thoughtful discussions, papers, and exams are important outcomes. We feel that one of the goals of the course is to have a number of important and complex questions left unresolved.

While conventional wisdom equates large class size with the lecture format and the modest-sized seminar with the discussion group, it has been our experience that lively and productive discussions with groups of fifty or more generate an intellectual momentum that continues in the hallways and dorms. With two discussion leaders who often disagree, the questions asked rarely lapse into mere rhetorical queries meant to lead the group to certain given conclusions. During any single discussion 25 to 40 percent of the class may participate; virtually all students eventually contribute to the discussions.

The last set of observations we should like to make about "Film Images of World War II" is that it has been a particularly rewarding class to teach. A great deal of that benefit has come about because of the team teaching structure. From the planning stages to the calculation of final grades, the course has involved us in discussions and arguments and a variety of mutually educating experiences. We listen to each other's lectures; we both read and comment on student papers and exams; we share the mundane duties of renting films, xeroxing, equipment care. During the semesters we aren't teaching the course, we keep each other posted on new materials that we might want to consider for the next time around and enjoy editing and modifying the course.

Like most teachers, we also take a good deal of our satisfaction from a course from our success in the classroom. That many of our students regard "Film Images of World War II" as the best course they have ever taken would be reward enough in itself; that it is also among the most exciting and enriching experiences of our teaching careers is perhaps not coincidental.

History/English 229　　　　　　　　　　　　　Cocks/Loukides
Film Images of World War II　　　　　　　　　Spring 1986

Syllabus

The purpose of this course is to explore history through film and film through history. The core of the course is the cataclysm of World War II as recorded by historians, filmmakers, and novelists. The approach of the course is eclectic and interdisciplinary. We will be looking at our subject from a variety of perspectives including politics, economics, aesthetics, sociology, technology, psychology, literature, military history, and film criticism. Those looking for a simple view of the war will be disappointed; those who can respond with flexibility of mind to a rich diversity and confusion of images, events, ideas, and interpretations will find the course a stimulating and enriching experience.

Required Texts: Saburo Ienaga, The Pacific War
Gordon Wright, The Ordeal of Total War
J.G. Ballard, Empire of the Sun
Jean-Francois Steiner, Treblinka
Joseph Heller, Catch-22
John Hersey, Hiroshima and some class handouts

Course Requirements:

Readings: Weekly assignments are to be completed before class on Tuesday so that you may view the films in an informed historical and literary context. In general, you are responsible for the main outlines, central arguments, and familiarity with the primary evidence. The readings are especially important since they will provide you with basic information and insights upon which classroom lectures and discussions will be based.

Films: You are responsible for the themes, plots, and the differences and similarities among them.

Lectures: Besides rich applause, genuine laughter (at the appropriate moments), and general wakefulness, you are responsible for the main outlines, critical arguments, and chief examples contained therein.

Discussion: By all means participate.

Evaluation	% of Grade
2 short (3-5 pp.) papers	20/30
1½-hr. mid-term examination	20
2-hr. final examination	30

Note: Detailed instructions for each paper will be distributed during the semester. The exams will consist of multiple choice questions on the readings and short answer and essay questions on the readings, films, and lectures.

Class will meet Tuesday and Thursday from 1-3 pm in Robinson 317 except where otherwise noted.

I   The Last European War: ". . . the strong do what they can and the weak suffer what they must . . . " (Thucydides, The Peloponnesian War)

    1/14   poster slide "Keep These Hands Off! Buy the New Victory Bonds" (USA)

            illustrated lecture   The 1930s. Plans, fears, and tensions in Europe. Film excerpts from Triumph of the Will (Germany, 1935), Grand Illusion (France, 1938), Fire Over England (Great Britain, 1937), and Alexander Nevsky (USSR, 1938).

            illustrated lecture   Film and Propaganda. What is propaganda and why did every major combatant nation allocate precious resources to the making of propaganda films? Illustrations include clips from The Great Dictator (USA, 1940), Triumph of the Will, and the U.S. government's "Why We Fight" series.

    1/16   audio prelude   Wagner, "Siegfried's Funeral March"

            poster slide   "This is the Enemy"   (USA)

            Prelude to War (USA, 1942); discussion

            READING: Ienaga, vii-xvi, 2-128; Wright, xiii-xiv, 1-16, 66-78

II Blitzkrieg: "Tanks! That's what I want!" (Adolf Hitler)

    1/21   audio prelude   Liszt, "Les Preludes"; Addinsell, "Warsaw Concerto"

            poster slide   "Komm' zu uns"   (Germany)

            lecture Blitzkrieg; illustrated lecture   War and Technology. Slides of ground, sea, and air weaponry. Excerpt from Spitfire (Great Britain, 1942).

    1/23   audio prelude   "Wenn Wir Fahren Gegen Engeland"; Beethoven, "Symphony #5"; Walton, "Spitfire Prelude and Fugue"; Coates, "Calling All Workers"; Churchill, "Their Finest Hour"

            poster slide   "Holding the Line"   (Great Britain)

            The Battle of Britain (USA, 1942) & Listen to Britain (Great Britain, 1942); discussion

            READING: Wright, 17-37, 44-65, 79-98; Manstein, "The Operation Plan Controversy" (cho)*; Freud & Billingham, "War and Children" (cho)

III The Battle of the Atlantic: " . . . full armed with weapons and with courage . . . you see your far-flung fleet come boiling in . . . " (Lucretius, That Nature of Things)

    1/28   audio prelude   Rodgers, "Song of the High Seas"

*cho=class handout

poster slide   "Your Britain. Fight For It Now." (Great Britain)

Lifeboat   (USA, 1944)

1/30   audio prelude   Dollinger, "Das Boot"

photo slide   U-boat battle station

The Boat   (West Germany, 1982); discussion   EVENING

READING: Wright, 170-73; Farber, "Among the Missing: Hitchcock" (cho); Steinbeck, "Letters on Lifeboat" (cho)

IV   The Eastern Front: "The enemy must not be left a single engine, or a single railway truck, and not a pound of bread nor a pint of oil." (Joseph Stalin, 3 July 1941)

2/4   audio prelude   Khachaturian, "The Bell"

poster slide   "Dutchmen, Fight Bolshevism in the Waffen SS" (Germany)

illustrated lecture   Operation Barbarossa. From Blitzkrieg to war of attrition. Excerpts from Die Frontschau (Germany, 1942), The Battle of Russia (USA, 1943); and Cross of Iron (USA, 1977).

2/6   audio prelude   Prokofiev, "Alexander Nevsky"; Shostakovitch, "Leningrad Symphony"

poster slide   "Follow This Worker's Example. Produce More for the Front!" (USSR)

Ballad of a Soldier   (USSR, 1960); discussion

READING: Wright, 37-43, 154-61, 194-96; Malaparte, "The Lessons in the Open" (cho)

V   The Arsenal of Democracy: "Well, Rick, you're not only a sentimentalist, but you've become a patriot."

2/11   audio prelude   Robinson, "Mussolini's Letter to Hitler" & "Hitler's Reply to Mussolini"; Miller, "In the Mood"

photo slide   Punch Bowl grave marker

Casablanca   (USA, 1943)

2/11   PAPER DUE

2/13   audio prelude   Lerner, "The Sun Will Soon Be Setting (For the Land of the Rising Sun)"; Friend-Tobias, "We Did It Before and We Can Do It Again"; Coots, "Goodbye Mama (I'm Off to Yokohama)"; Loesser, "Praise the Lord and Pass the Ammunition"; Roosevelt, "A Date That Will Live in Infamy"
discussion; illustrated lecture   War in the Pacific. Japanese victories 1941-42 and the turning point at Midway. Excerpt from A Town Like Alice on the fall of Singapore.

READING: Wright, 167-70; Ienaga, 129-80; Ballard, 3-287; Prange, "'Difficult But Not Impossible'" (cho); Mailer, "Argil and Mold" (cho)

VIa Heroes and Villains: "Do unto Japs as Japs do unto you--but first." (Peter Bowman, Beach Red)

    2/18 illustrated lecture Them and Us (Film and Propaganda, Part II). The evolution and role of stereotypes in feature and documentary films. Life Goes to the Movies: The War Years; Gung Ho! (USA, 1943), Stalag 17 (USA, 1953), Back to Bataan (USA, 1945), "Have You Killed a Jap Soldier Today?".

VIb Strategic Bombing: ". . . the suburbs on top of the cathedrals . . . locomotives on belfries!" (Louis-Ferdinand Celine, Castle to Castle)

    2/20 audio prelude Miller, "Air Corps Song" & "Pistol-Packin' Mama"

    photo slide B-24 over Ploesti

    illustrated lecture Total Air War. Evolution, practice, and limitations of the doctrine of strategic bombing. Excerpt from We'll Meet Again on the impact of American airmen on English society.

    The Memphis Belle (USA, 1944)

    READING: Wright, 174-82; Deighton, "Bomber" (cho)

VII Up Front: "'Do retreatin' blisters hurt as much as advancin' blisters?'" (Bill Mauldin, Up Front)

    2/25 audio prelude Miller, "There'll Be a Hot Time in the Town of Berlin" & "What Do You Do in the Infantry"; Schultze, "Lili Marleen"

    cartoon slide Mauldin, "Willie and Joe"

    Battleground (USA, 1950)

    2/27 discussion; guest lecture by Theron Snell, Kenyon College. The 978th Engineer Maintenance Company

    READING: Wright, 182-94, 196-203; van Creveld, "German and US Army Performance" (cho); Jones, "History" (cho)

VIII Victory in Europe: ". . . we shall succeed and we shall see it, this better world; and above all our children will see it."

    3/4 Rome, Open City (Italy, 1945)

    READING: Wright, 144-54; begin Steiner

    3/6 MID-TERM EXAMINATION

IX Homecoming: "You're home now, kid."

 3/18 audio prelude Moschwitz-Carr, "He Wears a Pair of Silver Wings"; Miller, "Flying Home"

 The Best Years of Our Lives (USA, 1946)

 3/20 discussion; Let There Be Light (USA, 1946)

 READING: Wright, 234-67; Warshow, "The Anatomy of Falsehood" (cho); Hammen, "At War with the Army" (cho)

X Hot and Cold Running War: "Alright, saddle up, let's get back in the war"

 3/25 audio prelude Rodgers, "Theme of the Fast Carriers"

 poster slide "Jap, You're Next" (USA)

 Sands of Iwo Jima (USA, 1949) w/With the Marines at Tarawa (USA, 1943)

 3/27 discussion; guest lecture by Jack Padgett: As a Marine on Okinawa

 READING: Ienaga, 181-92, 203-28; begin Heller

XI Holocaust: "A naked heap. . . . Behind thick glass." (Czeslaw Milosz, "From the Rising of the Sun")

 4/1 audio prelude Baez, "For Sasha"

 poster slide "The Eternal Jew" (Germany)

 illustrated lecture The War Against Civilians. Excerpts from Forbidden Games (France, 1952); Paisan (Italy, 1946); The Sorrow and the Pity (France, 1971); To Be or Not to Be (USA, 1983); The Pawnbroker (USA, 1964); and Shoah (France, 1985)

 illustrated lecture Literature and Film of the Holocaust. An exploration of the problems confronting the artist who attempts to deal with the mind-staggering dimensions of the systematic extermination of millions of human beings. Clips and citations from The Pawnbroker, Last of the Just, Mein Kampf (film), Shoah, Playing for Time, The Painted Bird. Bibliography and filmography posted.

 4/3 Kitty: Return to Auschwitz (Great Britain, 1980); discussion

 READING: Wright, 107-43; Steiner

XII Women and War: "'The girl he left behind' is still behind him."

 4/8 audio prelude Loesser, "First Class Private Mary Brown"; Browne-Devol, "Little Bo-Peep Has Lost Her Jeep"

 poster slide "Rosie the Riveter" (USA)

 guest lecture by Wes Dick & Bucky Halker: US Women and WWII; The Life and Times of Rosie the Riveter (USA, 1980)

	4/10	discussion; guest lecture by Henry Dyer, Control Officer, Southwest Pacific, 1943-46

READING: Havens, "Women and War in Japan, 1937-1945" (cho)

XIII The War Hero: "Rommel, you magnificent bastard, I read your book!"

4/15   Patton (USA, 1970)   EVENING

4/17   illustrated lecture   War is Fun. War films, including comedies, musicals, romantic adventures, epics, and melodramas, are perennial favorites at the box office. What are the filmic appeals of war and does the war film tell us anything about our cultural attitudes towards war? Clips from: South Pacific (USA, 1958), Operation Petticoat (USA, 1959), The Dirty Dozen (USA, 1967), and Battle Cry (USA, 1955)

READING: Wright, 204-33; Jones, "The Home Front"

XIV The 1960s. "One, two, three, what're we fightin' for?" (Country Joe and the Fish, "Feel Like I'm Fixin' to Die Rag")

4/22   audio prelude, Joe MacDonald, "The Fish Song"

Catch-22 (USA, 1970)

4/24   audio prelude   Lennon & McCartney, "Hey Bulldog" & "A Day in the Life"

Poster slide   "Holding the Line"   (Great Britain)

illustrated lecture   Anti-War Fiction and Film. The perception that, for the Allies, WWII was a just and necessary war against the real evils of Nazism and Japanese imperialism seems to undercut the moral validity of anti-war novels and films. A thematic exploration of several anti-war novels and films, including The Naked and the Dead, Catch-22, The Americanization of Emily (USA, 1964), Bridge on the River Kwai (Great Britain, 1957), How I Won the War (Great Britain, 1967), A Hard Day's Night (Great Britain, 1964), Fires on the Plain (Japan, 1959), and The Burmese Harp (Japan, 1956).

READING: Heller

XV The Bomb: "I am become Death, the destroyer of nations." (The Bhagavad-Gita)

4/29   audio prelude   Penderecki, "Threnody for the Victims of Hiroshima"

Hiroshima, Mon Amour (France-Japan, 1959)

5/1   prelude (concurrent): video excerpt from Godzilla (Japan, 1951); audio Harry/Destri, "Atomic"; Harnick, "The Merry Minuet"; Byrne, "Life During Wartime'; photo slide A-Bomb detonation

discussion; conclusion

READING: Ienaga, 192-202, 229-56; Wright, 99-106; Hersey; Ballard, 291-375; reviews of <u>Hiroshima, Mon Amour</u> (cho); Duras, "Waiting" (cho)

IMAGES OF BLACKS IN MOTION PICTURES: A SUGGESTED COURSE OUTLINE

15 WEEK SEMESTER

Edward C. Mapp, Ph.D.
Professor, Speech, Communications and Theatre Arts
Borough of Manhattan Community College, The City
University of New York

INTRODUCTION

The course will examine closely the assumptions about blacks perpetuated by a cross-section of motion pictures. Special attention will be devoted to black filmmakers who over the decades have been involved in the making of films in spite of limited resources and the continued resistance of the white dominated film industry. With few exceptions, white filmmakers have misrepresented or distorted the image of blacks according to their own particular fantasies. The course consists of lectures, screenings, and discussions. A final paper (thesis) on some aspect of "The Image of Blacks in Motion Pictures" is required. This project will allow students to pursue their own individual interests within the overall purview of the course. The course can be offered under the aegis of college/university programs in cinema, popular culture, black studies or American studies. The fifteen units outlined are easily adapted to a wide variety of teaching methods. How a particular instructor structures the course depends on such variables as running times of films selected for screenings, number of students and the scope and variety of other class assignments.

SUGGESTED TEXTS:

    Cripps, Thomas. *Slow Fade to Black: The Negro in American Film 1900 - 1942*. Oxford U. Pr. 1977

or

    Nesteby, James. *Images in American Films, 1896-1954: The Interplay between Civil Rights and Film Culture*. U. Pr. of America 1982.

UNIT 1   INTRODUCTION AND OVERVIEW

The devastating effect that a dominant culture can have on minorities is often reflected best through film. Motion pictures are a powerful weapon for social change. Does the medium of film actually influence or merely report the changing role of the black in society?

Screening:
Black History: Lost, Stolen or Strayed. 1968 or
Black Shadows on the Silver Screen.

UNIT 2   THE TWENTIES AND EARLIER

The Negro is depicted as buffoon. Whites in black face promulgate the stereotype of a lazy, ignorant, fearful, child-like Negro. The only balance provided to the negative image is seen in the black cast productions of the period. D. W. Griffith is a focus.

Screening:
Birth of a Nation. 1915
Scar of Shame. 1927

UNIT 3   THE THIRTIES AND REEL IMITATIONS OF LIFE.

During the Great Depression, a black underground film network was at work. Bill Robinson taught a curly-topped Shirley Temple to tap dance and black actresses Hattie McDaniels and Louise Beavers preferred playing maids for $7000 per week to being maids at $7.00 per week.

Screening:

Judge Priest 1934

Imitation of Life 1934

Harlem Rides the Range 1939

UNIT 4   EARLY INDEPENDENT BLACK PRODUCERS.

Segregated movie theatres existed throughout the United States including the Nation's capital. In response to the harsh reality of the situation, many talented black filmmakers produced and distributed films that have become classics. Some even wrote and directed these vehicles. Special attention is given to the work of Oscar Micheaux and Spencer Williams.

Screening:

Eleven P. M. 1925

Ten Minutes to Live 1932

Lying Lips 1939

Blood of Jesus 1941

UNIT 5   THE FORTIES BLACKS BATTLING A WHITE WAR

As the United States fought the Axis powers, Hollywood used blacks in "voice of conscience" roles and as token servicemen involved in the war. On the home front, Lena Horne sang in the phenomenon of the "disappearing musical production number." Toward the end of the decade, a new white liberalism began to define black consciousness.

Screening:

Casablanca 1942

Bataan, Crash Dive or Sahara 1943

Home of the Brave 1949

UNIT 6   ALL BLACK MUSICALS

No Al Jolson, you can't play "De Lawd" in The Green Pastures. This genre has consistently allowed the black performer to display a full range of instrumental, singing and dancing talents, admittedly in a segregated setting. One musical, Carmen Jones, earned for Dorothy Dandridge, who portrayed the title role, the distinction of being the first black actress nominated for an Academy Award in a leading role.

Screening:

Cabin in the Sky 1943

Stormy Weather 1943

UNIT 7   THE FIFTIES AND SOCIAL PROBLEMS HOME AND ABROAD

Racism rears its ugly head in films set in New York City, the Caribbean, South Africa and Chicago. Black performers play a broader range of characters including priest, prostitute, school teacher, soldier, maid and physician.

Screening:

Native Son 1951

Island in the Sun 1957

Young Man with a Horn 1950

UNIT 8   ROBESON AND POITIER OR SUPER SID AND PROGRESSIVE PAUL

The study of these two distinguished black actors is a contrasting analysis of two different approaches to the reality of limited access to motion picture roles of any significance. Attention is devoted to why America loved Poitier so and hated Robeson with equal passion.

Screening:

Sanders of the River 1935

Song of Freedom 1937

A Patch of Blue 1965

Guess Who's Coming to Dinner? 1967

Paul Robeson: Tribute to an Artist. Narrated by Sidney Poitier 1979

UNIT 9   THE SIXTIES OR FAREWELL TO UNCLE TOM

Keeping pace with the civil rights movement in the U.S., black militancy was on the march in cinema. The black man asks for the overdue payment of his promissory note of justice. Movie themes began to ask the question, if not now, when? This is also the eve of the black "superstud."

Screening:

To Kill a Mockingbird 1962

A Raisin in the Sun 1961

Hurry Sundown 1966

Uptight 1968

UNIT 10   THE SEVENTIES AND A STEP TOWARD EQUAL OPPORTUNITY

More black actors and actresses were being employed in films (exclusive of the black exploitation genre) than ever before. Many of the films were quality productions destined, regretfully, to be viewed by limited numbers, predominantly black. Some of the dramas and comedies were based on a valid "black experience."

Screening:

Sounder 1972

Lady Sings the Blues 1972

River Niger 1976

Claudine 1974

UNIT 11   BLAXPLOITATION OR THE FANTASY OF POWER

Warmed over Sam Spade in Blackface. The films feature lots of sex and violence having little to do with the realities of life. The black hero is seen beating or shooting people, tossing around in bed or pushing drugs. "Mr. Charlie" learns how to gross an easy $20 million by exploiting a minority starved for heroes and heroines. Is it better to be Shaft than Uncle Tom is the question. A succession of Shafts, Superflys, Coffys and Cleopatra Jones receive a warm reception from black audiences. This was inevitably a transition period.

Screening:
Shaft 1971
Superfly 1972
Coffy 1973

UNIT 12   THE EIGHTIES OR IS HOLLYWOOD COLOR-BLIND AT LAST?

A look at the advent of Whoopi Goldberg and Eddie Murphy and its impact on the image of blacks. Is the Oreo/Eskimo Pie syndrome still operative? The prevalence of the biracial partnership raises the question: Are Huck Finn and Jim still alive? These films suggest the kind of black-white friendships that America likes to think of as reality.

Screening:
48 Hours 1982
Beverly Hills Cop 1985
Jumpin' Jack Flash 1986

UNIT 13   CONTEMPORARY INDEPENDENTS OR INTERPRETING YOUR OWN IMAGE

The motion picture medium can be a powerful weapon for social change but the weapon remains only a "pipe dream" for blacks until more black producers assume control. The precedent was established in the early thirties. Attention is given to William Greaves, Bill Gunn, Spike Lee, Robert Townsend and Melvin Van Peebles.

Screening:

Sweet Sweetback's Baadassss Song 1971

From These Roots 1974

She's Gotta Have It 1986

UNIT 14   FOREIGN MADE--THE INTERNATIONAL IMAGE

A number of films have been made outside the United States, portraying blacks in a realistic way. Many of these were documentary in nature and received considerable acclaim. The works of Sembene, Gerima are among those to be considered.

Screening:

Black Orpheus 1959

Mandabi 1968

Bush Mama 1976

The Harder They Come 1973

UNIT 15   THE TEN BEST CANDIDATES

Any study of the images of blacks projected on the silver screen would be incomplete without discussion of a standard of quality. While unanimity is improbable certain films have engendered acclaim from a variety of critics. Attempts will be made to agree upon a list of ten.

Screening:

The Learning Tree 1969

Sounder 1972

Nothing but a Man 1963

Carmen Jones 1954

Popular Culture 350
The Western Film   Spring, 1985

Instructor: Jack Nachbar
Office: Popular Culture Building (corner of Wooster and S. College) 372 2981
Office Hours: 10-12 Monday; 1-2:30 Tuesday; 1-3 Thursday and by appt.

Texts: 1. JOURNAL OF THE WEST, October, 1983. (Pick up at Popular Press, in the rear of the Popular Culture Building)
2. Kinko Packet (Pick up at Kinkos. It might be necessary to call ahead)
3. HONDO by Louis L'Amour
4. THE VIRGINIAN by Owen Wister
5. THE WESTERN FILMS OF JOHN FORD by J. A. Place

General Course Structure:
Tuesdays - We will see a Western feature film. Those who can't make class in the morning or who wish to see the film twice, may see the same movie under more favorable viewing conditions in Gish Theater, Tuesday evenings at 8:00.

Thursdays - Lectures and discussions of readings, viewings and ideas.

In addition - "Enrichment" movies will be shown on Monday nights for those who love Westerns. These films, mostly on tape, will be shown in 300 University Hall at 7:30 (See handout for a schedule) You don't need to see these. Come, if you wish, and enjoy.

Course Requirements:

Tests: There will be three of these. 100 points each. The first two will be short essay and in class. (See schedule for exact times) The third essay will be a take-home test. It will be distributed about two weeks before the end of the semester. The final test will include the entire course, but the in-class tests will cover only the materials handled since the last test.

Journals of Ideas and Comparisons: 200 points. These will be made up of six entries turned in every four weeks for the first twelve weeks of the course. Each entry should be 1-2 typed pages. Journals are not summaries and they are not just personal reactions. They should be new ideas about materials you figure out on your own or they should be interesting comparisons between movies or between movies and our readings. (Note: This will be easy if you do 1-2 entries per week.)

Some Course Objectives:
1. To learn to more fully enjoy one of the twentieth century's great story forms.
2. To learn to place Western movies in their historical context in the history of film.
3. To analyze Western movies to discover how they relate to the ideas and values of the American movie audience.
4. To discover how changes in the form of the Western suggest changes in the American mindset.

Tentative Schedule   Western Movies   (Extras)

Monday Evenings   7:30   300 University Hall

January 21	D. W. Griffith's THE BATTLE AT ELDERBUSH GULCH (1913) Tom Ince's THE INVADERS (1912)
January 28	THE MAGNIFICENT SEVEN (1960) with Steve McQueen and Yul Brynner
Feb. 4	JESSE JAMES (1939) and THE RETURN OF FRANK JAMES (1941) both with Henry Fonda
Feb. 11	Howard Hawks' RED RIVER
Feb. 18	John Ford's RIO GRANDE (1951)
Feb. 25	COLORADO TERRITORY (1949) with Joel McCrea
March 4	HIGH NOON (1952) with Gary Cooper
March 11	HIGH PLAINS DRIFTER (1973 with Clint Eastwood Or A FISTFUL OF DOLLARS (1964)
March 18	NONE VACATION
March 25	BEND OF THE RIVER (1952) with James Stewart
April 1	Howard Hawks' RIO BRAVO (1959)
April 8	None (Vacation for Instructor)
April 15	Either RIDE THE HIGH COUNTRY or THE MAN WHO SHOT LIBERTY VALANCE (both 1962)
April 22	JOHNNY GUITAR (1954) or something else weird.
April 29	THE BALLAD OF CABLE HOGUE (1970)
May 6	(for diehard fans only) HEAVEN'S GATE (1980) the whole 3½ hr catastrophe.

Spring, 1985　　　Western Film　　Schedule Part I

The Western Formula, Definitions and Meanings

Week One
Tue. Jan. 15　　General Course Introd.　　　Assign: None
　　　　　　　　Film: GREAT TRAIN ROBBERY

Thur. Jan. 17　　Film: The Real West　　　　Assign: Kinko: Nachbar, "Focus"
　　　　　　　　The Western and History　　　　　　J. of West, 1-23

Week Two
Tue. Jan. 22　　Film: The Covered Wagon　　Assign: Kinko, Cawelti
　　　　　　　　　　　　　　　　　　　　　　　　　　F. J. Turner

Thur. Jan. 24　　The Western Formula　　　　Assign: Place, 2-9, 19-23
　　　　　　　　The Western Formula as
　　　　　　　　　Western Myth

Week Three
Tue., Jan 29　　Film: Stagecoach　　　　　　Assign: Place, 30-41
　　　　　　　　　　　　　　　　　　　　　　　　　Kinko, Capt. Narr.

Thur. Jan. 31　　Origins I: Indian Captivity　Assign: J. of West, 24-33
　　　　　　　　　Narratives
　　　　　　　　Stagecoach and the Formula

Week Four
Tue. Feb. 5　　Films: B Western Double Feature　Assign: Kinko: Kitses art.

Thur. Feb 7　　Expanding the Western Formula　Assign: Place, 74-91
　　　　　　　Discuss the B Western
　　　　　　　1st Set of Ideas Due

Week Five
Tud. Feb. 12　　Film: Jeremiah Johnson　　　Assign: Begin Hondo

Thur. Feb 14　　The Western and landscape　Assign: (For Test)
　　　　　　　　The Concept of Community in　Place 108-127, 146-159
　　　　　　　　　the Western

Week Six
Tue. Feb. 19　　Film: She Wore a Yellow Ribbon　Assign: Study for Test

Thur. Feb 21　　FIRST TEST　　　　　　　　Assign: Finish Hondo
　　　　　　　　Discussion of Yellow Ribbon

Spring, 1985   Western Film   Schedule Part II

The Western Hero and the American Hero

Week Seven
Tuesd. Feb. 26 FIRST TEST   Assign: Finish Hondo
                Discussion: YELLOW RIBBON   See SHANE in Gish
                and the ideal of Community   Tue: 8:00 pm
                                                               Wed: 2:30, 5:30, 8:30 pm

Thur. Feb 28   Briefly discuss journals   Assign: Kinko on Hart
                SHANE and the Western hero   pp. 43-58
                Compare Shane with Hondo

Week Eight
Tue. March 5   Film: HELL'S HINGES (1916)   Assign: Kinko Boone material
                Hart's farewell to the Screen   pp. 59-69

Thur. March 7   Discuss Daniel Boone as   Assign: Get caught up on Journals
                essential American hero.   Debate Assigned
                Origins II   Kinkos: Marsden pp. 33-37
                Hell's Hinges and Hart

                HAPPY VACATION TIME, PILGRIMS
        (But ya oughta be goin west to the Rockies instead a
         east to Florida. You're headin for retirement
                    instead a open options.)

Week Nine
Tues. March 19 The Great Debate: Marsden vs Warshow   Assign: Journal of West
                General discussion of issue as it   pp. 34-42
                relates to MAN FROM LARAMIE
                SECOND JOURNALS DUE

Week Ten
Tue. Mar. 26   Film: THE TALL T (1957)   Assign: Small Group Reports
                                                               Assigned
Thur. March 28 Final Discussion of the   Assign: Journal of West
                Western Hero   pp. 53-63
                Origins III: The Dime Novel

Week Eleven
Tue. April 2   Film: THE SEARCHERS (1956)   Assign: Study for Test
                Note: Not included on second
                test

Thurs. April 4 TEST NUMBER TWO   Assign: Kinkos: Durgnat and
                                                               Simon pp. 70-77
                                                               Journal of West 43-52

Note: No Regular Class Tuesday April 9 Instead come to showing of
THE WILD BUNCH at 8:00 PM in Gish Film Theater

Popular Culture 350   1985
The Western Film   Schedule, Part III
The Complexities of the Contemporary Western

Week Twelve
Tues. April 9   No Regular Class. See film   Assign: Begin THE VIRGINIAN
                THE WILD BUNCH in Gish   Review: "Hoppy"
                Theater at 8:00   J of W pp. 34-52

Thur. April 11 An Introduction to the   Assign: J of W pp. 64-71
                Contemporary Western (with   Continue VIRGINIAN
                allusions to THE SEARCHERS
                and THE WILD BUNCH)

Week Thirteen
Tues. April 16 Film: McCABE AND MRS. MILLER Assign: Continue VIRGIN.
                (1971)   Kinko 78-80

Thur April 18   Racism and Sexism in the   Assign: Finish VIRGIN.
                Western
                Origins, IV. Buffalo Bill

Week Fourteen
Tue. April 23   Film: THE SHOOTIST (1976)   Assign: Kinko pp. 6-10
                                                      Finish Journals

Thur April 25   JOURNAL #3 Due
                The Sense of Loss in the   Assign: Kinko pp. 70-77
                Contemporary Western.   (review)
                Take-Home Final Exam Assigned

Week Fifteen
Tues April 30   Film: BARBAROSA (1981)   Assign: Work on Test

Thur. May 2   Western Creeds in
                THE VIRGINIAN
                Final Thoughts
                Evaluation of Class and Movies

Week Sixteen   Final Examination Due Wednesday
                May 8 by Noon

                Also, One of the great Westerns,
                MONTE WALSH (1970) has been scheduled
                as a special exam week bonus. Exact time
                to be announced.

AL 310 American Film and Society
Dr. Douglas A. Noverr
Winter quarter, 1988
Office: 285 Bessey Hall   Office Phone: 353-2945
Office Hours: 3:00-4:30 Friday and 2:30-4:30 Tuesday and Thursday

I. COURSE TEXTS:

David L. Vanderwerken and Spencer K. Wertz, eds. Sports Inside Out: Readings in Literature and Philosophy. Forth Worth, TX: Texas Christian University Press, 1985.

Peter Gent, North Dallas Forty. New York: Ballantine Books, 1984. Novel originally published in 1973.

David Halberstam. The Amateurs. New York: Penguin Books, 1985.

Mark Harris, Bang the Drum Slowly. University of Nebraska Press, 1984. Novel originally published in 1956.

Bernard Malamud. The Natural. New York: Avon Books, 1980. Novel originally published in in 1952.

II. COURSE DESCRIPTION

This course will examine the connections between sports literature and sports films by focusing on five sports (football, boxing, rowing, Olympic track and field, and baseball) in their historical and social context. The course materials will focus on the problematic relationship between organized sport and society and on the role of sports in shaping values and character. Specific themes explored include the following: the dynamics of hero and legend creation, kinds of sports heroes, sport as myth and ritual, professionalism and amateurism, the black American experience in sports, sports and violence, and the aesthetics of sports. The class will be taught by the lecture-discussion method with the nine feature-length films and course readings serving as the basis for discussion.

III. COURSE EVALUATION

Evaluation will be based on two exams (midterm and final) and on a 8-10 page analytical and critical paper dealing with a particular sport and dealing with at least one major primary source work of sports literature and two films. The final grade will be 30% midterm exam, 40% final exam, and 30% paper.

IV. COURSE FILMS:

Jim Thorpe - All American (1951); North Dallas Forty (1979); Great White Hope (1970); Raging Bull (1980; The Boy in Blue (1985); Oxford Blues (1984); Chariots of Fire (1981); Bang the Drum Slowly (1973); The Natural (1984).

V CLASS SCHEDULE AND READING ASSIGNMENT SCHEDULE

Wed. Jan. 6th	Course overview and introduction of guiding concepts for course
Mon. Jan. 11th	Screening of <u>Jim Thorpe - All American</u> (Warner Brothers, 1951), directed by Michael Curtiz Running time: 107 mins.
Wed. Jan. 13th	Discuss <u>Jim Thorpe - All American</u> and readings on football in <u>Sport Inside Out</u> <u>Readings</u>: Irwin Shaw "The Eighty-Yard Run" (9-20); Michael Novak "Regional Religions" (188-196); Gerald R. Ford "In Defense of the Competitive Urge" (246-256); Edwin H. Cady "The Sort of Sacred, Sometimes Ritual" (308-318); Murray Ross "Football Red and Baseball Green" (716-724); Gary Guy "Ishmael in Arlis" (174-180); Ernest W. Speed "The Coach Who Didn't Teach Civics" (680-685)
Mon. Jan. 18th	Screening of <u>North Dallas Forty</u> (Paramount, 1979), directed by Ted Kotcheff Running time: 119 mins.
Wed. Jan. 20th	Discussion of film and Peter Gent novel, <u>North Dallas Forty</u> (1973); discussion of readings in <u>Sport Inside Out</u> <u>Readings</u>: Alex Michalos "The Unreality and Moral Superiority of Football" (238-240); John McMurtry "The Illusions of a Football Fan: A Reply to Michalos" (241-244); Dan Jenkins "Game-Face" (256-267) and "The Wool Market" (704-713); Drew Hyland "Playing to Win: How Much Should It Hurt" (280-289); Michael Novek "Sacred Space, Sacred Time" (725-732); James Dickey "For the Death of Vince Lombardi" (105-107)
Mon. Jan. 25th	Screening of <u>The Great White Hope</u> (20th Century Fox, 1970), directed by Martin Ritt Running time: 103 mins.
Wed. Jan. 27th	Discussion of <u>The Great White Hope</u> and the boxing career of Jack Johnson
Mon. Feb. 1st	Screening of <u>Raging Bull</u> (United Artists, 1980), directed by Martin Scorsese Running time: 128 mins.
Wed. Feb. 3rd	Discussion of <u>Raging Bull</u> and reading in <u>Sport Inside Out</u> and handouts <u>Readings</u>: Ernest Hemingway "Fifty Grand" (43-62)
Mon. Feb. 8th	Screening of <u>The Boy in Blue</u> (1985) *Midterm take-home examination due
Wed. Feb. 10th	Discussion of <u>The Boy in Blue</u> and David Halberstam's <u>The Amateurs</u> (1985)
Mon. Feb. 15th	Screening of <u>Oxford Blues</u> (United Artists/MGM, 1984), directed by Robert Boris Running time: 102 mins.
Wed. Feb. 17th	Discussion of <u>Oxford Blues</u> and David Halberstam's <u>The Amateurs</u> (1985)

Mon. Feb. 22nd	Screening of <u>Chariots of Fire</u> (British, 20th Century Fox, 1981), directed by Hugh Hudson Running time: 123 mins.
Wed. Feb. 24th	Discussion of <u>Chariots of Fire</u> and readings in <u>Sport Inside Out</u> <u>Readings</u>: Allen Guttmann "The Sacred and the Secular" (298-308); Paul J. Kuntz "Aesthetics Applies to Sports as Well as to the Arts" (492-509); Lynne Belaief "Meanings of the Body" (414-434); Hans Lenk "Action Theory and the Social Scientific Analysis of Sports Actions" (480-487)
Mon. Feb. 29th	Screening of <u>Bang the Drum Slowly</u> (Paramount, 1973), directed by John Hancock Running time: 98 mins.
Wed. Mar. 2nd	Discuss film and Mark Harris novel; discuss readings on baseball in <u>Sport Inside Out</u> <u>Readings</u>: Howard S. Slusher "Sport and Death" &752-761); Kathy L. Ermler "Two Expressions of Failure in Sport" (761-764); William Harper "The Philosopher in Us" (449-454); Rolfe Humphries "Night Game" (108) and "Polo Grounds" (714-715); Roland Garrett "The Metaphysics of Baseball" (643-663) * **Critical and analytical paper (8-10 pg.) due**
Mon. Mar. 7th	Screening of <u>The Natural</u> (Tri Star Pictures, 1984), directed by Barry Levinson Running time: 134 mins.
Wed. Mar. 9th	Discuss film and novel by Bernard Malamud; discuss readings on baseball in <u>Sport Inside Out</u> <u>Readings</u>: Glendon Swarthout "The Ball Really Carries in the Cactus League Because the Air Is Dry" (20-29); Roger Kahn "Lines on the Transpontine Madness: (181-188); George Grella "Baseball and the American Dream" (267-279); Jack Spicer "God is a big white baseball" (298); Jim Brosnan "The Fantasy World of Baseball" (636-643); Ring Lardner "A New Busher Breaks In" (685-704); John Updike "Hub Fans Bid Kid Adieu" (400-414)
Mon. Mar. 14th 12:45-2:45 p.m.	Scheduled final examination period ***Take-home examination due**

AL 310 Film and Society (Sports Film and Literature)
Dr. Noverr
Winter Quarter, 1988

Course Paper Requirements and Guidelines

1. The course paper should be 8-10 pages in length (double-spaced with conventional margins of one inch at the top, right, and bottom and one and one-half inches at the left). The paper should have a separate cover page that includes the paper's title (centered on the page) and your name, student number, and due date (Wednesday, March 2nd). The paper should also have a separate sheet of Sources Cited and Consulted, which should include information on the films and books or readings used in writing the paper.

2. The paper should be analytical and critical in its approach and format. You should make significant connections between the primary sources you are analyzing (two films and at least one work of sports literature). The paper should explore the dimensions and qualities of one sport of your choice.

3. The paper's topic should explore one (or possibly a combination of two) of the following concerns or points of focus.
   a. the concept of the hero in sport
   b. the challenges and joys of a particular sport for the athlete/participant
   c. the physical mechanics of a sport and its execution or performance qualities
   d. the theme of experience and maturity gained through sports
   e. cultural meanings of the sport to Americans
   f. individualism and team effort in a sport
   g. the athlete's adjustment to a life without sports
   h. the relationship between coach and athlete
   i. the dynamics and psychology of competition
   j. the meaning of time and space as dimensions within a sport
   k. emotional bonds and dependencies between teammates
   l. sport and the community
   m. aesthetic qualities of a sport
   n. sport as social ritual and religion
   o. injury, aging, and death in sports
   p. the language of a particular sport
   q. sport as fantasy
   r. sport and philosophy
   s. the social mythology of sport
   t. sport as a social ritual and religion
   u. sport and social values
   v. the meanings of amateurism or professionalism
   w. violence (physical and psychological) in a sport
   x. sport as a source of cynicism and disillusionment

4. Your paper should use, whenever possible, concepts and means of analysis available in the readings in <u>Sport Inside Out: Readings in Literature and Philosophy</u>, the anthology required in the course.

5. It is not necessary to use footnotes in your paper. Instead, use the Works Cited method of documentation. Following a direct quote, a summary or paraphrase of information taken directly from a source, or a specific reference to information or facts, put the author's last name in parentheses and give the page number (Halberstam, 56) or numbers. On the Works Cited and Consulted page provide full information on the source.

>   Halberstam, David. *The Amateurs*. New York: Penguin Books, 1985.

Put the entries in alphabetical order on the Works Cited and Consulted page. Use the film director's name for films. For example,

>   Hudson, Hugh. *Chariots of Fire* (20th Century Fox, 1981).

Keep direct quotes to a minimum and quote only the material specifically relevant to the point you are establishing.

6. You must use at least two films and related one major work of sports literature as your primary sources as well as utilize relevant readings from *Sport Inside Out*. Your goal is to synthesize materials, focus them, interrelate them, and develop their implications and meanings in a coherent and purposeful way.

7. By Monday, February 22nd (or earlier) you should submit a one-page descriptive prospectus for your paper. This prospectus should include the tentative title for your paper, a list of the films and work of sports literature you are using, and a statement of your focus and purpose in the paper.

Theater Arts 171, Film Genres: Science Fiction Vivian Sobchack (D124)
T/TH   10:45am-12:45pm   College 5, Rm. 148   Off. Hrs.: Wednesday and
T   7:30pm-11:00pm   Classroom 2 (SCREENINGS)   by appointment

REQUIRED TEXTS:
John Brosnan, Future Tense: The Cinema of Science Fiction (New York: St. Martin's, 1978).
Vivian C. Sobchack, The Limits of Infinity: The American Science Fiction Film (New York: A.S. Barnes, 1980).

RECOMMENDED TEXTS:
John Baxter, Science Fiction in the Cinema (New York: A.S. Barnes, 1970).
Thomas & Vivian C. Sobchack, An Introduction to Film (Boston: Little, Brown, 1980).
RESERVE READINGS: These are listed on the class date they are due for discussion and are indicated by (R). They will be on reserve in McHenry Library and there will only be 1 copy of each, so xerox or plan ahead to get the reading done.

ASSIGNMENTS, EXAMS & PAPERS: Class attendance is required as is attendance at the evening screenings. Be advised that the films will be open to the public and are likely to be popular. To ensure a seat, get there early (the classroom opens at 7:00pm). There will be no exams, but 3 assignments in addition to classroom participation and reading: 1) a critical film journal to be kept as an on-going project for the quarter and in which films, class discussions, and readings are dealt within an informal structure, 2) a term paper of 10-12 typed pages on a focused topic pertinent to class concerns, and 3) an in-class presentation of a nature to be determined with instructor.

SPECIAL FEE: There will be a $15.00 screening fee to cover film rentals for the course. Unless the fee is paid, you will not be able to register for Winter quarter and will receive no credit for TA 171.

SCREENINGS AND READINGS: These are listed by class period. Screenings (unless otherwise indicated) are always Tuesday evening.

TH   9/24/81   Introduction and Definitions: Science? Fiction? Genre?
               In-class Screening: A TRIP TO THE MOON (1902) Georges Melies
                                   STRANGER THAN SCIENCE FICTION (1969) ???
T   9/29   Reading: Susan Sontag, "The Imagination of Disaster" (R);
                        Sobchack & Sobchack, An Introduction to Film, Chapter 4, "Genre Films"
               Films: DESTINATION MOON (1950) 91 min/C/Prod. George Pal
                        THE THING (1951) 87 min/BW/Dir. Christian Nyby/Howard Hawks
TH   10/1   Topic: "Dual Impulses: Where it all Began, or the Moon is Better in the Movies"
               Reading: The Limits of Infinity, Chapter I.
T   10/6   Topic: "Cautionary Tales and Benevolent Dictators"
               Reading: The Limits of Infinity, Chapter II.
               Films: THE DAY THE EARTH STOOD STILL (1951) 92min/BW/Dir. Robert Wise
                        RED PLANET MARS (1952) 87 min/BW/With Peter Graves
TH   10/8   Reading: The Limits of Infinity, Chapter III. & Conclusion
T   10/13   Topic: "Visual Paranoia: SF and the Enemy Within"
               Reading: Vivian Sobchack, "The Alien Landscapes of the Planet Earth" (R)
                        Future Tense, pp. 9-71

TA 171

TH	10/15	Films: INVADERS FROM MARS (1953) 78 min/C/Dir. William Cameron Menzies INVASION OF THE BODY SNATCHERS (1956) 80min/BW/Scope/Dir. Don Siegal. With Dana Wynter & Kevin McCarthy. Reading: Brian Murphy, "Monster Movies: They Came from Beneath the Fifties" (R); Richard Hodgens, "A Brief, Tragical History of the Science Fiction Film" (R)
T	10/20/81	In-class Screening: LA JETTE (1962) 29min/BW/Dir. Chris Marker Reading: Jeff Rovin, "Ray Harryhausen" and "Twenty Million Miles to Earth," Chapters 4 & 9 in From the Land Beyond Beyond (R); Joel Uman, "The Monstrous World of Ray Harryhausen" (R); John D. Denne, "Society and the Monster" (R) Films: THE BEAST FROM 20,000 FATHOMS (1953) 80min/BW/FX:Harryhausen/ From a story by Ray Bradbury. 20 MILLION MILES TO EARTH (1957) 82min/BW/FX: Harryhausen
TH	10/22	Topic: "The Aesthetics of Collision--or Stomping Cities Flat" Reading: Andre Bazin, "The Virtues and Limitations of Montage" (R), Future Tense, pp. 74-105 (and review Limits of Infinity, pp. 136-145). JOURNALS DUE IN CLASS!!!
T	10/27	Topic: "Genre Theory" Reading: Tom Ryall, "The Notion of Genre" (R); Edward Buscombe, "The Idea of Genre in the American Cinema" (P.); Richard Collins, "Genre: A Reply to Ed Buscombe" (R) Film: FORBIDDEN PLANET (1956) 98min/C/Scope. With Robby and Robot.
TH	10/29	Reading: Andrew Tudor, "Genre: Theory and Mispractice in Film Criticism" (R); Edward S. Small, "A Note on Genre Film" (R); Charles F. Altman, "Towards a Theory of Genre Film" (R); Thomas G. Schatz, "New Directions in Film Genre Study (A Response to Charles F. Altman)" (R)
T	11/3	Topic: "Sex and Gender in the Science Fiction Film" Reading: Future Tense, pp. 118-138 Films: SHE DEVIL (1957) 77min/BW/Dir. Kurt Neumann. With Jack Kelly. I MARRIED A MONSTER FROM OUTER SPACE (1958) 78min/BW/With Gloria Talbot & Tom Tryon.
TH	11/5	Reading: Frank D. McConnell, "Song of Innocence: The Creature from the Black Lagoon" (R)
T	11/10	Topic: "Science Fiction and Auterusim" Reading: Bill Kelley, "Jack is Back" (R); An Introduction to Film, pp. 294-306 Films: THE INCREDIBLE SHRINKING MAN (1957) 81min/BW/Dir. Jack Arnold/Sc: Richard Matheson. With Grant Williams MONOLITH MONSTERS (1957) 77min/BW/Dir. John Sherwood.
TH	11/12	Topic: "The Subversion of the Familiar: SF and Surrealism" Reading: Martin Rubin, "Film Favorites: The Incredible Shrinking Man" (R); C.M. Stanbury II, "Monsters in the Movies: A Mythology of the Absurd" (R)
T	11/17	Topic: "SF Optimism: Big Budgets, Hardware and Technology" In-class Screening: HARDWARE WARS (1978) 13 min/C Reading: Future Tense, pp. 139-191 Films: HARDWARE WARS (1978) 13min/C/Dir. Ernie Fosselius & Michael Wiese ROBINSON CRUSOE ON MARS (1964) 110min/C/Scope/Dir. Byron Haskin
TH	11/19	Reading: Joan F. Dean, "Between 2001 and Star Wars" (R)
T	11/24	Topic: "SF Pessimism: Technological Update on 'Being Taken Over'" Reading: Future Tense, pp. 192-216 Film: TERMINAL MAN (1974) 104min/C/Dir. Mike Hodges. With George Segal and Joan Hackett.

TA 171

TH	11/26	THANKSGIVING RECESS
T	12/1	Topic: "The Language of Science Fiction" Reading: Larry Niven, "The Words in Science Fiction" (R) JOURNALS DUE!!! Film: A CLOCKWORK ORANGE (1971) 137min/C/Dir. Stanley Kubrick.
TH	12/3	Topic: "SF and Mainstream Cinema" Reading: Future Tense, pp. 239-290; FINAL PAPERS DUE!!!!

THEATER ARTS 171: FILM GENRES
(THE AMERICAN SCIENCE FICTION FILM)

Prof. Vivian Sobchack
Mailbox: Porter Steno Pool
Phone Msg: 429-2951

Summer Session II, 1987
T/TH 1:00-4:30 pm

COURSE FOCUS:

This course will focus on the American SF film in a comparative manner; we will be looking at films from both the 1950's and the 1970's-80's and contrasting their thematics and aesthetics in relation to the historical context in which they have emerged and enjoy their peak popularity. In general, however, we will be exploring the way in which each "Golden Age" of SF cinema responds differently to the genre's perennial concerns with various existential boundaries (those between human/non-human; animate/inanimate; self/Other; Us/Them; male/female; nature/culture; and even science/fiction)--and whether they are regarded as marking off discrete categories, or as permeable to transgression or open--indeed, reversible!

REQUIRED TEXTS:

camera obscura #15 (Special Issue on Science Fiction Film)

Sobchack, Vivian. Screening Space: The American Science Fiction Film. New York: Ungar, 1987.

ON RESERVE IN MCHENRY LIBRARY:

The following materials (as well as those above) are on 2 hr. reserve. Except for the first book which is a general text, the materials are on SF film or related to specific generic concerns.

Sobchack, Thomas & Vivian. An Introduction to Film, 2nd Edition. Boston: Little, Brown, 1986. (This text will be particularly useful to those of you who have little experience of critical studies in cinema. See Chapter 9 for a brief overview of issues discussed in the entire book and for a guide to writing critical papers about film.)

*****

Baudrillard, Jean. "The Ecstasy of Communication." Trans.
John Johnston. In The Anti-Aesthetic: Essays on Post-
Modern Culture. Edited by Hal Foster. Pt. Towsend, WA:
Bay Press, 1983, pp. 126-134.

Brosnan, John. Future Tense: The Cinema of Science Fiction. New
York: St. Martin's Press, 1978.

Jameson, Fredric. "Post Modernism, or The Cultural Logic of Late
Capitalism." New Left Review #146 (July-August 1984),
pp. 53-92.

Peary, Danny, ed. Omni's Screen Flights/Screen Fantasies: The
Future According to Science Fiction Cinema. Garden City,
NY: Doubleday, 1984.

Slusser, George and Eric S. Rabkin, eds. Shadows of the Magic
Lamp: Fantasy and Science Fiction in Film. Carbondale,
IL: Southern Illinois Press, 1985.

COURSE REQUIREMENTS:

In addition to class attendance and general participation,
students will be required to do one in-class presentation
(individually or in small groups--depending upon class size) on
a relevant topic of their choice, and a final paper of 10-15
double-spaced, typed pages on a topic of their choice. (This
paper is to be handed in at the last class meeting.) No late
papers will be accepted! It is also in your best interest to
check both presentation and paper topics with the instructor.

FILMS BY WEEK:

There will be two feature film screenings per week: one representative of the 1950's (the first "Golden Age" of SF cinema) and one
representative of the renaissance (or second "Golden Age") of SF
cinema in the 1970's-80's. In addition, and when time permits,
selected clips will be shown from other relevant films. Unfortunately,
videotapes cannot be placed on reserve for screening in McHenry
Library; you will be dependent upon your own resources for
additional screenings of any of the class films: i.e., private
VCR's and tape rental.

T 7/28: The Day the Earth Stood Still (Robert Wise, 1951), 92 min.
TH 7/30: The Brother from Another Planet (John Sayles, 1984), 109 min.

T 8/4: The War of the Worlds (Byron Haskin, 1953), 85 min.
TH 8/6: The Last Starfighter (Nick Castle, 1984), 100 min.

T 8/11: The Invasion of the Body Snatchers (Don Siegel, 1956), 80 min., Flat version.
TH 8/13: Blade Runner (Ridley Scott, 1982), 124 min.
T 8/18: I Married a Monster from Outer Space (Gene Fowler, Jr., 1958), 78 min.
TH 8/20: Starman (John Carpenter, 1984), 115 min.
T 8/25: Close Encounters of the Third Kind: The Special Edition (Steven Spielberg, 1977), 135 min., Flat version.
TH 8/27: Repo Man (Alex Cox, 1985), 92 min.

Other relevant films from which clips may be shown (and which you can rent on video) are: The Thing (Christian Nyby/Howard Hawks, 1951), Them! (Gordon Douglas, 1954), Forbidden Planet (Fred Wilcox, 1956), The Incredible Shrinking Man (Jack Arnold, 1957), The Monolith Monsters, 1957, Star Wars (George Lucas, 1977), Liquid Sky (Slava Tsukerman, 1983), The Terminator (James Cameron, 1984), Back to the Future (Robert Zemeckis, 1985), and Radioactive Dreams (Albert F. Pyun, 1986).

Professor Jon Tuska

SYLLABUS for IMAGES
OF THE AMERICAN WEST

24 June 1985　　　Orientation. The three modes of Western fiction.
　　　　　　　　　Clip from SAHARA (Columbia, 1943) and clip from
　　　　　　　　　LAST OF THE COMANCHES (Columbia, 1952). The
　　　　　　　　　first program from IMAGES OF INDIANS.
　　　　　　　　　Assignment: Read the Introduction and the first
　　　　　　　　　　　　　　　two chapters from THE AMERICAN
　　　　　　　　　　　　　　　WEST IN FILM.

25 June 1985　　　The Concept of Historical Reality.
　　　　　　　　　THE GREAT TRAIN ROBBERY (Edison, 1903)
　　　　　　　　　d. Edwin S. Porter [9 minutes]
　　　　　　　　　SHOOTIN' MAD (Sperry, 1918)
　　　　　　　　　d. Jesse L. Robbins [22 minutes]
　　　　　　　　　Assignment: Read the General Introduction to
　　　　　　　　　　　　　　　THE AMERICAN WEST IN FICTION.

26 June 1985　　　The Idea of the Western Hero.
　　　　　　　　　RIDER OF DEATH VALLEY (Universal, 1932)
　　　　　　　　　d. Albert Rogell (77 minutes)
　　　　　　　　　Assignment: Read the six stories in the first
　　　　　　　　　　　　　　　part of THE AMERICAN WEST IN FICTION
　　　　　　　　　　　　　　　and in THE AMERICAN WEST IN FILM.

1 July 1985　　　 The Role of the Frontier in 19th Century American
　　　　　　　　　Fiction.
　　　　　　　　　THE LAST OUTLAW (RKO, 1936)
　　　　　　　　　d. Christy Cabanne [62 minutes]
　　　　　　　　　Assignment: Read the chapters on Jesse James
　　　　　　　　　　　　　　　and Billy the Kid from THE
　　　　　　　　　　　　　　　AMERICAN WEST IN FILM.

2 July 1985　　　 The Legendry of Western Outlaws and How to
　　　　　　　　　Interpret It.
　　　　　　　　　STAGECOACH (United Artists, 1939)
　　　　　　　　　d. John Ford [96 minutes]
　　　　　　　　　Assignment: Read the chapters on "Wild Bill" Hickok

	AND Wyatt Earp from THE AMERICAN WEST IN FILM.
3 July 1985	The Legendry of the Western Lawman and How to Interpret it. THE DESPERADOES (Columbia, 1943) d. Charles Vidor [86 minutes] Assignment: Read the six stories in the second part of THE AMERICAN WEST IN FICTION.
8 July 1985	Discussion of the films and fiction so far. Assignment: Read the remaining chapters in part three of THE AMERICAN WEST IN FILM.
9 July 1985	The Role of Women on the Frontier in History and in Fiction and Film. BEAUTY AND THE BANDIT (Monogram, 1946) d. William Nigh [71 minutes] Assignment: Read the chapter on Women in THE AMERICAN WEST IN FILM.
10 July 1985	Presentation of mid-term book reports orally in class as well as in written form. Assignment: Read the six stories in the third part of THE AMERICAN WEST IN FICTION.
15 July 1985	Images of Indians in Western fiction and films. BATTLE AT ELDERBUSH GULCH (Biograph, 1913) d. D. W. Griffith [19 minutes] IMAGES OF INDIANS: Program #2 Assignment: Read the chapter on Images of Indians but not the Epilogue from THE AMERICAN WEST IN FILM.
16 July 1985	The concept of _auteurisme_ in film criticism. RIDE LONESOME (Columbia, 1959) d. Budd Boetticher [75 minutes] Assignment: Read the chapters on John Ford and Howard Hawks from THE AMERICAN WEST IN FILM.

17 July 1985   The ideology of film and the concept of narrative
                   rhythm in fiction and film.
                   DECISION AT SUNDOWN (Columbia, 1957)
                   d. Budd Boetticher [95 minutes]
                   Assignment: Read the chapters on Henry Hathaway,
                        Anthony Mann, and Budd Boetticher
                        from THE AMERICAN WEST IN FILM and
                        the six stories in the fourth part
                        of THE AMERICAN WEST IN FICTION.

22 July 1985   Discussion of the fiction read so far in class.
                   Assignment: Read the Introduction to WESTWARD
                        THE WOMEN.

23 July 1985   The legacy of the Indian wars through the Vietnam
                   war.
                   TWO RODE TOGETHER (Columbia, 1961)
                   d. John Ford [109 minutes]
                   Assignment: Read the chapter on Sam Peckinpah
                        and the Epilogue to THE AMERICAN
                        WEST IN FILM.

24 July 1985   THE BALLAD OF CABLE HOGUE (Warner's, 1970)
                   d. Sam Peckinpah [120 minutes]
                   Assignment: Read the first six stories in
                        WESTWARD THE WOMEN.

29 July 1985   Discussion of the first six stories in WESTWARD
                   THE WOMEN.
                   Assignment: Read the remaining six stories in
                        WESTWARD THE WOMEN.

30 July 1985   JEREMIAH JOHNSON (Warner's, 1972)
                   d. Sydney Pollack [108 minutes]

31 July 1985   Discussion of the remaining six stories in
                   WESTWARD THE WOMEN and a summing up of the course.

Texts:
> THE AMERICAN WEST IN FILM: CRITICAL APPROACHES TO THE WESTERN by Jon Tuska
> THE AMERICAN WEST IN FICTION edited with an Introduction by Jon Tuska
> WESTWARD THE WOMEN edited with an Introduction by Vicki Piekarski

Grading:
> 30% of your grade will be based on class attendance and contribution. 30% of your grade will be based on your mid-term. 40% of your grade will be based on your final examination. Final examinations are due on 2 August at Noon in my box at the Summer Sessions office.

Contact Information:
> My telephone number is 232-0238. If you have a question, please do not hesitate to call me.

ENG 781
Spring 1987   Gregory A. Waller

Genre Criticism and the American Horror Film

This course will be organized as an in-depth study of 1) the historical transformation and rich heterogeneity of the American horror film from the 1930s to the 1980s and 2) the theory and practice of genre criticism. Readings will include Freud's **Civilization and Its Discontents** and several articles that exemplify different contemporary critical approaches to horror (ideological, feminist, psychoanalytic, mythic, structuralist, etc.). Using horror as a test case, we will examine certain basic questions about the definition, function, cultural significance, and historical transformation of genres (question that apply to the study of literature as well as film and popular culture). Readings on genre will include Todorov's **The Fantastic**, Neale's **Genre**, and selections from a number of other studies.

Films will be shown outside of class at times to be announced. Written work will include a research paper, one or two oral presentations, and probably several short exercises.

Screening Schedule

Date   Film

Jan. 19 (M) DRACULA (1931)
     21 (W) FRANKENSTEIN (1931)
     26 (M) THE WOLF MAN (1941)
Feb. 2 (M) CAT PEOPLE (1942)
      9 (M) INVASION OF THE BODY SNATCHERS (1956)
     16 (M) NIGHT OF THE LIVING DEAD (1968)
     18 (W) THE TEXAS CHAIN SAW MASSACRE (1974)
     23 (M) ROSEMARY'S BABY (1968)
     25 (W) THE EXORCIST (1973)
Mar. 2 (M) PSYCHO (1960)
      9 (M) HALLOWEEN (1978)
     11 (W) A NIGHTMARE ON ELM STREET (1984)
Apr. 6 (M) DON'T LOOK NOW (1973)

Remainder of films selected by seminar participants

Apr. 13 (M) DAWN OF THE DEAD
     15 (W) THE SHINING
     20 (M) VIDEODROME
     22 (W) CAT PEOPLE (1982)
     27 (M) PEEPING TOM

Texts: Grant, Barry Keith. **Film Genre Reader** (U of Texas Press)
        Freud, Sigmund. **Civilization and Its Discontents** (Norton)

Todorov, Tzvetan. _The Fantastic_ (Cornell U Press)
Neale, Stephen. _Genre_ (British Film Institute)

Readings (all texts marked * are on reserve in the library)

Jan. 27 Hess, _Film Genre Reader_, 41-49
     29 * R. H. W. Dillard, "Even a Man Who Is Pure in Heart," in _Man and the Movies_ (Penguin) ed. W. R. Robinson, pp. 60-96.

Feb. 3 * J. P. Telotte, _Dreams of Darkness_ (U of Illinois Press), pp. 1-39.
     5 Kawin, _Film Genre Reader_, 236-57

    10 _Civilization and Its Discontents_

    19 * Robin Wood, "An Introduction to the American Horror Film," in _Planks of Reason_, ed. Barry K. Grant (Scarecrow Press), 164-200.

Mar. 5 * Dennis Giles, "Conditions of Pleasure in Horror Cinema," in _Planks of Reason_, pp. 38-52.

        * Linda Williams, "When a Woman Looks," in _Re-Vision: Essays in Feminist Film Criticism_, ed. Mary Ann Doane (American Film Institute), pp. 83-99.

    10 Vera Dika. "The Stalker Film"

Mar. 24 _Film Genre Reader_, pp. 3-40, 102-113
     26 _Film Genre Reader_, pp. 50-101, 114-128.
     31 _Genre_

Apr. 2 _The Fantastic_, pp. 3-23.
     7 _The Fantastic_, pp. 24-175.

Fall 1987

ARTS AND LETTERS 310
SECTION 2

THE HOLLYWOOD MUSICAL

1933-1983

"Part of the reason some of us love musicals so passionately is that they give us a glimpse of what it would be like to be free."—Jane Feuer

Instructor: Bill Vincent
Office: 521 Kedzie
Hours: 9:00-10:00 a.m. MW, 11:30 a.m. to 12:30 p.m. TTh, and by appointment
Phone: 355-9534

Grading Criteria: Grades will be curved on the basis of total points:

    1. 30 points: Two 750-page papers (15 points each)
    2. 30 points: Three ten-point quizzes
    3. 10 points: Class Participation
    4. 50 points: Final Examination

Assigned Text: Jane Feuer, THE HOLLYWOOD MUSICAL: Read Chapter One by Oct. 8; Chapter 2 by October 15; Chapter 3 by Oct. 22; Chapter 4 by October 29; and Chapter 5 by Nov. 5.

Films:

Sept. 29, 30	FOOTLIGHT PARADE (Lloyd Bacon, 1933)
Oct. 6, 7	SWING TIME (Pandro Berman, 1936)
Oct. 13, 14	CABIN IN THE SKY (Vincente Minnelli, 1943)
Oct. 20, 21	MEET ME IN ST. LOUIS (Vincente Minnelli, 1944)
Oct. 27, 28	AN AMERICAN IN PARIS (Vincente Minnelli, 1951)
Nov. 3, 4	SINGIN' IN THE RAIN (Gene Kelly, Stanley Donen, 1952)
Nov. 10, 11	HELP! (Richard Lester, 1965)
Nov. 17, 18	CABARET (Bob Fosse, 1972)
Nov. 24, 25	NEW YORK, NEW YORK (Martin Scorsese, 1977)
Dec. 1, 2	PENNIES FROM HEAVEN (Herbert Ross, 1983)

Course Goals: The Hollywood musical is nearly 60 years ols. From BROADWAY MELODY (1929) to DIRTY DANCING (1987), the genre has undergone a number of transformations but has remained nonetheless constant in certain of its fundamental aspects. The musical is generally conceived as entertainment by its creators and perceived as entertainment by its audience, but that fact should not blind us to the fact that beneath the shimmering surface of the genre-- swimming around in its depths as it were--are more profound aspects which deserve careful analysis. What we shall be fishing for this term are the following elusive creatures:

1. The aesthetic dimension:
2. The generic dimension:
3. The sociological dimension:
4. The psychological dimension:
5. The mythological dimension:

ARTS AND LETTERS 310: THE HOLLYWOOD MUSICAL

MEET ME IN ST. LOUIS

Date: 1944
Director: Vincente Minnelli
Producer: Arthur Freed
Studio: MGM
Screenplay: Irving Brecher and Fred Finklehoffe, from a novel by Sally Benson
Music and Lyrics: Hugh Martin and Ralph Blane; Mills and Sterling, Freed and Brown
Cinematography: George Folsey
Editor: Albert Akst
Art Direction: Cedric Biggons, Lemuel Ayers, Jack Martin Smith
Costumes: Irene Sharaff
Characters (and Cast): Esther Smith (Judy Garland), Anna Smith (Mary Astor), Alonzo Smith (Leon Ames), Rose Smith (Lucille Bremer), Tootie Smith (Margaret O'Brien), Agnes Smith (Joan Carroll), Grandpa (Henry Davenport), Alonzo Smith, Jr. (Henry H. Daniels), Katie (Marjorie Main), John Truett (Tom Drake), Lucille Ballard (June Lockhart), Mr. Neely (Chill Wills), Colonel Darly (Hugh Marlowe)
Time and setting: St. Louis, Missouri—1903
Musical Numbers: "Meet Me in St. Louis," "The Boy Next Door," "Skip to my Lou," "Under the Bamboo Tree," "The Trolly Song," "You and I," "Have Yourself a Merry Little Christmas"

ANALYSIS

1. Historical/biographical: MEET ME IN ST. LOUIS was Vincente Minnelli's third film, and his first in color. Born into a theatrical family and with a strong interest in art, he went to Chicago at the age of sixteen. There he, like Chester Kent in FOOTLIGHT PARADE, became involved in between-the-films stage extravaganzas as production designer for the Balaban-Katz theatre chain. When Balaban-Katz was gobbled up by Paramount, he moved to New York as production designer for Paramount's stage shows. In New York, he began as well to design a few Broadway shows and attracted critical attention for his daring uses of color and starting surrealistic techniques. When the Depression killed the Paramount touring shows in 1933, he became art director for Radio City Music Hall and began to design musicals for the Schuberts. In his private life, he was a member of the set centering on the household of Ira and Lee Gershwin, a set which included the likes of George Gershwin, Moss Hart, Dorothy Parker, Harpo Marx, Lilian Hellman, Dashiell Hammett, Oscar Levant, and Yip Harburg. It was Harburg who introduced Minnelli to Arthur Freed in 1940. Freed offered him $300 a week to come to Hollywood and learn movie-making. Minnelli was astonished by the offer and accepted: "My instinct told me Arthur was a great showman . . . Today, whenever film cultists point to my contributions in the progress of the movie musical, I plead not guilty. The true revolutionary was Arthur . . . He gave his creative people extraordinary freedom."

Minnelli was to remain under exclusive contract to MGM for 24 years—the longest director-studio connection in film history. MGM, with "more stars that in Heaven" and a dedication to the production of lavish and polished entertainments, proved uniquely equipped to give Minnelli the perfect outlet for his talents.

The elements of Minnelli's style, already apparent in CABIN IN THE SKY, become fully realized in MEET ME IN ST. LOUIS. He insisted, for example, upon a full integration of character, plot, music, decor, mise en scene, and mise en frame into a stylistic and dramatic whole. He uses color with an artist's sense of its effect and in combinations which conventional Hollywood wisdom said were impossible. Sets and decor were designed to reflect the influence of a famous artist: "I felt the whole picture should have the look of Thomas Eakins' paintings, though not to the point of imitation . . ." One other major element of his style is his lyrical use of the moving image. He was dedicated to long takes and flowing, often intricately choreographed camera movements. The resultant "Minnelli style" made his musical films among the most successful in film history.

2. Aesthetic:
   A. Directing and Editing:
      1. Mise en scene:
         a. Color: Concentrate upon Minnelli's use of color. What kinds of effects does he achieve? How does the use of color enhance the mood of the film?
         b. Decor: What are the effects achieved by the sets and decorations?
         c. Costumes: What effects?
      2. Mise en frame: how does he compose his shots within the frame?
      3. Camera movement: Note the lyrical style. Plot the camera movements within a particular scene--for example, the scene where Esther and Tom turn out the lights or the "Trolley Song" scene, or the opening "Meet Me in St. Louis" scene. How does the camera movement enhance the mood of the film?
      4. Pacing and editing: What is the effect of the long takes? How does the film use close-ups? Types of edits.
   B. Writing:
      1. Dialogue: Focus upon its tone and its effect: is it "naturalistic"? If so, why?
      2. Narrative:
         a. Structure: How well does the seasonal structure work? Is this the classical narrative pattern?
         b. Content: The first script incorporated a standard melodramatic blackmail plot. Why does this film not need that? What is this film about? How is it about the audience in 1944?
         c. Characters: The demands of the narrative and the mood dictate a particular kind of characters. What kind?
   C. Music and Dancing:
      1. How are the musical numbers shot?
      2. What is the overall effect that is aimed for? Note uses of "bricolage," non-choreography, and non-singing.
      3. Many of the songs used are from the turn-of-the-centruy. How are they made more palatable for 1944 audiences?
   D. Acting and Performance:
      1. Minnelli's chief problems: how to elicit a performance from a sulky Judy Garland and how to control an overly theatrical performance from Margaret O'Brien. How well does he succeed?
      2. What kinds of performances does this kind of film require?
      3. Judy Garland: How does Minnelli cater to her status as star? What is the nature of her star persona? Why do we like her? (Read Feuer on Garland: pp. 117-122)
   E. Diegesis: Where are we as spectators? How does this film pull into the

diegesis without using the substitute audience discussed by Feuer? In other words, what are the diegetic "hooks"?

3. Generic: The classical Hollywood musical of the 1940's. How has the genre changed since the films of the 1930's? Which do you like better, and why?

4. Sociological:
   A. What values does this film embrace? Are they real values or tinsel ones?
   B. How does this film refelct the fact that it was made during World War II?
   C. In general, what function does "nostalgia" serve and when is it most likely to predominate?
   D. Societal roles: women, parents, grandparent, courtship

5. Thematic/Mythic/Psychological:
   A. Redemption: Who is redeemed from what and how?
   B. Ritualistic enactment of coming of age, courtship, and other societal ceremonies. How does this factor enhance our enjoyment of the film? What does this factor tell us about the fundamental "trajectory of audience desire" which fuels the film musical?
   C. The myth of "the American Dream:" What is it and how is it reflected in this film? Why is it necessary psychologically?

Fall 1987

ARTS AND LETTERS 310: THE HOLLYWOOD MUSICAL

SINGIN' IN THE RAIN

"You're nothing but a shadow on the screen . . . a shadow. You're not flesh and blood."

Date: 1952
Directors: Gene Kelly and Stanley Donen
Producer: Arthur Freed
Studio: MGM
Screenplay: Adolph Green and Betty Comden
Cinematography: Harold Rossen
Editing: Adrienne Fazan
Choreography: Gene Kelly and Stanley Donen
Music: Nacio Herb Brown
Lyrics: Arthur Freed
Musical Direction: Lennie Hayton
Art Direction: Cedric Gibbons and Randall Duell
Costumes: Walter Plunkett
Setting: Hollywood, 1927
Characters (and actors): Don Lockwood (Gene Kelly), Cosmo Brown (Donald O'Connor), Kathy Selden (Debbie Reynolds), Lina Lamont (Jean Hagen), R. F. Simpson (Millard Mitchell), Roscoe Dexter (Douglas Fowley), Zelda Zanders (Rita Moreno), dancer in "Gotta Dance" number: Cyd Charisse
Musical Numbers: "Fit as a Fiddle," "All I Do Is Dream of You," "Make 'Em Laugh," "Beautiful Girl," "You Were Meant For Me," "Moses Supposes," "Good Mornin'," "Singin' in the Rain," "Would You," "Gotta Dance" Ballet: "Broadway Melody" and "Broadway Rhythm," "You Are My Lucky Star"

ANALYSIS

1. Historical/biographical: SINGIN' IN THE RAIN was the second collaboration as co-directors/co-choreographers of Gene Kelly (b. 1912) and Stanley Donen (b. 1924). The two had met during the Broadway run of PAL JOEY in which Kelly starred and Donen was in the chorus. They renewed their friendship in Hollywood in 1942 on the set of FOR ME AND MY GAL, in which Kelly was making his film debut and Donen was once again in the chorus. Their first film together was ON THE TOWN in 1949. In 1951, Donen made his solo debut as a director before he and Kelly collaborated on SINGIN' IN THE RAIN. They were to make one more film together--IT' ALWAYS FAIR WEATHER (1955). Thereafter, each was to go his own way--Kelly to such musicals as INVITATION TO THE DANCE (1956) and HELLO DOLLY! (1969); Donen to musicals including SEVEN BRIDES FOR SEVEN BROTHERS (1954), THE PAJAMA GAME (1957), DAMN YANKEES (1958), as well as straight films, the best of which are INDISCREET (1958), CHARADE (1963), and the vastly underrated TWO FOR THE ROAD (1967).

SINGIN' IN THE RAIN was made in part to celebrate the first quarter century of Hollywood musicals and looks back to those first hectic days after the introduction of sound revolutionized the industry. Ironically, although its makers were probably totally unaware of it, the film was also a celebration of a dying genre and a doomed industrial system. For 1952 was the year of Lucy's baby on I LOVE LUCY, an event which captured the imagination of the American public and symbolized television's triumph as the dominant mode of popular entertainment.

This triumph was to prove devastating for the Hollywood studio system. The precipitous decline in the numbers of films that now could be made in the face of drastically diminishing audiences meant that even a studio the size of MGM could no longer afford to keep vast numbers of actors and technical artists under contract. The studio with "more stars than in Heaven" soon had to begin cutting back. Not only did personnel have to be let go, but vast areas of the back lot--the all-purpose sets which could be reused again and again--could no longer be maintained.

The musical was particularly hard-hit. The public's thirst for musicals may already have been declining after the great glut of the 1948-1952 period. In any case, when the audiences began staying home to watch TV, musicals suffered particularly. The numbers of musicals declined; and aside from a few original successes-- SEVEN BRIDES FOR SEVEN BROTHERS, A STAR IS BORN and GIGI, for example--Hollywood tried to insure success by making only "pre-sold" properties--films based on Broadway hits. Just as in the first five years after the introduction of sound, a great many careers dies, among them the careers of Debbie Reynolds and Donald O'Connor (not to mention Leslie Caron, Howard Keel, Jane Powell, Kathryn Grayson, Esther Williams, and a host of others), while people like Kelly, Astaire, and Garland had to turn to dramatic roles to survive at all. Directors like Minnelli and Donen had to move into other genres. Perehaps the most startling aspect of these declining years was the introduction of the very device which SINGIN' IN THE RAIN ridicules--the substitute voice. These years could be called the Marni Nixon years, since it was her singing voice which was substituted for the likes of Deborah Kerr (THE KING AND I), Natalie Wood (WEST SIDE STORY and GYPSY), and Audrey Hepburn (MY FAIR LADY). One might suggest that there is no clearer indication of the death of the classic musical genre than this practice of hiring actors rather than singers and dancers to appear in the Broadway-clone films. In fact, when you think about it, the past twenty-five years have produced only one star who has been able to sustain herself on musicals alone--Barbra Streisand.

2. Aesthetic:
  A. Direction:
    1. Mise en Scene
    2. Mise en Frame:
      a. compositions
      b. camera movements: How does the Kelly-Donen style differ from the Minnelli style?
      c. angles
      d. motivation: Are the shots motivated?
    3. Diegesis: extra-diegetic elements; hooks; positioning of the spectator
  B. Editing:
    1. Pacing
    2. Edits: What kinds? What effects?
    3. Note the principle of cutting on movement
    4. Montage sequences
  C. Writing:
    1. Dialogue: naturalistic or expressionistic?
    2. Narrative structure: Classic structure?
    3. Characters: realistic or stereotypical? Believable?
    4. Tone: What is the overall tone of the film? What attitude does it take towards the film of the past?
  D. Acting and Performance: What are the advantages and disadvantages of casting Debbie Reynolds? Why does Cyd Charisse make a guest appearance?

E. Music and Dancing:
   1. Once again, a film filled with "old standards." How well does this work? Does it suggest that the Hollywood musical is running out of inspiration?
   2. How are the songs varied?
   3. How well do the songs fit the plot?
   4. Compare the "Gotta Dance" Ballet with the "American in Paris" Ballet.

3. Generic:
   A. This film marks a definite stage in generic development--the self-reflective stage. That is to say that it looks back on the practices and conventions of the first (naive) stage of the genre and by exposing them as artifice conceals and authenticates its own artifice. To put it another way, this is a film which enlists the audience as its ally by saying, "Those silly fans back then could not see how artificial those musicals were. We modern sophisticates, on the other hand, are not to be taken in." We might call this the emperor's new clothes syndrome: by pointing out the emperor's nakedness, we assert that we have clothes on. In fact, we are all naked under our clothes. The self-reflective stage of generic development is just as much a product of artifice and illusionism as the two earlier stages (naive and classical).

   Let us then propose these three stages: 1) the naive, during which there are as yet no set conventions and expectations on the part of the audience (presumably, these develop as a result of a. audience response, b. the filmmakers' intentions, and c. accumulated experience with the genre on the part of the filmmaker); 2) the classical, during which a more or less complete and comprehensive set of "rules" and "truths" about the genre and its audience dominate the creative process and the conditions of spectatorship; 3) the self-reflective stage in which (some of) the earlier "rules" and "truths" of the genre are exposed and ridiculed so as to salvage and conceal more essential "rules" and "truths"--i.e. to enable the genre to survive.

   The irony here, of course, is that SINGIN' IN THE RAIN does not operate on a much different set of rules and truths than did the films of the naive or classical periods. In fact, it has to go back in part to one of the earliest strategies--the "backstage" setting--to justify its own musical conceits and avoid a rupture of the symbiotic relationship between the audience and the diegesis. (Ask yourself what kinds of numbers have to be justified by the backstage element and what kinds don't need to be because we are willing to accept them as extensions the filmic reality.)

4. Sociological/Political: Aside from some superficial observations on the excesses of fandom, this film would seem to be as far removed as possible from any kind of political/ideological statement: the real world of 1952 simply does not seem to intrude anywhere. Perhaps that is one clue to its continuing popularity. Film theorists tell us, however, that it is precisely when Hollywood is being least "political" that we should be most wary of its political/ideological intentions. Proposition: SINGIN' IN THE RAIN is a film which upholds the hegemony of a capitalistic, white, male, heterosexual establishment, that its primary function is a sedative one, that its generic self-reflectiveness tends to authenticate what in fact is a totally false view of the world in which most of its audience

must live.
5. Mythic/psychological:
    A. Redemption of the hero from what? By what? Compare Lise and Kathy.
    B. The role of the androgynous best friend: first Adam Cook, now Cosmo Brown.

IV. EUROPEAN AND WORLD FILM

Film R6016y, LATIN AMERICAN CINEMA Annette Insdorf
Thursdays, 1:15-5:00, 511 Dodge Hall Spring 1988

Texts:

Randall Johnson, Cinema Novo x Five: Masters of Contemporary Brazilian Film
Randall Johnson and Robert Stamm, BrazilianCinema

Roy MacBean, Film and Revolution (recommended)

Syllabus

Jan. 28 LUCIA (Cuba, 1969), dir. Humberto Solas

Feb. 4 PORTRAIT OF TERESA (Cuba, 1979), dir. Pastor Vega

Feb. 11 CAMILA (Argentina, 1984), dir. Maria Luisa Bemberg

Feb. 18 BLOOD OF THE CONDOR (Bolivia, 1979), dir. Jorge Sanjines

Feb. 25 THE JACKAL OF NAHUELTORO (Chile, 1969), dir. Miguel Littin

Mar. 3 BARRAVENTO (Brazil, 1962), dir. Glauber Rocha (first paper due)

Mar. 10 GANGA ZUMBA (Brazil, 1963), dir. Carlos Diegues

Note: March 17 or 17, see MAN FACING SOUTHEAST at the Cinema Village

Mar. 24 MACUNAIMA (Brazil, 1969), dir. Joaquim Pedro de Andrade

Mar. 31 HOW TASTY WAS MY LITTLE FRENCHMAN (Brazil, 1971), dir. Nelson Pereira dos Santos

Apr. 7 TENT OF MIRACLES (Brazil, 1977), dir. Pereira dos Santos

Apr. 14 GAIJIN (Brazil, 1979), dir. Tizuka Yamasaki

Apr. 21 PIXOTE (Brazil, 1981), dir. Hector Babenco

Apr. 28 THE CITY AND THE DOGS (Peru, 1985), dir. Francisco Lombardi
(second paper due)

NEW YORK UNIVERSITY

V51.0506--German Dept.
(Cross-listed as:
   V30.0506--Drama;
   V50.0506--Interdepartmental
     Program;
   V51.0506--Lit. in Translation)
Tues. 2:50-5:20 (Film showing)
Thurs. 2:50-4:05 (Lecture)
West Room, Avery Fischer Center:
  2nd Floor, Bobst Library

New German Cinema
Spring 1987
4 Points
Prof. Richard McCormick
Office: Room 428,
     19 University Pl.
Phone: 598-3269/2428
Office Hours: 11-12 Tues.
           2-4 Wed.

A STRUGGLE FOR ALTERNATIVE VISIONS:
THE "NEW GERMAN CINEMA"
IN SOCIO-HISTORICAL AND AESTHETIC CONTEXTS

"The old film is dead. We believe in the new."

    In 1962 young West German filmmakers boldly proclaimed their determination to create a new cinema which would both challenge their society politically and undermine the domination of commercial cinema over its "ways of seeing." Out of this determination, what we now know as the "New German Cinema" has developed. We will examine this cinema in its endeavor to produce alternative visions, using an interdisciplinary approach which places this struggle into both socio-historical and aesthetic contexts.

    How can films dedicated to "alternative visions" reach an audience shaped by its experience with commercial films (made in Hollywood for the most part)? How can a cinema intended to subvert commercial logic survive financially? Can freedom of expression be guaranteed by government subsidy? These questions have plagued--but also enriched--the New German Cinema from the beginning. Its dilemma has encompassed a variety of contradictory positions between which filmmakers have had to negotiate compromises: between cinematic experimentation and "accessible narratives," between oppositional politics and the politics of government funding agencies, between political goals and aesthetic ones. These contradictions have shaped the history of the New German Cinema.

    The course aims to equip students with sufficient socio-historical background to evaluate the films in terms of such contradictions, as well as to provide the fundamentals of film analysis and contemporary film criticism, so that the formal structures of the films can be understood. By the end of the course, students should be able both to do a "close reading" of a film and to place it within the larger historical context defined by the aesthetic and political debates in West German society to which the films respond.

COURSE OUTLINE: Film and Lecture Topics

I. Introduction: Overview of German Film History: 2/5/87.

    1. "New German Cinema"--between Hollywood and German history: Rainer Werner Fassbinder's The Marriage of Maria Braun (1979: 120 min.) as paradigm. Showing: 2/10; lecture: 2/12.

II. In the Beginning was the Past: "Young German Cinema," 1962-71.

    2. Coming to terms with the past: literary adaptation. Volker Schlöndorff's Young Törless (1966: 87 min.). Showing: 2/17; lecture: 2/19.

    3. Increasing politicization and the Weimar tradition: the "Workers' Film." Christian Ziewer's Dear Mother, I'm OK (1971: 91 min.). Showing: 2/24; lecture: 2/26.

III. Escape from the Political? Turning Inward, 1972-77.

    4. The Expressionist legacy: Caligari as conquistador. Werner Herzog's Aguirre (1972: 93 min.). Showing: 3/3; lecture: 3/12.

    5. "Bildungsroman" as road movie: Wim Wenders's The Wrong Move (1974: 103 min.). Showing: 3/10; lecture: 3/12 & 19.

    6. Feminist exploration of everyday reality: undermining the "private/public" dichotomy. Helke Sander's The All-Round Reduced Personality (REDUPERS) (1977: 100 min.). Showing: 3/17; lecture: 3/19 & 3/31.

IV. Midterm Summary: 3/31 & 4/2.

V. Germany after Autumn: The Re-Presentation of History, 1977-80.

    7. Backtracking: earlier cinematic experimentation in juxtaposing public and private, personal and historical realities. Brechtian montage and West German reality in Alexander Kluge's Yesterday Girl (Abschied von gestern, 1965: 88 min.). Showing: 4/7; lecture: 4/9.

8. Artists Collaborating for an "Alternative Public Sphere." Kluge, Fassbinder, Schlöndorff, Heinrich Böll, Edgar Reitz, et al.: <u>Germany in Autumn</u> (1978: 124 min.). Showing: 4/14; lecture: 4/16.

9. History and Feminist Autobiography: Helma Sanders-Brahms's <u>Germany, Pale Mother</u> (1980: 130 min.). Showing: 4/21; lecture: 4/23.

VI. New Directions: Aesthetics and Politics of the Body, 1980-?

10. The Avant-Garde Vision: Ulrike Ottinger's <u>Ticket of No Return</u> (<u>Bildnis einer Trinkerin</u>, 1980: 108 min.). Showing: 4/28; lecture: 4/30.

11. Sexuality, Repression, and the Cold War: Marianne S.W. Rosenbaum's <u>Peppermint Peace</u> (1983: 100 min.). Showing: 5/5; lecture: 5/7.

VII. Has the "New German Cinema" Survived? Course Summary and Conclusion(s): 5/12, 14, 19.

ASSIGNED READINGS:

1. * Eric Rentschler: <u>West German Film in the Course of Time: Reflections on Twenty Years Since Oberhausen</u> (Bedford Hills, NY: Redgrave, 1984).

2. * Louis Gianetti: <u>Understanding Movies</u>, 3rd ed. (Englewood Cliffs, NJ: Prentice-Hall, 1982). (Not required for students with sufficient background in film studies.)

3. $ Hans Günther Pflaum and Hans Helmut Prinzler: <u>Cinema in the Federal Republic of Germany. The New German Film: Origins and Present Situation. A Handbook</u> (Bonn: Inter Nationes, 1983).

4. Xeroxed articles and hand-outs to be distributed in class.

RECOMMENDED READINGS:

1. * John Sanford: <u>The New German Cinema</u> (New York: Da Capo, 1980).

2. * Gerald Mast and Marshall Cohen, eds.: <u>Film Theory and Criticism</u>, 3rd ed. (New York: Oxford U. Press, 1985).

3. Klaus Phillips, ed.: <u>New German Filmmakers From Oberhausen Through the 1970s</u> (New York: Frederick Ungar, 1984).

4. Eric Rentschler, ed., German Film and Literature: Adaptations and Transformations (New York: Methuen, 1986).

5. Timothy Corrigan: New German Film: The Displaced Image (Austin: U. Texas, 1983).

6. James Franklin: New German Cinema: From Oberhausen to Hamburg (Boston: Twayne, 1983).

* = available in bookstore
$ = in course reader

REQUIREMENTS:

1. 2 film reviews, approx. 1 p. each (typed); the first is due by Mar. 10, and can deal with any one of the first 4 films shown in the course, or with any "New German" film seen outside of class (subject to approval of instructor). Second review is due no later than May 19, and must deal with either Doris Dörrie's Men or Margarethe von Trotta's Rosa Luxemburg (both of which must be seen outside of class).

2. Opening class discussion of film on Thursday with one or two other students--at least once.

3. Midterm Paper (essay based on sequence analysis); 5 pp. minimum. Due April 14.

4. Final Examination: choice of essay questions plus sequence analysis.

McCormick
New German Cinema
Spring 1987

FINAL EXAM

Part I. Write an essay based on one of the seven general areas suggested below. You must discuss at least four films in your essay, and they must be chosen according to the directions specified in the directions for the topic on which you elect to write.

1. The Representation of History: Discuss the role history--German and otherwise--plays within four of the following films. What period(s) of history is (are) thematized? Are allusions made to other periods than those obviously thematized? What formal strategies are used to depict certain historical realities? How do these strategies compare from film to film? Which strategies do you consider more effective? Why? What does the use of history in each film signify about the historical period in which the film itself was made?
  You must write on at least 3 films from the following group: Germany in Autumn, Germany Pale Mother, Yesterday Girl, The Marriage of Maria Braun, or Peppermint Peace. The fourth film may also come from that group, or can be chosen from the following films: Wrong Move, Young Törless, Aguirre.

2. Political Film: Discuss four of the following films in terms the way politics is thematized within them, or how it structures their projects. Are there differing conceptions of "politics" informing some of the films? Which films have apparent political goals? How do the aesthetic strategies employed in the films relate to politics in general, and to achieving specific goals? What is the relation of the "means" and the "ends" in these films? How successful are they? What relation is there between the apparent political intention behind each film and your interpretation of its political significance? What relation is there between each film and the political climate in West Germany when the film was made?
  You must discuss Dear Mother I'm OK, and Germany in Autumm. The other two films must be chosen from the following group: Maria Braun, Germany Pale Mother, REDUPERS, Wrong Move, Peppermint Peace.

3. Germany as Mise-en-scene: Discuss the function of the settings within four films, especially with regard to their meaning as physical representations of German (social, political, psychological) realities. Do not ignore the differing aesthetic strategies in the films, since they obviously play a determining role in how any physical or social reality is depicted within a film. You can restrict your discussion to films which depict

urban environments: REDUPERS, Ticket of No Return, Yesterday Girl, Maria Braun. Or you can limit your discussion to two or three of those films, contrasting them to one or two films which do not depict an urban environment exclusively--or at all: Peppermint Peace, Wrong Move, Aguirre.

4. Gender Roles and Perspectives: what significance does the gender of a character have for the meaning of a particular film? How is gender depicted? Is this problematic from certain perspectives--including your own? Discuss the function of gender within four films in terms of its thematization (or apparent absence), and in terms of narrative perspective (grounded in a character), directorial perspective, or the perspective of a potential or real spectator (including yourself, if you like). The orientation towards the spectator would include consideration of genre expectations which the film might in some ways call forth but also in part frustrate.

Of the four films you discuss, at least two must be from the following group: Germany Pale Mother, REDUPERS, Peppermint Peace, Ticket of No Return. You must also discuss at least one of the following two films: Yesterday Girl and Maria Braun. You may also write on one of the following: Aguirre, Törless, Wrong Move.

5. Documentary vs. Fiction: this is a formal dichotomy which much film theory and many films of the 60s and 70s have attempted to undermine. Why? How successful have the filmmakers been who tried to do so? What relation might these aesthetic goals have to the political goals of the filmmakers, and to the historical context in which they worked? Use these questions to guide your discussion of the juxtapositions, fusions, and/or simulations of documentary and fictional footage--and techniques--(or lack thereof) in four films. Besides describing the specific mixture of both in each film and discussing their function and significance therein, you may also want to cite Kluge's theory about documentary and fiction.

Discuss at least three of the following films: Yesterday Girl, Germany in Autumn, REDUPERS, Germany Pale Mother, Dear Mother I'm OK. You may discuss one of the following: Maria Braun, Rosa Luxemburg, Wrong Move.

6. Avant-Garde vs. Realism: Position four films of your choice along the spectrum between the avant-garde and realism, with two of the films closer to the avant-garde, and two closer to realism. Use this as the basis of your discussion of the films. Why do you position them as you do? What elements of distantiation are present--or lacking--in each film? Does this have an effect in accord or in contrast with a filmmaker's apparent intent in using or avoiding such technique? Do you see these films as validating avant-garde or realistic strategies?

You may find it useful in your discussion to cite theories of Brecht, Godard, and/or Kluge, or to use Metz's "story/discourse" distinction, whether to agree with or to problematize them. You may also structure your argument so as to undermine the very dichotomy between these two supposed poles (avant-garde/realism)--e.g. by accepting rhetorically the conventionally understood spectrum between them, and showing how four films which seem to fit on that spectrum actually expose it as a fallacy. Or you may argue convincingly that these distinctions are valid and should not be lost.

7. New German Cinema Between Hollywood and the Avant-Garde: the NGC has been seen--and has seen itself--as an attempt to create a cinema which creates "new ways of seeing" without simply being an elitist art cinema, and which is popular without being manipulative, as dominant commercial cinema is seen as being. Choosing four films of your choice, discuss the various positions within this range of alternatives which the films you choose illustrate. How successful is each film in terms of the goals of the NGC? On the basis of the four films you choose (this should influence your choice), how successful has the NGC as a whole been in terms of its goals? If you like, you may also develop an argument as to the present state (or non-existence) of the NGC, basing it on your discussion of the four films. (You may allude to other films as well, of course, but discuss four films thoroughly.)

Part II: Sequence Analysis. Write an essay based on your analysis of the sequence which I will show 3 times. Analyze the sequence both in terms of:

a) the various codes employed--and whether or not they are foregrounded so as to be distinct from or in tension with each other, or whether they fuse together into a harmonious effect which effaces them. And what is their significance for a reading of this particular sequence?

b) the relation of the sequence to the formal style, aesthetic project, and political or historical significance of the film as a whole, in terms of your reading of the film.

College Course File

THIRD WORLD CINEMA
ROBERT STAM

Culturally rich, formally innovative, and politically progressive, Third World Cinema forms a vital current within World Cinema. Although the cinematic traditions of many countries which we now recognize as belonging to the Third World—notably those of India, Egypt, Brazil, and Argentina—go back to the first decades of this century, it was only in the sixties that Third World Cinema as a self-aware movement emerged on the international film scene by winning prizes and critical praise in Europe and North America. In the wake of the pioneering work of Brazil's Cinema Novo and the independent neo-realist-inflected productions of Satyajit Ray, dynamic film movements appeared in such countries as Algeria, Senegal, Cuba and Chile.

Despite the artistic excellence and historical importance of much of Third World Cinema, however, the subject is often ignored by standard film histories and cinema studies curricula. When not ignored, it is treated with a certain condescension, as if it were merely the "shadow" of the "real" cinema of Europe and North America. Because of such attitudes, a course in Third World Cinema presents a number of special challenges in that the teacher is obliged to clear away the "rubble" of misconceptions in order to lay the groundwork for appreciation of the films. Many students, for example, have very imprecise notions about the exact definition of the Third World, often confusing its true definition—the ensemble of colonized, neo-colonized, and de-colonized nations whose political and economic structures have been shaped by the colonial process—with some vague economic notion (the "poor" or "non-industrialized" nations), or with a geographical schema (the nations of Asia, Africa, and Latin America), or with an ethnic ("non-white") or cultural ("backward") classification. These notions are imprecise, I point out, because Third World nations are not necessarily poor (Kuwait, Venezuela, and Mexico are rich in petroleum), nor non-industrialized (Brazil has been industrialized for decades), nor non-White (Argentina is predominantly white), nor culturally backward (witness the brilliance of contemporary Latin American literature).

The teacher of Third World Cinema, then, is often obliged to "deconstruct" a series of mistaken assumptions on the part of the first-world student. As part of this deconstruction, I have found a number of strategies useful. I ask students about their source of information concerning the Third World, whether it is a) personal experience as a Third World person; b) personal contact with Third World peoples or countries; or c) through the

---

ROBERT STAM is an Associate Professor in the Department of Cinema Studies at New York University. He is co-editor (with Randal Johnson) of *Brazilian Cinema* (Ass. University Press, 1982). His *Reflexivity in Film and Literature: From Don Quixote to Jean-Luc Godard* will be published by UMI in January 1985.

Copyright © 1984 by Robert Stam

mass-media. The point is that the Third World seldom represents itself; it is represented by others, mediated by Hollywood. Dan Rather, or *The New York Times*. One of the purposes of the course, then, is to allow the Third World to speak for itself through its films. In this context I emphasize the distorted images of Third World peoples generated by First World Cinema. Many of the misconceptions concerning Third World peoples derive from the long parade of lazy Mexicans, shifty Arabs, savage Africans and exotic Asiatics that have disgraced our movie screens. Africa was portrayed as a land inhabited by cannibals. Mexicans were reduced to "greasers," and slavery was idealized. Hundreds of Hollywood westerns turned history on its head by making Native Americans appear to be intruders on what was originally their land, thus providing a paradigmatic perspective by which the First World came to view the Third World.

Colonialist discourse, I argue, pervades not only the mass-media, but also the specific realm of film criticism. The most celebrated film critics in the print and electronic media, for example, display a kind of tendentious ignorance concerning Third World Cinema. Some, like Andrew Sarris, invite a few elite members of the Third World into a pre-existing pantheon, while arguing that North American Cinema is "the only cinema worth studying in depth." Others, like Pauline Kael in "The Future of the Movies," blame Third World audiences, "starved for entertainment," for consuming the client Eastwood films that Hollywood has unceremoniously "dumped" on Third World markets. Richard Schickel, on the Public Television series "Films of Propaganda" (a series which mingled *Triumph of the Will* with *Lucia* and *Far From VietNam*), claimed incorrectly that Cuba had produced no major film since *Lucia*. And critics like Bosley Crowther demonstrate a kind of racism of perception and vocabulary, describing the Brazilian film *The Given* *Word* as one in which "pagans" (i.e., practitioners of the Afro-Brazilian religion called *candomble*) "wiggle-dance" (i.e. do the samba) as they "stage a stomping swirling riot" (i.e. react against police repression to try to save the protagonist). In such instances, ethnocentric expectations inform the very perceptions of the critic who is literally incapable of seeing what is in the film.

Finally, I stress the fact of our connectedness to the Third World. Not only are many American cities such as New York, Los Angeles or San Francisco "Third World Cities" with large black, hispanic and third-world immigrant populations, but also all Americans are connected with the Third World if only because our tax dollars go to Nicaraguan contras, or because we buy shirts made in Taiwan or South Korea, or because we all depend on raw materials and resources from the Third World. I further emphasize the question of cultural reciprocity. Given the generally unilateral flow of information from First to Third World, "they" tend to know "us" better than we know them. Brazilian popular music, for example, constituting one of the richest musical traditions in the world, combining Africanized polytrhythms, Europeanized melodies and poetic lyrics, is rarely heard on North American radios, while American top-forty hits dominate the air waves in Brazil. This lack of reciprocity, I argue, has little to do with the intrinsic value of the two traditions, and has everything to do with the projection of political and economic power.

Another challenge facing the teacher of a course on Third World Cinema is the lack of a basic text. The only book that offers some level of generality is Teshome Gabriel's *Third Cinema in the Third World: The Aesthetics of Liberation*, a valuable text, but unfortunately priced out of the range of most students. There are worthwhile books on specific Third World Cinemas: Barnouw and Krishnswamy's

Indian Cinema (Oxford). Jay Leyda's *Dianying: Electric Shadows: An Account of Films and the Film Audience in China,* and Johnson and Stam's *Brazilian Cinema.* A number of BFI publications are dedicated to Third World Cinema, notably *Chilean Cinema* (edited by Michael Chanan), *Algerian Cinema* (edited by Hala Salmane), and *Twenty-Five Years of the New Latin American Cinema* (edited by Michael Chanan). There are also a number of special BFI Dossiers, notably Numbers 2 *(Santiago Alvarez),* 3 *(Electric Shadows: 45 Years of Chinese Cinema);* 5 *(Indian Cinema),* and 6 *(African Films: The Context of Production).* Julianne Burton's *The New Latin American Cinema: An Annotated Bibliography 1960-1980,* finally, is invaluable in a course which almost inevitably features a high proportion of Latin American films. Apart from these sources, the teacher is generally obliged to rely on either back issues or xeroxed reproductions of articles from journals which regularly feature work on Third World Cinema, notably *Screen, Jump Cut, Cineaste, Film Quarterly, Film Library Quarterly, Framework, Critical Arts, Cinetracts,* and *Journal of the University Film and Video Association.*

Although all film courses inevitably have a political dimension, a Third World Cinema course is political through and through; to be apolitical is to condemn the course to triviality. (The term "Third World" is political in origin, since it was initially coined by analogy to the "third estate" at the time of the French revolution, and extended to metaphorize the struggle against colonialism.) For this reason, I also assign two books not specifically devoted to the cinema, but which provide a conceptual framework as well as contextual information in terms of the basic anti-colonialist thrust of the course. Frantz Fanon's *The Wretched of the Earth* (Grove Press) is perhaps the most eloquent anti-colonial treatise ever written. The book has the further advantage of bearing direct relevance to certain films such as *Battle of Algiers* and *Xala,* to the point that such films seem to offer filmic demonstrations of specific passages in Fanon. (For those disturbed by Fanon's emphasis on the therapeutic role of violence, Albert Memmi's *The Colonizer and the Colonized* [Beacon Press] will serve similar purposes). Given the course's high proportion of Latin American films, I also assign Eduardo Galeano's *The Open Veins of Latin America.* A passionate and beautifully written essay on the economic servitude of Latin America; the Galeano text displays the strengths (and the occasional weaknesses) of what is commonly called "dependency analysis." As an accessible and cogent introduction to Latin America, the book is extremely valuable.

In terms of methodology, my approach is, first of all, *textual,* having to do with film-as-film. I see film texts, following Metz, as the product of the interweaving of specifically cinematic codes (lighting, editing, camera movement) with more widely shared artistic codes (narrative structure, genre conventions), together with broadly disseminated cultural and ideological codes (the role of carnival in Brazilian culture, the presence of Hindu mythology in Indian film). My analytical method is synthetic, drawing on the descriptive categories of contemporary film theory and criticism (Metz, Bellour, Mulvey) as well as on the tradition of literary theory and exegesis (Auerbach, Barthes, Bakhtin, Jameson.) In my discussion of individual films, I characterize its particular style of narration as well as on the mechanisms and contradictions of the overall design.

My approach is, secondly, *intertextual,* that is, it deals with the relations between the films under discussion and the other texts that have preceded them. In the case of Third World Cinema, the intertext englobes a progressively more inclusive set of categories: 1) the immediately play of allusion and citation within a specific national tradition (*The World of Apu* alludes to the commercial Indian "mythologicals"); 2) influence of specific films from outside the national tradition (*Macunaima* cites Busby Berkeley's *Footlight Parade*); 3) the more diffuse stylistic impact of broader movements such as Italian Neo-Realism or the French New Wave (*Vidas Secas* shows traces of Neo-Realism); 4) the presence of non-filmic texts in the films themselves, in the form of plays (the Dias Gomes source-play for Duarte's *The Given Word*) or novels (the Desnoes novelistic source for *Memories of Underdevelopment*); 5) In the broadest sense, intertextuality refers to the larger discursive practices of a culture, within which each single work is situated. In this sense, the films might echo the "already said" of journalists, politicians, popular poets, musicians or philosophers.

Since textual and intertextual analysis hardly exhaust a film's signification, my approach is also *contextual*. Third World films are informed by their ambiant cultures, shaped by history, inflected by events. The 1964 *coup d'état* in Brazil, for example, sharply modified cinematic productions. I also explore the importance of state regulations and censorship for Third World film industries, as well as the consequences of Hollywood domination of distribution. To link the textual and contextual, I draw on Lucien Goldmann's notion of "homologies" between narrative structure and historical moments, as well as on Fredric Jameson's idea of "competing class discourses" within the text. Metz' concept of the "three industries" (the industry proper, the mental machinery of the spectator, and critical machinery or "linguistic appendage"), with its implicit call for a multi-disciplinary approach embracing the economic-historical, the psychoanalytic, and the linguistic-critical, is also germane.

My approach, finally, deals with the *spectator-in-the-text*. How do these films implicate or address the spectator? Is the spectator assumed to be from the First World, as with *Battle of Algiers*, or assumed to be Third World, as with *Macunaima*? How would a Cuban spectator see *Memories of Development* as compared with a first-world intellectual? Is the spectator of the film assumed to be male, female, or both? How does the film conform to, frustrate, or subvert our conventional expectations? What are the ideological assumptions and institutionalized expectations that we bring to Third World films and how do they affect our experience of the films?

My Third World Cinema course is built around a tripartite structure. The beginning of the course is designed to communicate the conceptual framework of the course: the struggle against colonialism. (I am quite aware that this framework is only one of many possible frameworks, but it is one that I find particularly appropriate and effective). The course then proceeds to discuss those national cinemas with a long tradition of filmmaking—India, Egypt, Mexico, Argentina, Chile, Brazil—and finishes by discussing those cinemas which have gained importance more recently, in the wake of Independence or Revolution (Senegal, Cuba). Within each national cinema, I proceed from historical overview to the analysis of specific films and filmmakers. Throughout, I emphasize the question of a "Third World Aesthetic," the search for production methods and a style appropriate to the economic conditions and political circumstances of the Third World, whether it is called a "Third Cinema" (Solanas-Getino), "an aesthetic of hunger" (Glauber Rocha), or "an imperfect cinema" (Julio Garcia Espinosa). To what extent do the films draw on national culture to forge an authentic style? (*Macunaima* draws on Amerindian legends, for example, and *The Mummy* draws on Egypt's pharonic past).

To what extent do the films imitate. subvert or simply ignore what we have come to call "dominant cinema?"

In addition to the films discussed in this course file. such countries as India. Egypt. Brazil and Argentina have also produced a popular cinema, especially in Latin America. However, because of the difficulty of obtaining prints of these works. I have not covered them in this article.

I. COLONIAL CONFRONTATIONS: THE BATTLE OF ALGIERS

The first class is taken up with questions of definition of essential terms. such as "Third World." with the distorted images fostered by First World Cinema. and with the basic conceptual framework of the course. I explain the historical origins of the Third World concept. and why Third Worldism reached its zenith in the late sixties. I stress the quixotic nature of the tasks of speaking of the Third World *in general*. in a situation where the cultural differences within a single country such as India are often as significant as those separating. for example. Spain from France.

An effective opening film. I have found. is Pontecorvo's *Battle of Algiers* (1966). perhaps the first European film to treat the subject of colonialism and wars of liberation from the point-of-view of the oppressed. After speaking about the image of the Arab in First World films. I stress that the film was a co-production with the Algerians. a fact that helped Pontecorvo avoid some of the ethnocentric blunders that marred his later *Burn*. Apart from illustrating many of the themes developed in *The Wretched of the Earth* — the physical and psychological brutality of colonialism. the myth of "assimilation." the therapeutic role of politicized struggle. the film also raises interesting questions concerning "objectivity" (is it possible or even desirable?). focalization (does the film focalize a single hero or a collective entity?). and of narrative and aesthetic strategies (does the documentary style work? Is the film Hollywoodean in form. or does it ultimately subvert Hollywood codes of suspense and spectacle?).

Readings

Stam. Robert and Louise Spence. "Colonialism. Racism. and Representation." *Screen* Vol. XXIV. Number 2 (March-April 1983).
Fanon. Frantz. *The Wretched of the Earth.* New York: Grove Press. 1963. pp. 1-106.
Spence. Louise and Robert Stam. "Racism in the Cinema: Proposal for a Methodological Investigation. *Critical Arts: A Journal for Media Studies,* Vol. II. Number 4 (Spring 1983).
Fanon. Frantz. "This is the Voice of Algeria." in Mattelart. Armand and Seth Siegelaub. *Communication and Class Struggle,* Vol. II (New York: International General. 1983). pp. 211-219.
Also Recommended: Joan Mellen. *Filmguide to the Battle of Algiers* (Indiana Univ. Press). Solinas' *Gillo Pontecorvo's The Battle of Algiers* (Scribners). and Salmane's *Algerian Cinema* (BFI).

II THE TRADITION: INDIA AND SATYAJIT RAY

Since it is often mistakenly assumed that Third World Cinema began in the sixties. I stress that many Third World countries feature filmmaking traditions going back to the silent period. The "golden age" of Brazilian Cinema. for example. occurred from 1908-1911. when production reached 100 fiction films per year. and decline set in only after the Hollywood take-over of the distribution circuits in the wake of World War I. Indian Cinema goes back to 1897. with the first film made by an Indian. through the first fiction feature in 1913 (*Rajah Harischandra*) and the first sound film (*Alam Ara*) in 1931. Currently. Indian Cinema constitutes one of the world's major industries. with ten million spectators per day and an annual production of feature films ranging from seven-hundred to a thousand per year. In 1977, India exported films to eighty-eight countries. While most of Indian film production has been dismissed as commercial escapist entertainment based on a star system and the voices of "playback singers," it is important to remember that American commercial cinema too was often treated with scorn by intellectuals. The films should also be seen in the context of the specific cultural codes of Sanskrit-Hindi art, which makes no rigorous distinction between fantasy and reality, where stylization is the norm and in which the nine "rasa" or moods (such as love, anger, sacrifice) are musically orchestrated.

Since Indian commercial films are not generally available in sixteen millimeter in the United States, I show Satyajit Ray's *The World of Apu*, partially because it includes a film-within-the-film, a "mythological," which conveys some sense of the commercial productions, even though the Ray film is itself conceived in the very different spirit of the auteurist "New Cinema," a movement characterized by relatively low-budget, non-industrial and non-escapist films featuring location shooting and little-known actors. I discuss *The World of Apu* in terms of specifically cinematic questions (the deployment of deep space, the subtle use of the noise and music tracks), as well as cultural and ideological questions (the cultural code of an arranged marriage based on astrological influences, the question of a specifically Indian "pacing," and the political limitations of Ray's "humanism").

A Third World Cinema course could easily feature two or more Indian films within a semester. I would have liked to include some of the films of Mrinal Sen, for example, such as *A Day Like Another* and *In Search of Famine*, but they were not in distribution. In any case, Indian Cinema presents fascinating material having to do with cultural diversity (the difference between a Bengali film and a Tamil film is as great as that between, say, a British and an Italian film), language (in a country with over 1500 languages, of which fifteen are recognized by the constitution), and the political role of the cinema (where Tamil Cinema became an ally of the Dravidian movement, and where Tamil stars or "film heroes" at times became important political figures.). But for more on such issues I point the students to the wealth of written material on Indian Cinema.

Readings:

Barnouw, Erik and S. Krishnaswamy. *Indian Film.* New York: Oxford University Press, 1980.
BFI Dossier Number 5. *Indian Cinema,* edited by Paul Willemen and Behroze Gandhy, British Film Institute (1982).
Robin Wood. *The Apu Trilogy.* New York: Praeger, 1971.
Ray, Satyajit. *Our Films, Their Films.* New Delhi: Orient Longman, 1976).
Lenglet, Philippe and Aruna Vasudev, editors. *Indian Cinema Superbazaar.* New Delhi: Vikas Publishing House. 1983.

II. EGYPTIAN CINEMA AND NATIONAL CULTURE

Like India, Egypt has a proud cinematic tradition, going at least as far back as the twenties (and earlier, if one counts European filmmakers based in Egypt), and, again like India, has often been an important regional influence, exercising a kind of hegemony within the Arab world. Most Egyptian films have been musical comedies or melodramas, at least prior to the Nasser revolution in 1952, after which there emerge more socially conscious films. One of the major Egyptian directors is Youssef Chahine, whose *Cairo Station* (also called *Gates of Iron,* 1958) shows the somewhat belated influence of Italian

Neo-realism. Chahine's later *Alexandria Why?* (1979) meanwhile, is an autobiographical and reflexive film concerning Chahine's adolescent dreams of becoming a Hollywood director. Set during World War II, the film contains spoofs of the different European communities as seen through Egyptian eyes, and brings up the issue of cultural colonialism through Hollywood films. *Alexandria Why?* ends with the protagonist's arrival in New York Harbor, where the Statue of Liberty, made up to look like a prostitute, throws him a salacious wink.

Another effective film is Shadi Abdel-salam's *The Mummy* (also called *Night of Counting the Years*, 1969). The film portrays the conflict that arises, within a mountain tribe, when archeologists discovered the legendary cachet of royal mummies in 1881. Since the tribe had traditionally lived off stealing from the tombs, they are faced with the dilemma of revealing or not revealing the innermost secrets of the tombs. This story becomes a springboard for a discussion of the conflicts and contradictions rending Egyptian nationality, of the relation between city and country as well as that between the Pharonic past and the Arabized Islamic present. The style of the film, with its Jansco-like camera movements, its choreographed movement in the shot, and its impeccable sense of composition, is perfectly appropriate to the theme of the film and its message of pride and dignity.

Readings:

Khan, M. *An Introduction to the Egyptian Cinema*. London: Informatix, 1969.
Said, Edward W. *Orientalism*. New York: Pantheon, 1978.
Salles Gomes, Paulo Emilio. "Cinema: Trajectory within Underdevelopment," in *Brazilian Cinema* (Cranbury: Associated University Presses, 1982).
Shochat, Ella, "Egypt: Cinema and Revolution," *Critical Arts: A Journal for Media Studies*, Vol. II, No. 4 (Spring 1983).

IV. MEXICO: HOLLYWOOD AND ITS ALTERNATIVES

Like Egypt, Mexico has a long industrial tradition and has been an exporter of films to other countries, in this case to Latin America. The Mexican industry is highly Hollywoodeanized, and indeed Hollywood itself has frequently been involved within the Mexican industry, favoring it against its rival Argentina, for example, during the Second World War because of Argentina's ambiguous neutrality. To give some sense of the commercial tradition within Mexico, I show a segment from Bunuel *Los Olvidados* (1950) as an example of a film made within the studio tradition, but which nevertheless subverts the codes of the Mexican melodrama (with its idealized mothers, sentimentalized poor, and asocial approach). I would also show Paul Leduc's *Reed: Insurgent Mexico* (1971) as an example of an alternative, more politicized cinema influenced by other Third World currents. Apart from its special interest for American students because of the John Reed connection, the film raises a number of issues: the representation of the Mexican revolution (a frequent subject of Hollywood films), the focalization of the Reed character, the meld of documentary and fiction strategies.

Readings:

Michel, Manuel. "Mexican Cinema: A Panoramic View," *Film Quarterly*, Vol. XVIII, No. 4 (Summer 1965).
Trevino, Jesus Salvador. "The New Mexican Cinema," *Film Quarterly*, Vol. XXXII, No. 3 (Spring 1979).
Ryan, Susan. "Film Across the Border: The Interaction of the Mexican and American Motion Picture Industries," *Critical Arts: A Journal for Media Studies*, Vol. II, No. 4 (Spring 1983).
Galeano, Eduardo. *The Open Veins of Latin America*, pp. 1-70.
Also Available: Carl J. Mora. *Mexican Cinema*. Berkeley: University of California Press, 1982.

V. ARGENTINA: FROM AUTEURISM TO MILITANCY

Argentina has a fairly well-developed industrial infrastructure and a long cinematic tradition going back to the turn of the century. As in Brazil, Argentinian Cinema was strong already in the teens of this century, with an annual production averaging thirty films per year. With the advent of sound, Argentina began to supply the Latin American market with Spanish-speaking films. The genres included tango films, like Luis Moglia Barth's *Tango* (1933), historical epics like Mario Sofici's *Viento del Norte* (1937), and socially conscious films like Hugo del Carril's *Las Aguas Bajan Turbias* (1959). In the fifties Leopoldo Torre-Nilsson begins making his sardonic portraits of the Argentinian upperclass. The sixties see the development both of New-Wave-style auteurist films, like Rodolfo Kuhn's *The Sad Young Men*, and of militant, often clandestinely-made, documentaries by Raimundo Gleyzer, Gerardo Vallejo, Grupo Cine de la Base, and Grupo Cine-Liberacio. In the late sixties, there emerges the underground "parallel cinema" of Edgardo Cozarinsky and Miguel Bejo. To give some sense of the range of Argentinian Cinema, I would show, finances permitting, a segment from one of the Torre-Nilsson/Beatriz Guido collaborations such as *Fin de Fiesta* (1960) along with the First Part of one of the key "Third Worldist" films, Solanas-Getino's *La Hora de Los Hornos* (1968). The latter film has a double usefulness, first as an example of the militant Argentinian cinema of the late sixties, and secondly as a didactic audio-visual treatise on the subject of cultural colonialism. The film orchestrates a multiplicity of styles and strategies, along with revolutionary homages to tricontinental culture heroes (Che Guevara, Frantz Fanon, Ho Chi Minh, and, more problematically, Peron). The film also raises a number of issues for discussion: the convergence in the film of the two avant-gardes, the political and the aesthetic; the relation between the process of production and the text itself; the various textual and extra-textual strategies deployed to turn passive film consumers into active accomplices; the authors' failure to analyze the contradictions of Peronist populism; the problematic mixture of anti-authoritarian language and demogogic manipulation of the spectator.

Readings:

Burton, Julianne, "The Camera as 'Gun': Two Decades of Culture and Resistance in Latin America," *Latin American Perspectives*, Issue 16, Vol. V, No. 1 (Winter 1978).

Birri, Fernando, "Cinema and Underdevelopment," in *Twenty-Five Years of the New Latin American Cinema*, ed. Michael Chanon, London: BFI, 1983.

Stam, Robert, "*Hour of the Furnaces* and the Two Avant-Gardes," *Millenium Film Journal*, Nos. 7/8/9 (Fall/Winter 1980-1981).

Galeano, Eduardo. *The Open Veins of Latin America*, pp. 71-148.

Solanas, Fernando and Octavio Getino. "Towards a Third Cinema," in Bill Nichols, *Movies and Methods* (Berkeley, 1976).

VI. CHILE: NEO-COLONIAL CONFRONTATIONS

Although Chile, like Argentina, has a long cinematic tradition, it reached a special effervessence during the Allende period in the early seventies. My choice is to show Part One of Patricio Guzman's epic documentary *The Battle of Chile* (1975), not only because it illustrates certain theses of Galeano in *The Open Veins of Latin America*, but also because it makes for an illuminating comparison with *The Hour of the Furnaces*, in terms of slightly different political positions (left Peronism versus leftism *tout court*), production methods (collaborative in both cases, clandestine versus semi-clandestine), and cinematic strategies (an emphasis on montage and voice-over in *Hour of the Furnaces*, as opposed to less commentary and more respect for actual space and time in *Battle of Chile*). The comparison should lead to lively discussion among the students concerning which film is more effective in conveying a left political message and which cinematic strategies account for this effectiveness.

Readings:

Galeano. Eduardo. *The Open Veins of Latin America*, pp. 149-187.
Burton, Julianne. "Politics and the Documentary in People's Chile. An Interview with Patricio Guzman on *The Battle of Chile*," *Socialist Review*, No. 35 (September/October, 1977), reprinted in pamphlet form by the New England Free Press, Sommerville, Mass.
Special Section on Chilean Cinema, *Cine-tracts*, Vol. 9, No. 3, 1981.

VII. BRAZIL: COCONUT MILK IN COCA COLA BOTTLES

Brazilian Cinema has been one of the most vital and innovative of the Third World cinemas, displaying a wider stylistic range than other countries, a range that goes from a commercial comic tradition (*chanchada*) to the politicized auteurism of Cinema Novo, through the avant-garde "aesthetic of garbage" through soft-core porn (*Pornochanchada*) and militant documentaries. My selection of films attempts to convey this variety and also offers typical samples of the work of specific periods. I begin with Anselmo Duarte's *The Given Word* (1962) because it gives an idea of the kinds of films that preceded Cinema Novo. Anselmo Duarte was formed both by the *chanchada* tradition, in which he was a star and where he learned filmmaking, and by the Europeanized Vera Cruz studios in Sao Paulo, where he worked as an actor. *The Given Word* constitutes an example of what Glauber Rocha once called "coconut milk in Coca Cola bottles," in the sense that it combines Brazilian pro-filmic elements— *capoeira*, samba, candomblé—with a highly Hollywoodean style which relies on point-of-view editing, smooth cutting, commentative music, classical framing, dissolves for passage of time and so on.

The Given Word centers on the vow of its protagonist to bring a cross to the Church of Saint Barbara in gratitude for the miraculous cure of his donkey. The priest refuses him entrance because the vow was proffered at an Afro-Brazilian candomblé shrine. Anti-clerical rather than anti-Christian, the film contrasts the sincere Christ-like faith of the protagonist with the ossified Catholicism of the priest. The film evokes a kind of revolution by having the people take over an institution, yet the "revolution" consists, ultimately, only in gaining entrance to a more ecumenically tolerant Catholic Church.

Readings:

Galeano. Eduardo. *The Open Veins of Latin America*, pp. 188-224.
Johnson, Randal and Robert Stam. *Brazilian Cinema*, pp. 1-51 ("The Shape of Brazilian Film History"); pp. 270-280 "Vera Cruz: A Brazilian Hollywood").
Stam, Robert. "Slow Fade to Afro: The Black Presence in Brazilian Cinema," *Film Quarterly*, Vol. XXXVI, No. 2 (Winter 1982-83).

VIII. BRAZIL: HUNGER AND AESTHETICS

Cinema Novo cohered as a movement in the early sixties, when it made its first feature films and formulated its political and aesthetic ideas. The directors shared their strong opposition to commercial Brazilian cinema, to Hollywood films, to Hollywood aesthetics, and to the domination of Hollywood distribution chains. Rather than exploit the conviviality of *chanchada* or the derivative classiness of

Vera Cruz, the Cinema Novo directors searched out the dark corners of Brazilian life, the places where the country's social contradictions appeared most dramatically. Nelson Pereira dos Santos' *Vidas Secas* (1963), based on a classic novel by Graciliano Ramos, exemplifies the goals and aesthetic strategies of first-phase Cinema Novo. The film, which concerns the oppression of peasants in the Northeast, embodies what Rocha later called "an aesthetic of hunger," not only in the sense that hunger is the film's subject, but also in that the film is metaphorically "hungry" in its production methods and style. Rather than emphasize picturesqueness of sentimental "folk values," Dos Santos presents images and sounds as harsh and uncompromising as the barren setting of the film.

Readings:

Galeano, Eduardo. *The Open Veins of Latin America,* pp. 225-283.
Johnson, Randal and Robert Stam. "The Cinema of Hunger: Nelson Pereira dos Santos' *Vidas Secas,"* in *Brazilian Cinema,* pp. 120-127.
Rocha, Glauber. "An Aesthetic of Hunger," in *Brazilian Cinema,* pp. 67-71.
Recommended: Graciliano Ramos. *Barren Lives.* New York: Alfred Knopf.

IX. BRAZIL: CANNIBALISM AS METAPHOR

Joaquim Pedro de Andrade's *Macunaima* (1969), based on the twenties novel by Mario de Andrade, is the filmic heir of Rabelais, of the European avant-garde, and of the Brazilian "carnivalesque" film. It also illustrates the third, or so-called "cannibal-tropicalist" phase of Cinema Novo, in which Brazilian filmmakers resurrected the cannibalist metaphor popular among the Brazilian modernists of the twenties, as a critique of a world in which social, political, economic, and sexual relationships are basically cannibalistic. The first Cinema Novo film to be truly popular in both cultural and box-office terms, *Macunaima* offers a dialectical demonstration of how to reach the public without compromising a left political vision of Brazilian society. The film also raises the following issues for discussion: the use of allegory and political indirection within a situation of extreme censorship and political repression, the need to know Brazilian cultural codes in order to appreciate the film, the usefulness of Bakhtin's category of the "carnivalesque" for the understanding of such a film, the problem of "positive" and "negative" images in a text where virtually all the characters have an element of the grotesque, and the deployment of the music track to make ironic comments on the image.

Reading:

Johnson, Randal. "Cinema Novo and Cannibalism: *Macunaima,"* in Johnson and Stam, *Brazilian Cinema,* pp. 179-190.
Vieira, Joao Luiz. "From *High Noon* to *Jaws:* Carnival and Parody in Brazilian Cinema," in *Brazilian Cinema,* pp. 256-269.
Stam, Robert. "On the Carnivalesque." *Wedge: An Aesthetic Inquiry,* No. 1 (Summer 1982).

X. SENEGAL: THE PITFALLS OF NATIONAL CONSCIOUSNESS

The final portion of the course deals with countries where the cinema emerged in full force only after independence or revolution. Since Independence, Senegal, especially in the person of Ousmane Sembene, has become one of the strongest film-producing countries in Sub-Saharan Africa. I show two films by Sembene: *Black Girl* (1966) and *Xala* (1974). The former film deals with the exploitation of a young Senegalese woman hired in France as a maid, while the latter deals with the symbolic "xala" (impotence) of El Hadji, a representative of Senegal's neo-colonial business elite. The woman protagonist of *Black Girl* stands at the point of convergence of multiple oppressions: as black, as woman, and as maid. The film raises significant questions of focalization, point-of-view, and the role of symbolic objects. *Xala*, meanwhile, is a filmic realization, in brilliant satirical form, of Fanon's insights concerning "the pitfalls of national consciousness," especially the process by which an African elite takes over the positions formerly occupied by the colonizers. Some of the issues raised by the film include: the allegorical role of El Hadji's three wives as representing distinct stages in Africa history, the metaphorical ramifications of the "xala," and the positive roles of El Hadji's daughter Rama and the Dakar beggars. Sembene, I argue, synthesizes humor and caricature with political consciousness in a dialectical critique of the ills of post-Independence Senegal.

Readings:

Fanon, Frantz. "The Pitfalls of National Consciousness," *The Wretched of the Earth*, pp. 148-205.
Gabriel, Teshome. *Third Cinema in the Third World*, pp. 57-93.
"Resolutions of the Third World Filmmakers Meeting in Algiers, 1973," and "Interview with Ousmane Sembene," in Gabriel, appendix.
BFI DOSSIER NUMBER 6, *African Films: The Context of Production*, ed. Angela Martin, London: BFI, 1982.

XI. CUBA: REVOLUTION AND THE BOURGEOIS INTELLECTUAL

In a country where there had been virtually no film industry worthy of respect, revolutionary Cuba created one of the most dynamic centers of film production in Latin America. Tomas Gutierrez Alea's *Memoires of Underdevelopment* (1968), an adaptation of a novel by Edmundo Desnoes, ironically dissects a bourgeois intellectual unable to adapt to revolutionary Cuba. Forsaking socialist realism for a collage aesthetic which draws on the diverse filmic "new waves" and on the international avant-garde, Alea treats his alienated protagonist with a mixture of ironic understanding and dialectical critique. Some of the issues raised by the film include: the effectiveness of the film's collage technique, the relation between the documentary and the fiction segments of the film, sexual politics and the critique of voyeurism, and the deployment of reflexivity.

Reading:

Myerson, Michael. *Memories of Underdevelopment: The Revolutionary Films of Cuba.* New York: Grossman, 1973. (Out-of-print but available in libraries—contains script of the film, emphasizing dialogue and major scene changes).
Burton, Julianne. "Revolutionary Cuban Cinema," *Jump Cut*, No. 19 (December 1978).
————. "Individual Fulfillment and Collective Achievement"—An Interview with Tomas Gutierrez Alea," *Cineaste*, Vol. VIII, No. 1 (Summer 1977)
————. "*Memories of Underdevelopment* in the Land of Over-Development," *Cineaste*, Vol. VIII, No. 1 (Summer 1977).
Chanan, Michael, "Introduction" to *Twenty-Five Years of the New Latin American Cinema* (London: BFI, 1983).
Recommended: Edmundo Desnoes, *Memories of Underdevelopment*

XII: CUBA: MACHISMO, MARGINALISM, AND THE REVOLUTION

The question of machismo informs a number of Cuban films, from Solas' *Lucia* through Vega's *Portrait of Teresa* and Alea's *Up to a Certain Point*. Sara Gomez' *One Way or Another* (1977) is one of the few films treating this theme to be actually directed by a woman. Although *One Way* or *Another* focuses on the problem of social marginalism, the question of machismo comes in through the story of the evolving relationship between Mario, a worker from a marginal district, and Yolanda, a teacher of middle-class origins drafted to teach in the district. The film uses the metaphor of slum clearance and construction in a film which operates a certain "deconstruction." Gomez weaves fictional and nonfictional segments, professional and non-professional players, in a multi-levelled reflexion on the relations between the sexes, between classes, between generations, and among workers, in a film which Julia Lesage correctly describes as "dialectical, revolutionary, feminist." Some of the issues worth discussing include: Does the film's emphasis on romance compromise the film's feminism? What is the film's attitude toward Afro-Cuban religion and toward "marginalism" generally? How does the film treat the ethics of one worker "informing" on another? How do the documentary and fictional segments relativize and mutually critique one another?

Reading:

Lesage, Julia. "One Way or Another: Dialectical, Revolutionary, Feminist." *Jump Cut,* No. 20 (May 1979).

Kuhn Annette, *Women's Pictures: Feminism and Cinema,* London: Routledge & Kegan Paul, 1982, pp. 162-167.

I hasten to add as a final note that the preceding represents a highly personal mix of films, based on personal preferences and affinities. One might easily spend more class time on Indian Cinema, or less on Brazil. One might include China or the Phillipines. Many specific substitutions are possible as well. Pontecorvo's *Burn,* despite its limitations, might serve as a didactic introduction to the themes of the course. Glauber Rocha's *Barravento* or Rui Guerra's *The Guns* might be substituted for *Vidas Secas* as examples of first-phase Cinema Novo. *Emitai* might substitute for *Xala,* and both *Lucia* and *Portrait of Teresa* would be worthy substitutions in the Cuban section. Littin's *The Promised Land* could replace *The Battle of Chile.* The course as formulated lacks militant documentaries dealing with current struggles in Central America and in Southern Africa (a lack easily compensated in cities where such films are shown frequently and can be recommended to students). My emphasis has been on major Third World industries and on the fiction film, neglecting documentary, to a certain degree, and the avant-garde. One final practical note: most of the Third World films are distributed by the following distributors: Cinema Guild, Grove Films, Icarus Films, Libra Cinema Five, New Line, New Yorker Films, Mypheduh Films, The Southern Africa Media Center, Hurlock Cine-World, and Third World Newsreel.

(continued from page 12)

[8] Metz, *op. cit.,* pp. 128-129.

[9] Stephen Crofts and Olivia Rose. "An Essay Towards *Man With a Movie Camera,*" *Screen* 18, no. 1 (Spring 1977), 21. The complexity of Vertov's film has encouraged numerous excellent close readings, and the film stands as the most closely analyzed documentary in film studies. The Crofts and Rose essay is a comprehensive examination of the film.

[10] I am grateful to Vance Kepley Jr. for first indicating the formal interest of the beer hall sequence to me. This essay has further benefited from Professor Kepley's comments on an earlier draft.

(continued from page 20)

tor's assumption of the name "America", representing people of all occupations, national origins, and religious beliefs. Broadcast over CBS in November 1939, Robeson's performance immediately popularized the work. But his "theatrical" performances of the piece in Harlem and Washington over the next few years had a polemical edge: a visibly black American was asserting his right to represent all. Similarly Robeson's appearance in the epilogue to *Native Land* may have brought a social specificity to his role as commentator that was masked in the original text.

Film 6016x, Seminar in International Film: FRENCH CINEMA FROM THE 1930s
   THROUGH THE NEW WAVE   Annette Insdorf
Thursdays, 1:30-5:10   511 Dodge Hall Columbia University
                                                       Fall '88
Texts: Jean-Luc Godard, Pierrot le Fou
       James Monaco, The New Wave
       Roy Armes, French Cinema

Sept. 8 Shorts: A DAY IN THE COUNTRY, Jean Renoir
                 LES MISTONS, François Truffaut
                 LA JETÉE, Chris Marker

Sept. 15 L'ATALANTE and ZÉRO DE CONDUITE, Jean Vigo

Sept. 22 LES VISITEURS DU SOIR, Marcel Carné

Sept. 29 RULES OF THE GAME, Jean Renoir

Oct. 6   THE RAVEN, Henri-Georges Clouzot

Oct. 13   ORPHEUS, Jean Cocteau

Oct. 20   LA RONDE, Max Ophuls

Oct. 27   to be announced   first paper due

Nov. 3   NIGHT AND FOG and HIROSHIMA MON AMOUR, Alain Resnais

Nov. 10   PIERROT LE FOU, Jean-Luc Godard

Nov. 17   TWO ENGLISH GIRLS, François Truffaut

Dec. 1   MY NIGHT AT MAUD'S, Eric Rohmer

Dec. 8   SANS SOLEIL, Chris Marker   second paper due

Reading assignments are made weekly, including xeroxed material

ITALIAN FILM FROM 1945 TO THE PRESENT

Jared M. Becker

A.

A course on post-World War II Italian cinema inevitably begins with questions about the films that come to be labelled "neorealist":

1. "Neorealism" represents a historical puzzle, in that this vigorous film movement emerged simultaneously with the end of the war, whereas cinema in Germany had no real revival till much later. The strength of the Italian Resistance and the populist or apparently leftist elements of Fascist culture help explain this anomaly.

2. Some sources or influences for "neorealism": 19th century realism in Italian literature and its importance for Visconti; United States culture during the Depression and its reception among Italian intellectuals; the model of Soviet film-making (Eisenstein and Pudovkin), which, however, diverges stylistically from "neorealism"; continuities between Fascist-era films and film theory and "neorealist" practice.

3. A seminal definition of "neorealism": André Bazin's writings in the late 1940s on Rossellini, De Sica, and Visconti. Bazin's distinction between the propaganda film and the "neorealist" film (De Sica's Bicycle Thieves); the latter maintains the appearance of an accidental string of events and thus is more powerful politically than the propaganda film. Bazin's remarks on the "neorealist" refusal of Eisensteinian montage and its emphasis instead on the "mise-en-scène" (e.g. length of the shot in Visconti's La terra trema). The ultimately aesthetic nature of every realism, according to Bazin--and hence the space given to illusion in "neorealism."

4. Inasmuch as "neorealist" directors defined themselves as "anti-Fascist," it may be of use to examine Fascist censorship practices as a means to understanding some of the content of their films. Regularly banished from Fascist film production are portrayals considered to incite class conflict; "neorealist" films, on the other hand, frequently present painful juxtapositions of social classes. Fascist films often have a Puritanical streak; but "neorealist" films can choose an unwed mother as a protagonist (Rossellini's Open City) or use a crime of passion as a vehicle for social commentary (Visconti's Ossessione, a 1942 film generally regarded as a precursor of "neorealism"). The Fascist censor is reluctant to permit dialect, in line with the regime's aversion to regional, as

against national, culture; "neorealist" directors, however, often embrace dialect, whether the Sicilian of Visconti's _La terra trema_ or the Roman dialect of Rossellini's _Open City_.

B.

Sample analysis of a "neorealist" film--Rossellini's _Open City_:

1. Relationship between the documentary and the film director's fiction: the historical figure of Don Morosini, an Italian partisan priest executed by the Nazis, and _Open City_'s Don Pietro.

2. Tension between "realism" and "artifice" in Rossellini's film. The director's statements against manipulative montage, his rejection of the studio as the source of falsehood in film making, his avoidance of a detailed screenplay and his acceptance of improvisation. On the other hand, _Open City_ is often given structure through _artful_ juxtapositions: the comedic last rites administered by Don Pietro when he conceals weapons from a Nazi search party, and the tragic last rites given to Pina after she has been machine-gunned; and consider the artifice of the Nazi headquarters, where the torture room lies on one side,

while an elegant salon for German officers is found on the other.

3. Rossellini's two female characters as part of his diatribe against the artificial and his praise of the "natural": Pina, the heroic lower-class Roman, pregnant but unmarried, loving toward son and fiancé, all in all a paradigm of populist "naturalness"; Marina, the showgirl, corrupted by drugs and surrounded by the atmosphere of decadence prevailing in the German command, a token, in short, of all that is "artificial" and thus contemptible.

4. Open City as a reflection of Italy's political situation in the immediate postwar months (1945): the alliance between Don Pietro, the priest, and Manfredi, the Communist, both of whom are killed by the Nazis. The temporary union of Catholic and leftist factions dissolves within a few years of the war's close and is not part of the repertory of films like De Sica's Bicycle Thieves (1948) or Visconti's La terra trema (1948).

C.

Fellini and the Italian auteurs appearing in the wake of "neorealism" :

1. The demise of "neorealism" in the early 1950s: the Cold War and Italian government opposition to the perceived leftism of "neorealist" films (Giulio Andreotti's attack on De Sica); Rossellini's abandonment of the Resistance as subject, following the "War Trilogy" (Open City, Paisan, Germania anno zero); Alberto Asor Rosa's critique of the inherent weaknesses of "neorealist" populism in Scrittori e popolo (1964-5).

2. Resistance to "neorealism" in Fellini's La strada (1954): the Felliniesque love of spectacle, show, and the artificial as opposed to the typical "neorealist" disdain for contrivance; the director's refusal of characters representing social or political categories (i.e. the unemployed urban worker of De Sica's Bicycle Thieves) and La strada's focus instead on nearly mythical or fantastic characters (Zampanò the Beast, the Fool, the innocent simpleton Gelsomina); Fellini's polemics with prescriptive critics like Guido Aristarco, who denounced La strada as a throwback after the advances of "neorealism."

3. Antonioni and Pasolini as critics of the limitations of "neorealism": Antonioni's interest, by the late 1950s, in middle class angst rather than the Resistance or working class politics; Pasolini's 1965 essay "The Cinema of Poetry" as a manifesto of the post-"neorealist" director's right to a subjective, "poetical" vision. Note, however,

that both Antonioni and Pasolini--unlike Fellini--continue to have strong political interests in their film-making, even if their political positions transcend those of the "neorealist" era: consider the implications of the mournful industrial landscape of Antonioni's Red Desert (1964) or his sympathetic, if awkward, portrait of US student unrest in 1968 (Zabriskie Point); Pasolini, likewise, has an aggressively political viewpoint even as he drops the "neorealist" working class for the Roman "sub-proletariat" in Accattone (1961) or renders The Gospel According to Matthew in film (1964).

4. Formal experimentation in post-"neorealist" Italian cinema: Fellini's expressionistic montage and framing in La dolce vita; Pasolini's references to painters (Morandi in Accattone, Piero della Francesca in The Gospel According to Matthew); the appearance of dreams and the use of a psychological rather than a realistic narrative sequence in Fellini's 8 1/2; the manipulation of color in Antonioni's Blow-up; the complex sound track in Fellini, Pasolini, and Antonioni.

D.

Sample analysis of a post-"neorealist" *auteur* film--Fellini's 8 1/2 (1963):

1. Introduction to Fellini's idiosyncratic world: spectacle and showmanship as his preferred vehicles for analyzing human behavior; his problematic relationship to the Catholic Church, a constant source of imagery if not an uncontested moral guide; the persistence of the autobiographical mode in his work, from portrayals of youth in a small town (I vitelloni, but also the much later Amarcord), to the excitement and glamor of Rome (La dolce vita, Roma), to the convoluted self-representation of 8 1/2; Fellini's sexual politics--recurring images of machismo and of abused females.

2. The two censors who appear as antagonists to Fellini's alter ego Guido in 8 1/2: Daumier, the intellectual script advisor whose criticisms seem to echo those of a real-life Fellini critic, Guido Aristarco; the Catholic Church, which places so many strictures on the film-maker's representation of his sexual life and quest for worldly happiness.

3. Guido/Fellini's counter to these two censors lies outside the sphere of either the Church or the anti-artistic intellectual: the Magician, who presides over the most lyrical, untroubled evocation of the past in 8 1/2, the return to childhood in Romagna, and then reappears at the close of the film as the guiding spirit for the

thaumaturgical concluding show, the dance around the circus ring.

4. Female characters in 8 1/2 and Fellini's sexual politics: the constellation of women around the male protagonist--wife, mistress, mother, childhood sex symbol-- as evidence of a male egocentricity and double standard. Yet Fellini also critiques the self-centered male by showing the various females resisting the roles assigned to them (the harem revolt, Claudia's inability to be the actress Guido desires, Rossella's acerbic comments).

5. Formal properties of Fellini's 8 1/2: how the director effects transitions between dream and waking state, or between present and past; expressive camera movements (the long tracking and panning shot to introduce the spa; selection of significant physiognomies (the physical similarity of the actors who play Daumier and the Cardinal, the two censors); ironic use of Wagner's "Ride of the Walkyries" on the sound track.

E.

Revisitation of the Fascist era in Italian film, beginning ca. 1970:

1. Film reconsiderations of Fascism in this period are an international development; consider, for example Louis Malle's Lacombe, Lucien (France) and Fassbinder's Marriage of Maria Braun (Germany). In Italy, films representative of this tendency are Visconti's The Damned; Bertolucci's Spider's Stratagem, The Conformist, and 1900; Lina Wertmuller's Love and Anarchy and Seven Beauties, Fellini's Amarcord; Liliana Cavani's Night Porter and La pelle; Pasolini's Salò; the Taviani Brothers' Night of the Shooting Stars; and Ettore Scola's Una giornata particolare.

2. Corollary Italian revisions of thinking on Fascism: the historian Renzo De Felice's argument for a Fascist regime that won wide popular consent; general disaffection with the "neorealist"-era conception of a heroic Resistance supposed to represent political forces far more powerful than Fascism.

3. General characteristics of film revisions of Fascism: interest in representing Fascist characters or those who consented to Fascism, rather than Resistance figures; prevalence of sexual analyses of Fascism, or sexual metaphors for Fascist behavior (e.g. Visconti's The Damned, Bertolucci's The Conformist, Wertmuller's Seven Beauties)

F.

Sample analysis of a post-1970 Italian film that revisits Fascism--the Taviani Brothers' Night of the Shooting Stars (1982):

1. Origins of Paolo and Vittorio Taviani's interest in Fascism and Resistance: early interest in Rossellini, especially Paisan; a 1954 short about the fate of their home town, San Miniato, in July, 1944; their long-standing preoccupation with representing progressive and reactionary movements in Italian history (Allonsanfan).

2. Revisionary history in Night of the Shooting Stars: the American army of liberation remains largely out of sight (compare its omnipresence in Paisan); the Catholic Church is timid and inadequate in confronting Nazis (compare Don Pietro in Open City); a significant portion of Italian characters are represented as Fascists (compare Rossellini's choice of just a few villainous Italian collaborators in Open City and Paisan); legendary versions of the Resistance are gently called into question by the "Homeric" battle scene (compare the "neorealist" era's unequivocal conviction in a heroic and saintly Resistance).

3. The populism of Night of the Shooting Stars: Galvano as representative of the simple, worthy people of the town; his success in leading fellow citizens to safety, contrasted with the ineffectual efforts of the Church and the frivolity of the lawyer; the consummation of Galvano's love for his wealthier cousin as a metaphor for the triumph of populist humanity and class reconciliation.

4. Technical questions: casting to emphasize the similarity between Fascists and townspeople who flee Fascism; the frame device at beginning and end of the film, suggestive of the directors' critical distance from the "neorealist" era; wipes and contrastive editing--signs of the Tavianis' post-"neorealist" aesthetics.

G.

SAMPLEREADING LIST FOR ITALIAN FILM:

André Bazin: What is Cinema? (vol. 2) "An Aesthetic of Reality;" "La terra trema;" "Bicycle Thief;" "De Sica: Metteur en Scène;" "Umberto D;" "Cabiria;" and "In Defense of Rossellini."

Mira Liehm: Passion and Defiance: Italian Film from 1942 to

the Present. Chapters I through V ("Obsession" through "Neorealism Is Like...")

David Overbey, ed. Springtime in Italy: A Reader on Neorealism. Introduction, D. Overbey; Ch. 4: "A Thesis on Neorealism," C. Zavattini; Ch. 12 "Truth and Poetry: Verga and the Italian Cinema," M. Alicata and G. De Santis.

Peter Bondanella, ed. Federico Fellini: Essays in Criticism. Part 2. Perspectives on Individual Films: Sections 6-10 (La strada); Section 14 (La dolce vita); Sections 15-17 (8 1/2).

Pier Paolo Pasolini, "The Cinema of Poetry" and Umberto Eco, "Articulations of the Cinematic Code," both in Bill Nichols, ed. Movies and Methods.

Roy Huss, ed. Focus on Blow-up.

Millicent Marcus, Italian Film in the Light of Neorealism. Ch. 13, "Bertolucci's The Conformist: A Morals Charge."

Bruno Bettelheim, "Surviving," in the book of the same title.

H.

SAMPLE FILM LIST:

1. Roberto Rossellini, **Open City**.
2. Vittorio De Sica, **Bicycle Thief**.
3. Luchino Visconti, **La terra trema**.
4. Federico Fellini, **La strada**.
5. Federico Fellini, **La dolce vita**.
6. Federico Fellini, **8 1/2**.
7. P. P. Pasolini, **The Gospel According to Matthew**.
8. Michelangelo Antonioni, **Blow-up**.
9. Bernardo Bertolucci, **The Conformist**.
10. Lina Wertmuller: **Seven Beauties**.
11. Paolo and Vittorio Taviani, **Night of the Shooting Stars**.

FILM HISTORY
ABOUT THE CONTRIBUTORS

LEO BRAUDY is Leo S. Bing Professor of Literature at the University of Southern California and Professor of English. He has also taught at Johns Hopkins University, Columbia University, and Yale University. His major works in film studies include Great Film Directors: A Critical Anthology, edited with Morris Dickstein; The World in a Frame: What We See in Films; Jean Renoir: The World of His Films; and Traffaut's "Shoot the Piano Player": A Collection of Critical Essays. Other major books include The Frenzy of Reknown: Fame and its History. He has received numerous honors and awards for his books and research, and he has served on the editorial boards of numerous scholarly journals in the areas of literature and film. Since 1984 he has served on the Executive Committee of the Modern Language Association Film Division.

JARED M. BECKER is an assistant professor of Italian language and literature at Columbia University. His numerous publications include translations and a major study titled Eugenio Montale (1986), and he is currently completing a book on Gabriele D'Annunzio and beginning work on a study of Luigi Pirandello. He teaches a course titled "Italian Film from Neorealism to the Present.".

EDWARD D. C. CAMPBELL, JR., received his Ph.D. from the University of South Carolina and is currently editor of the Virginia State Library and Archives quarterly, Virginia Cavalcade, as well as the author of numerous studies of film, including The Celluloid South: Hollywood and the Southern Myth (1981).

JIM CASH is a professional screenwriter and Adjunct Professor at Michigan State University, where he offers courses in the history of motion pictures and screenwriting techniques. With Jack Epps, Jr., he has co-authored the original screenplays for the films Top Gun, Legal Eagles and The Secret of My Success.

GEOFFREY COCKS is Professor of History at Albion College in Michigan. He is the author of Psychotherapy in the Third Reich: The Goring Institute (Oxford, 1985), co-editor of Psycho/History: Readings in the Method of Psychology, Psychoanalysis, and History, (Yale, 1987), co-editor of German Professions, 1800-1950 (Oxford, 1989), and author of "The Hinting: Holocaust Imagery in Kubrick's The Shining," Psychohistory Review (1987).

JACK C. ELLIS is professor of film and former chair of the department of radio, television, and film, Northwestern University. Founder of film studies at Northwestern in 1956, he also has taught film at the University of California at Los Angeles, New York University, and the University of Texas at Austin. He is author of A History of Film (1979, rev. ed. 1985), cocompilator of The Film Book Bibliography 1940-1975 (1979), and coeditor of Cinema Examined (1982). He is past president of the Society for Cinema Studies and was editor of its journal, Cinema Journal, from 1976 to 1982. His articles in various journals have been mainly on screen education and on the career and influence of John Grierson. His latest book is John Grierson: A Guide to References and Resources, (1986).

LOUIS GIANNETTI is a professor of English and film at Case Western Reserve University. His books include Understanding Movies (Prentice-Hall, 4th ed., 1987); Flashback (with Scott Eyman, Prentice-Hall, 1986); Masters of the American Cinema (Prentice-Hall, 1981); and Godard and Others: Essays in Film Form (Fairleigh Dickinson U.P. and Tantivy Press, 1975). Among the courses he has taught: Intro to Film, American Cinema Since 1940, International Cinema Since 1940, History of Cinema to 1940, Teaching Film (graduate seminar), Italian Cinema, the American Studio System, American Film Comedy, Images of Women in the American Cinema, and others.

DOUGLAS GOMERY is author of <u>The Hollywood Studio System</u>, <u>Film History: Theory and Practice</u> (with Robert C. Allen), <u>High Sierra: Screenplay Series</u>, and <u>The Will Hays Papers</u>. Currently he is on the Boards of the Theatre Historical Society and the American Film Institute.

BARRY KEITH GRANT is Associate Professor of film and popular culture at Brock University, St. Catharines, Ontario, Canada. He has edited several books of film criticism and is the author of numerous essays on film and popular music in such journals as <u>Jump Cut</u>, <u>Journal of Popular Film and Television</u>, <u>Persistence of Vision</u>, <u>Literature/Film Quarterly</u>, and <u>Cineaction</u>. He is currently working on a book on the films of Frederick Wiseman.

MIRIAM HANSEN teaches film and literature at Rutgers University. She has published a book on Ezra Pound and numerous articles on film, in particular on early as well as recent German cinema, on Griffith and Valentino, and on the Frankfurt School (Benjamin, Adorno, Kluge). Her book on spectatorship in American silent film, <u>Babel and Babylon</u>, is forthcoming from Harvard University Press. Her recent article titled "Pleasure, Ambivalence, Identification: Valentino and Female Spectatorship" was published in <u>Cinema Journal</u> 25 (Summer 1986).

ANNETTE INSDORF is known primarily as a film professor, critic, lecturer, translator and television personality. She is Director of Undergraduate Film Studies at Columbia University, where she holds the title of Professor as well as Chairman of the Doctoral Program in Film and Theater. She has been teaching film history and criticism at Yale University since 1975. Dr. Insdorf is the author of <u>Indelible Shadows: Film and the Holocaust</u>, published by Random House in 1983 to critical acclaim. Her previous book is <u>Francois Truffaut</u>, a study of the French director's work, published by William Morrow in 1979. She is a frequent contributor to The New York Times Arts and Leisure Section, and her articles have appeared in <u>The Los Angeles Times</u>, <u>The San Francisco Chronicle</u>, <u>Premiere</u>, <u>Film Comment</u>, <u>Elle</u>, <u>Cineaste</u>, <u>The Boston Globe</u>, <u>American Film</u> and <u>Rolling Stone</u>.

E. ANN KAPLAN directs the Humanities Institute at the State Univesity of New York at Stony Brook, where she is also a Professor in English. She has published widely in film, feminist theory, and television studies. Her books include <u>Women and Film: Both Sides of the Camera</u> (Methuen, 1983), and <u>Rocking Around the Clock: Music Television, Postmodernism and Consumer Culture</u> (Routledge, 1987). She is finishing a book on Motherhood and Representation (Routledge, forthcoming), and plans to write a book about early women film directors.

BRUCE KAWIN is Professor of English and Film Studies at the University of Colorado at Boulder. He recently completed two screenplays (<u>Grifters</u> and <u>The Gold Tiberius</u>), a book of poems (<u>Geometry of Dawn</u>), and an introductory film textbook (<u>How Movies Work</u>). He has also written three books on Faulkner and three books on narrative theory (<u>Telling It Again and Again</u>, <u>Mindscreen</u>, and <u>The Mind of the Novel</u>).

DANIEL J. LEAB is Professor of History at Seton Hall University and Editor of <u>Labor History</u>. He has also taught at Columbia University, the University of Pennsylvania, and Cologne University. His books include a history of blacks in American movies, a study of the formation of the American Newspaper Guild, and the <u>Labor History Reader</u>. He is currently engaged in a study of how the movies fought the Cold War, and articles on that subject have appeared in the <u>Journal of Contemporary History</u>, <u>Encounter</u>, and the <u>Historical Journal of Film, Radio, and TV</u>.

PAUL LOUKIDES is an Associate Professor of English at Albion College where he teaches courses in film history, film and American culture and creative writing. He and Geoffrey Cocks have recently completed work on an anthology of readings about WWII using sources from each of the major combatant nations.

EDWARD C. MAPP is Professor of Speech, Communications and Theatre Arts at Borough of Manhattan Community College, The City University of New York. Professor Mapp writes a column "Black Media Beat" for Movie/TV Marketing. Later this year, a second edition of his Directory of Blacks in the Performing Arts will be published by Scarecrow Press, publisher of his 1972 book Blacks in American Films.

RICHARD W. MCCORMICK is Assistant Professor in the German Department at the University of Minnesota, Twin Cities. He has published articles on Wim Wenders, Helke Sander, and Helma Sanders-Brahms. He is co-editor of Gender Perspectives on German Cinema, a study of gender in German film of the 1920s. He teaches such courses as German Women Filmmakers, New German Cinema, Weimar Cinema.

JACK NACHBAR is Professor of Popular Culture and Director of the Film Studies Program at Bowling Green State University. His numerous publications on film include Focus on the Western and Western Films: An Annotated Critical Biography, and he has served as co-editor of the Journal of Popular Film and Television since its inception as the Journal of Popular Film in 1972. He has also edited and compiled important books in the area of popular culture: The Popular Culture Reader, edited with Christopher D. Geist (1983); and Currents of Warm Life: Popular Culture in American Higher Education, compiled and edited with Mark Gordon (1980).

JIMMIE L. REEVES is Visiting Assistant Professor of Communication at the University of Michigan. He teaches courses in media criticism, media history, and dramatic scriptwriting. Since receiving his Ph.D. from the University of Texas in 1984, he has published several scholarly articles and reviews, the most recent appearing in Wide Angle.

ADAM REILLY left a monastic order of the Catholic Church to earn his M.A. in Cinema Studies from New York University. Prior to his death in 1987, he was Cinema Director of the Denver Center for the Performing Arts; earlier, he was Director of the American Film Institute Theater at the Kennedy Center in Washington, and head of publicity for Time-Life Films and for Contemporary Films. He is author of Harold Lloyd: King of Daredevil Comedy.

DAVID H. SHEPARD directs the Film & Television Study Center and is Adjunct Associate Professor of Cinema-Television at the University of Southern California. He also owns Film Preservation Associates, a specialized laboratory, and was formerly Special Projects Officer for the Directors Guild of America, Vice President of Blackhawk Films, and Associate Archivist from the AFI Collection at the Library of Congress. His films have won several Emmys and an Oscar.

ROBERT SKLAR is Professor of Cinema Studies at New York University. He is the author of Movie-Made America: A Cultural History of American Movies (1975) and Prime-Time America: Life on and Behind the Television Screen (1980), as well as many essays and articles on film, television and other cultural subjects.

TOM SOBCHACK is Professor of English and Film at the University of Utah. His publications include numerous articles as well as An Introduction to Film and the forthcoming Critical Approaches to Film: An Introduction to Film Criticism. He is currently working on a book on British silent film.

VIVIAN SOBCHACK, Associate Professor of Theater Arts, teaches Film Studies at the University of California, Santa Cruz. Past President for the Society for Cinema Studies, she has published widely on cinema in numerous periodicals and anthologies. Her current books are An Introduction to Film, 2nd Ed and Screening Space: The American Science Fiction Film.

ROBERT STAM is an Associate Professor in the Department of Cinema Studies at New York University. His many publications on film include Brazilian Cinema, edited with Randal Johnson, and Reflexivity in Film and Literature: From Don Quixote to Jean-Luc Godard.

JON TUSKA is the author of The Filming of the West (1976), The Vanishing Legion: A History of Mascot Pictures 1927-1935 (1982), Billy the Kid: A Handbook (1983), and The American West in Film: Critical Approaches to the Western (1985), among numerous other books. He edited The American West in Fiction (1982) and was Co-Editor-in-Chief on the Encyclopedia of Frontier and Western Fiction (1983) and The Frontier Experience A Reader's Guide to the Life and Literature of the American West (1984). He wrote, produced, and appeared on the ten-part series "They Went Thataway" (PBS, 1970), a history of the Western film, and has since been the special film consultant on numerous television series and productions, including "Images of Indians" (PBS, 1980) and, most recently, "Billy the Kid" (PBS, 1988). He has lectured widely on various aspects of the American West in history and legend at universities and historical societies and has taught his course "Images of the American West" at Lewis & Clark College, the University of Portland, and Portland State University. He is a resident of Portland, Oregon.

WILLIAM A. VINCENT is Professor of Humanities at Michigan State University, where he has taught since 1965. He teaches courses in history and the visual arts and has taught courses on Fellini, Hitchcock, the Hollywood Musical, Contemporary World Cinema, and Introduction to Film. He devised Michigan State's highly successful Film In Britain summer program.

GREGORY A. WALLER is an Associate Professor in the Department of English at the University of Kentucky, where he teaches courses in film and popular culture. His publications include The Living and the Undead: From Stoker's "Dracula" to Romero's "Dawn of the Dead" and American Horrors: Essays on the Modern American Horror Film. His most recent articles include "Re-placing The Day After" in Cinema Journal 26 (Spring 1987) and "Flow, Genre, and the Televison Text" in Journal of Popular Film and Television 16 (Spring 1988).

ANDREA S. WALSH is Assistant Professor of Sociology and Adjunct Assistant Professor of Screen Studies at Clark University, Worcester, MA. She teaches courses on the sociology of mass communications and film. She has written Women's Film and Female Experience 1940-1950, as well as other articles on popular film, advice literature and television. Currently she is writing a history of popular images of aging in American film from the silent era to the present.

ABOUT THE EDITORS

ERIK S. LUNDE is currently Professor of American Thought and Language at Michigan State University, where he received his initial appointment in 1970. A Harvard graduate, Professor Lunde received both the M.A. and Ph.D. degrees (in 1966 and 1970) in American history from the University of Maryland. Professor Lunde has also taught at Marquette University, the University of Wisconsin-Milwaukee, Kalamazoo College and The University of Michigan. A member of the Film Studies faculty at Michigan State since 1975, Professor Lunde has offered courses in writing and film, the films of Alfred Hitchcock and the silent film. Professor Lunde is the author of Horace Greeley in Twayne's United States Authors series (number 413) and of several articles in American history and film. With Truman Morrison, he has co-hosted a local television series entitled Conversation.

DOUGLAS A. NOVERR teaches film courses at Michigan State University in the Department of American Thought and Language and in the Film Studies Thematic Program. He has published articles and delivered papers on disaster films, the sports film, and the western. The author of numerous articles in the areas of American literature, American art history, popular culture, and sports history, Professor Noverr has co-authored three books: The Games They Played: Sports in American History, 1865-1980 (with Lawrence E. Ziewacz), The Relationship of Painting and Literature: A Guide to Information Sources (with Eugene L. Huddleston), and Sport History - Selected Reading Lists and Course Outlines (with Lawrence E. Ziewacz).